NEOPLATONISM
AND INDIAN PHILOSOPHY

NEOPLATONISM AND INDIAN PHILOSOPHY

Paulos Mar Gregorios, editor

INTERNATIONAL SOCIETY FOR NEOPLATONIC STUDIES

Volume 9 in *Studies in Neoplatonism: Ancient and Modern*
R. Baine Harris, General Editor

STATE UNIVERSITY OF NEW YORK PRESS

Published by
State University of New York Press, Albany

© 2002 State University of New York

All rights reserved

Printed in the United States of America

No part of this book may be used or reproduced in any manner whatsoever without written permission. No part of this book may be stored in a retrieval system or transmitted in any form or by any means including electronic, electrostatic, magnetic tape, mechanical, photocopying, recording, or otherwise without the prior permission in writing of the publisher.

For information, address State University of New York Press,
90 State Street, Suite 700, Albany, NY 12207

Production by Michael Haggett
Marketing by Fran Keneston

Library of Congress Cataloging-in-Publication Data

Neoplatonism and Indian philosophy / Paulos Mar Gregorios, editor.
    p. cm. — (Studies in Neoplatonism; v. 9)
    Includes bibliographical references and index.
    ISBN 0-7914-5273-5 (alk. paper). — ISBN 0-7914-5274-3 (pbk. : alk. paper)
    1. Neoplatonism—Congresses. 2. Philosophy, Indic—Congresses.
    3. Philosophy, Comparative—Congresses. I. Paulos Gregorios, 1922– II. Series.

B517.N459 2001
186'.4—dc21   2001049177

10 9 8 7 6 5 4 3 2 1

Table of Contents

Preface 5
    R. Baine Harris

A Word of Thanks 9
    Paulos Mar Gregorios

Does Geography Condition Philosophy? On Going
Beyond the Occidental-Oriental Distinction 13
    Paulos Mar Gregorios

Plato, Neoplatonism and Their Parallel Indian Ideas 31
    D. P. Chattopadhyaya

The Omnipresence of Being, The Intellect-Intelligible
Identity and the Undescending Part of the Soul 45
    Atsushi Sumi

The Oriental Influences Upon Plotinus' Thought: An
Assessment of the Controversy Between Bréhier and
Rist on the Soul's Relation to the One 71
    Roman T. Ciapalo

Plotinus and Interior Space 83
    Frederic M. Schroeder

Unity and Multiplicity: Reflections on Emanationism as
a Philosophical Theme in the Context of Neoplatonism 97
    P.K. Mukhopadhyaya

Being and Knowing in Plotinus 107
    Lloyd P. Gerson

Platonism in Late Classical Antiquity
and Some Indian Parallels 127
    Henry J. Blumenthal

The *Sadhana* of Plotinus and Sri Aurobindo 153
    Arabinda Basu

Plotinus' Neoplatonism and the Thought
of Sri Aurobindo 163
    John R.A. Mayer

The Theoria of Nature in Plotinus and the
Yoga of the Earth Consciousness in Aurobindo 173
    Daniel Kealey

The Four Dimensional Philosophy of Indian
Thought and Plotinus 189
    I.C. Sharma

Plotinus' Criticism of Materialism 199
    Christos Evangeliou

Plotinus and Vedanta 211
    S.R. Bhatt

Plotinus and Sankara: Some Significant
Affinities and Divergences 215
    G.C. Nayak

Man's Predicament—The Unique Indian Experience
and the Neoplatonic Tradition 223
    Gopal Chandra Khan

Rationality and Ritual in Neoplatonism 229
    Robert M. Berchman

Participants 269

Contributors 273

Preface

R. Baine Harris

Most Western scholars are not aware of the complexity, richness, and antiquity of Indian Philosophy. It is one of the oldest, if not the oldest, continuous philosophical traditions in history, antedating the speculations of the early Greeks, Egyptians, and Babylonians in its origin, and covers most of the whole spectrum of possibilities for philosophical speculation. Most of it is related to Hinduism in some way, but there are also significant Buddhist, Muslim, Christian, and atheistic philosophers within it. Some Western Scholars have some knowledge of the six major philosophical systems that allow a wide variety of philosophical interpretations of Hinduism, but are not aware of the various schools of thought within them or the wide variety of non-Hindu Indian philosophers.

Most philosophers, including most Indian philosophers, seem to be content to work mainly within their own given inherited philosophical traditions, with only minor concern for comparative philosophy. Due to recent advances in rapid transportation and communication East and West are now meeting and entwining their own economic and even political destinies with each other in ways not imagined a hundred years ago. However, this has not occurred in philosophy and religion. Eastern thought still remains eastern and Western thought still remains western and the "twain" have not really met. Most people, including philosophers, still remain suspicious of foreign philosophies and religions and are quite content to remain with their own traditional ways of thinking. Only a very few philosophers in the West and in the East have been concerned to make serious studies of the philosophical thinking of other major cultures.

In light of these facts, the meeting of a few American, British, Canadian, and Japanese philosophers with a group of eminent Indian philosophers in a conference held in New Delhi during the last few days of 1992 and the first few days of 1993 is of some significance. It was not only a genuine exercise in comparative philosophy for the participants, it was also a small step forward in aiding East and West to meet philosophically. Although I had a role to play in the organizing of this conference, I was not able to be one of the participants, since I was busy having a heart attack at the time, a rite of passage that seems to come to all the men in my family when they reach a certain age. The conference was ably conducted by Paulos Mar Gregorios, who was then the Metropolitan of the Syrian Orthodox Church of Northern India and the President of the Indian Section of the International Society for Neoplatonic Studies and a past president of the Indian Philosophical Congress and the World Council of Churches. He was assisted by Professor John Mayer of Brock University in St. Catharines, Ontario, and Professor Christos Evangeliou of Towson University. Numerous Indian organizations provided various forms of support, financial and otherwise and Dr. Gregorios mentions them in his introductory essay to this volume. Dr. Gregorios was able to complete most of the editing of this volume just a few weeks before his death, and I spoke with him by telephone about it less than a week before his death. Both the conference and the book are the product of his efforts and this book is now offered to the public in his memory.

The theme of the conference was "Neoplatonism and Indian Philosophy." Its stated aim was to note elements in certain Indian philosophies that appear to be very similar to Neoplatonism. Another concern was the controversy among Neoplatonic scholars about the influence of Indian philosophy on Plotinus, a topic on which Dr. Gregorios himself had some firm opinions, as he mentions in his own extensive introductory essay, and one also quite ably dealt with in some of the other papers. I have often wondered if philosophical notions must have one historical source from which they are historically transmitted or may occur in various places at various times as the result of a certain way of logicizing. Regardless of which is cause and which is effect, elements of Plotinus' monism are found in parallel ways of thinking of Indian writers throughout India's long history, and it is important to note these similarities.

All of the participants who have communicated with me concerning the conference have been commendatory of the way Dr. Gregorios and his associates conducted the conference, some even saying it was the finest conference they have ever attended. All agree that another similar conference should be held either in India or in some other country within the next few years. I do hope that some younger minds will come forth with the knowledge, energy, and enthusiasm to carry on this cause now that Dr. Gregorios for sure, and I, for the most part, are out of the picture.

July 21, 1998
R. Baine Harris
Norfolk, Virginia
Old Dominion University

A Word of Thanks

Paulos Mar Gregorios
Editor

We owe a word of thanks to many. We can acknowledge here only a few of those who have made this volume possible. First to the International Society for Neoplatonic Studies and its indefatigable Executive Director, Professor R. Baine Harris of Old Dominion University in Norfolk, Virginia. He initiated the preparatory work for the Second International Seminar on Neoplatonism and Indian Thought, held at Teen Murti Bhavan (Nehru Memorial Museum and Library), New Delhi, from December 29, 1992 to January 3, 1993. He also did all the international work of organizing the Seminar, though he was prevented from personally attending due to ill health. Without his untiring effort, the Seminar would not have taken place.[1]

Equally important for the New Delhi Seminar was the support of the Indian Council for Philosophical Research, New Delhi. They gave us a substantial grant covering more than half of the organizers' cost of the Seminar and co-sponsored it. We wish to express our special gratitude to Professor R. Balasubramaniam, the Chairman and Professor Bhuvan Chandel, the Member-Secretary, who gave us all possible support and encouragement. Professor Balasubramaniam chaired the Valedictory session and gave us a scholarly presidential address. We are especially indebted to Dr. Ranjan Ghosh, the Director of ICPR, who personally and with great skill and dedication, handled the major part of the organisational work. To him and to the students from Jawaharlal Nehru University and Delhi University who helped him in the organisational work we owe a deep debt of gratitude.

Three other organisations bore the rest of the cost, and we are grateful to them: the Sarva Dharma Nilaya, New Delhi; the All India Association for Christian Higher Education; and the Manavata Mandir, Hoshiarpur (Dr. I. C. Sharma). We are grateful also to the other co-sponsoring bodies, namely the Indian Philosophical Congress, the International Society for Indian Philosophy, the Akhil Bharatiya Darshan Parishad, the Jamia Millia Hamdard, the Nehru Memorial Museum and

Library, and the Indira Gandhi National Centre for the Arts. Sri Ravindra Kumar, himself a consummate scholar, helped us most generously with the free use of the Seminar Room and other facilities at Teen Murti Bhavan.

I want to express my special thanks to Professor John R. A. Mayer of Brock University, who co-chaired the Seminar with me, and to Professor Christos Evangeliou of Towson University, Towson, Maryland, Acting General Secretary of the International Society for Neoplatonic Studies.

Special thanks are due to several Indian philosophers who gave valuable addresses, the texts of which are not available, for various reasons, for inclusion in this volume. I want to mention especially Professor K. Satchidanada Murty's memorable keynote address on the One, Professor Richard Sorabji's stimulating lecture on, "Porphyry and Iamblichus on Animals", and Dr. Girija Vyas' (at that time Minister of State for Information in the Government of India) opening remarks as National Organising Chairman about the wide variety of Indian thought. Several of the papers read during the Seminar could also not be included in this volume.

Some of the papers have been edited; the Editor asks pardon for any slips in editing. Most of the papers are left as presented, with some subsequent changes made by the authors. The Editor believes that this volume, with all its imperfections, constitutes a major contribution to the comparative study of Indian thought and Neoplatonism. The papers in this volume suggest both that the matter is important enough for further research, and also that there is need to reexamine the questions we ask and the presuppositions with which we approach the topic. We also saw, during the Seminar, how Westerners, non-westerners, and Indians can sharpen their own conceptualisations by such inter-cultural dialogue.

Dr. Paulos Mar Gregorios
Editor
New Delhi
February, 1994

Endnote

1. The First International Conference on Neoplatonism and Indian Thought was held at Brock University, St. Catharine's, Ontario, Canada in October 1976. The papers from this first conference are in R. Baine Harris, editor, *Neoplatonism and Indian Thought*, ISNS, Norfolk, Virginia, and SUNY Press, Albany, 1982.

Does Geography Condition Philosophy? On Going Beyond the Occidental-Oriental Distinction
An Introduction to the Second International Seminar on Neoplatonism and Indian Thought

Paulos Mar Gregorios

The question has been raised time and again, and supposedly discussed threadbare, as to whether there are any demonstrable oriental influences in the thought of Plotinus. As I suggested at the beginning of the New Delhi Seminar in my brief remarks from the Chair, is it not time that we had a good look at the question itself? What are the assumptions that lie behind the question as it is formulated?

Let us begin by asking ourselves what we actually mean by the term "oriental". To what geographical region does it apply? Would it apply, for example, to the ancient Roman Province or διοίκησις of Oriens? If it does then the whole of the West Asian region of the Roman Empire would be meant, (the Diocesan (Διοίκησις) or Diocese means a group of Roman provinces under a Prefect or Viceroy) with the capital at Antioch-on-the-Orontes. In such a case the word *Oriental* would not include India in the scope of its meaning. But we know that even in Roman usage, the word meant everything East of the Bosporus, or sometimes everything outside of Europe. "Oriental" is a very European word. We do well to be careful in the use of this word, particularly in view of the cultural Connotations it carries. Sometimes it is parallel to calling the Germanic people "barbarians". It is basically the same spirit, of which we have examples in this volume, by which some Indian scholars sometimes dismiss western thought too lightly, without any major effort to understand it.

Most people, when they reflect on regional philosophies, think primarily of three groups: Western (mainly Euro-American, Classical, Medieval, and Modern Critical) philosophies; South Asian (including Ancient Pre-Vedic, Hindu, Jain and Buddhist) philosophies; and Far Eastern, (Taoist, Confucianist and Chinese Buddhist) philosophies. Certainly there were other philosophies not included in that threefold grouping. Even if there were not, the term "Oriental" would have to include the two latter groups, i.e., everything that is not Occidental philosophy would be *Oriental*!

To deny any oriental influence whatsoever in Plotinus is to deny even the influence of Egypt, where Plotinus was presumably born (in Lycopolis, either the one on the Nile Delta, or in the city of that name in Upper Egypt). He was brought up there as a child and he lived there for a good number of years of his adult life; Egypt certainly cannot legitimately be considered part of the Occident. I think we have to be just as circumspect in our denials as in our affirmations, as philosophers worth our salt. Let us then be done with loose statements in this matter, and state categorically: *There is no historical or philosophical ground whatsoever for the affirmation that the thought of Plotinus is totally free from all Oriental influence.*

I presume that the blurb on the Second Edition of *Plotinus* (7 volumes) translated by Professor A. H. Armstrong in the *Loeb Classical Library*[1] is not the work of Professor Armstrong himself. In any case someone who has more authority than the present writer should advise the Harvard University Press that it will be in the interests of scholarly accuracy to delete from the front and back flap of all seven volumes of future editions or reprints the unnecessary and incorrect statement: "There is no real trace of Oriental influence on his thought".

Let us proceed further to see what we can legitimately say in this matter. In order to do so, we will be on surer ground if we abandon the term *Oriental* altogether, for it was used by the Westerners (Europeans) to denote whatever lay east of their continent; its meaning was vague and imprecise; since Europeans had practically no west before the 15th century, it meant, for many Europeans, just what was not part of their world. It was what was east from the European perspective; the word *oriental* also came to have, perhaps only since the colonial period, a pejorative connotation: for many Europeans, what was not European was somehow inferior.

Besides, even today, both Egypt and Syria are still included by many in the Middle East and would therefore have to be regarded as part of the region denoted by the word *Oriental*. It would be much too laborious and from the start unfruitful to try to disprove all Syrian (e.g. Nemesius) and Egyptian (Ammonius Saccas, Alexandrian culture), and Jewish (Philo) influence on Plotinus. In so far as Plotinus was born and brought up in Egypt, he has to be regarded as an Oriental if that term is to be used at all. Talking about oriental influence on Plotinus is therefore, strictly speaking, nonsense.

So what we want to talk about is the influence of specifically Indian thought on Plotinus, not any so-called oriental influence' on him.

Now, Indian thought is a fairly wide ocean, as anyone with even a cursory knowledge of India's vast and deep philosophical heritage should know. Summaries of Indian philosophical thought have been attempted by many competent and not so competent scholars, both Indian and foreign. Even the best among them admittedly do not do equal justice to the Carvaka, Jaina and multi-schooled Buddhist as well as several Tantric schools of Indian philosophical experience, practice and reflection. In view of this formidably wide scope of Indian thought, it would not be very precise to speak of the influence of 'Indian Thought' in general on Plotinus. If someone has a positive affirmation to make about such influence, that affirmation would gain in clarity and refutability or critical examinability, if a particular aspect of Indian thought could be specified as having influenced Plotinus.

Perhaps we should consider the appropriateness of attaching any geographical labels at all to various schools of global philosophy. Every school we know is indebted to some school outside of its geographical region, either by way of ideas and categories adapted, or in terms of a polemic that generates new ideas.

If philosophy is some form of universal truth why should geography condition it? We have all to learn to shed some of our geographical and racial parochialisms in this regard. In our time we are called upon to regard all regional philosophies as the common heritage of all humanity, and to develop the notion of a global Common Human Tradition, which encompasses all the major trends in the heritage of humanity. All of us are called upon to focus on our common human identity, and our common global heritage, and to seek new human global philosophical perspectives duly enriched by as many regional philosophies as we can access.

Now we have to ask a third question as to what precisely we mean by 'influence'. If for example, the present writer, who is an Indian by birth but trained in the West, has read two books on Chinese philosophy, would he be regarded as having been influenced by Chinese thought? If again as a student at Oxford, he participated in an intensive three-month seminar on "The Tacit Dimension of Knowing" led by the Hungarian émigré, Professor Michael Polanyi, should he be regarded as influenced by Hungarian thought? Influence is rather too vague a concept to define or measure precisely.

I presume that no one disputes the fact attested by Porphyry that Plotinus was profoundly influenced by the teachings of Ammonius Saccas, whose lectures he attended for eleven long years, after having sampled and rejected those teachers in Alexandria who were recommended to him as the best in that city. Plotinus himself may have regarded Plato and Socrates as his basic saints or gurus and guides. Porphyry tells us that the only feasts Plotinus observed were the traditional feasts of Plato and

Socrates. But Ammonius was his living mentor, his preferred teacher. To affirm one is not to deny the other. If one has to speak about 'influence', we are fully justified, by the available evidence, in stating that Ammonius exerted a strong influence on Plotinus. One may even say that the influence of Ammonius was a decisive factor in Plotinus' reinterpretation of Pythagoras, Plato, Aristotle and the Stoics.

I know that the question, "Who was Ammonius Saccas?" will probably elicit a yawn from some of you. That is also a question that has been discussed "threadbare". Even at the risk of a few yawns and frowns, let us see where we stand at the end of the threadbare discussion.

It has been suggested by one imaginative speculator that the name Ammonius Saccas is a latinisation or hellenisation of the Sanskrit "Muni Sakya" or *Sakyamuni*, which is a well known form of appellation for the Lord Buddha. If that were only demonstrable, we could have regarded Ammonius, whatever his nationality, as a Buddhist monk, who took on for himself one of the many names by which the Master was called. This was actually put forward by no less a scholar than Cardinal Daniélou, in his lectures on 'The Fourth Century' at the Sorbonne fifty years ago. Unfortunately it is probably only about as true as the other proposal that Pythagoras, or in Greek Πυθαγόρας, was a Buddhist monk and that his Greek name was simply a Buddhist monastic name he chose for himself, meaning Putha (original Pali or Prakrit which was then Sanskritized as *Buddha*) of the marketplace, taking *agoras* as genitive of Greek ἀγορὰ (=market). Let us leave aside these entertaining speculations, and get back to the question, "who was this Ammonius Saccas?" What in his teaching, according to Porphyry, made Plotinus say, "this is what I was looking for!" (τοῦτον εζήτουν).

I am unable to answer either of these questions. What can be said has been said by H. R. Schwyzer and E. R. Dodds and other careful scholars.[2] Ammonius lived ca 175-243 A D, while Plotinus lived 204/5-270, both for substantial periods in Alexandria. Ammonius was thus thirty years senior to Plotinus, who began his study of philosophy in Alexandria in 232, when he was twenty-seven.

According to Longinus, cited by Porphyry, Ammonius was the greatest linguistic and literary scholar (φιλολογώτατος) of his time, and no one had come anywhere near him in learning. Longinus himself, according to Porphyry "the most discerning critic of our time" (κρτικώτατος) was a fellow student with Plotinus of Ammonius, and calls Ammonius both *Platonikos* (Πλατωνικός) and *Peripatetikos* (Περιπατητικὸς)[3] But Ammonius wrote nothing, and told his disciples not to put in writing anything he said.

For eleven years Plotinus studied with Ammonius. We still need a proper exegesis of that key sentence of Porphyry's:

Καὶ ἀπ' ἐκείνης τῆς ἡμέρας συνεχῶς τῷ Ἀμμωνίῳ παραμένοντα τοσαύτην ἕξιν ἐν φιλοσοφίᾳ κτήσασθαι, ὡς καὶ τῆς παρὰ τοῖς Πέρσαις ἐπιτηδευομένης πεῖραν λαβεῖν σπεῦσαι καὶ τῆς παρ' Ἰνδοῖς κατορθουμένης.

"And from that day continually staying with Ammonius, (Plotinus) acquired such a mastery of philosophy, that he became eager to gain knowledge of the teaching prevailing among the Persians, as also among the Indians."

Now, putting all that together this is what I get. Ammonius was both a great scholar and a great philosopher, well versed in Plato and Aristotle, as well as in the whole Greek tradition. Plotinus thought so highly of his teaching, in comparison with that of others available in Alexandria at that time, that he not only said the very first day: "This is what I was looking for", but also continued with Ammonius for eleven long years. If any single living teacher influenced Plotinus more than others, it was Ammonius. Ammonius, being an all round scholar, initiated Plotinus into the niceties and nuances of the teachings of Parmenides, Pythagoras, Plato, Aristotle and the Stoics, so that the latter achieved a good grasp of philosophy in general.

So far I hope everyone agrees. Whether Ammonius was also well versed in Persian and Indian thought Porphyry does not clearly say. What he does say is that the mastery of philosophy which Ammonius imparted to Plotinus was such that it kindled in the latter a great zeal to get better acquainted with Persian and Indian thought. That zeal impelled the nearly forty year old Plotinus to join Gordian's military expedition to Persia, not because he was interested in Romans conquering Persia or India, but because his teacher had told him that he must find out more about Persian and Indian thought. Obviously Gordian's expedition was a failure, and Plotinus had to flee for his life and came and settled down in Rome.

Shall we then say that, after that initial failure, Plotinus gave up every effort to know something about Persian and Indian thought? There certainly were, already by the first century, Brahmins and Buddhists in Alexandria. Did he ever try to contact them? Was literature from India and Persia available in the Alexandrian *Museion*? By the time we come to the third century, Buddhists have established themselves in Alexandria, with a *Vihara* or place of teaching of their own. Do you have reason to think that Plotinus gave up the effort to know something of Persian and Indian thought after the Gordian expedition failed? Or did he continue to pursue that interest in Rome, where all roads met, including the ones from Alexandria, Persia and India? I leave these questions with you, and do not want to draw any specific conclusions at this point, except to point out that:

    1. Ammonius Saccas taught philosophy in such a way to his student Plotinus that the latter felt it necessary to go and acquire some competence in Persian and Indian thought;

    2. If the above is true, then Ammonius Saacas had some knowledge of Persian and Indian philosophy, which he most likely imparted to Plotinus as his student.

Let us now raise a fourth point. When Armstrong, or anyone else for that matter, says for example that "There is no trace of Oriental influence on his (i.e., Plotinus') thought" his/her argument must be that, if all elements in the *Enneads* can be explained as originating within the Hellenistic tradition, then there is no need to hypothesize "Oriental influence". But are such scholars, including Armstrong, assuming that the Hellenistic tradition itself is uncontaminated by anything coming from East of the Bosporus? A cursory examination would reveal that the Hellenic culture and religion were 'Oriental', in the sense of just as much Asian-African as European, through and through.

Hellenistic Religion

By Hellenism is meant that form of Greek culture which was shaped in and spread from the Eastern Mediterranean from the time of Alexander (the first Western empire-builder ca 330 BCE) for about four centuries. When the Romans took over the Empire in the first century BCE, Hellenism went into a down-swing, till it was resurrected and reinstated as Byzantine culture in the middle of the fifth century. When Plotinus lived and wrote, Hellenism was expressed mostly in the many attempts to revive, reintegrate and revise the ancient Greek religion and thought of Parmenides and Heracleitus, Pythagoras and the other Pre-Socratics, as well as Socrates, Plato and Aristotle, the Stoics and others.

    Soon after Alexander, Alexandria, the Capital of Egypt, in Africa replaced Athens of Europe as the cultural capital of Hellenism. In that process Alexandrian Hellenism had absorbed many Asian-African (Syrian, Babylonian and Egyptian as well as others) elements; it thus became more cosmopolitan in its outlook and could no longer be regarded as strictly European.

Neither was Alexandrian Hellenism a secular philosophy. It was fully a religious system in which many philosophies flourished side by side. When Ptolemy I founded the city of Alexandria, its core was the Μουσείον, a community of learned and gifted men, headed by a Priest of the Muses. The community had its own ceremonies and rituals, and offering of sacrifices. The theurgical tradition soon became part of Hellenic culture and philosophy.

Hellenism was thus not just rational philosophy. Fundamental to it was the religious perspective, integral to all genuine philosophical reflection leading to experiential knowledge of Transcendent Reality. Plotinus was no exception. This religious perspective in Classical as well as in Hellenistic Greek culture expressed itself in three major areas, which one can discern in Socrates and Plato as well as in the Neoplatonist school as a whole:

1. the cult of the gods and daimons in temples and shrines dedicated to them;

2. the Gnostic and Mystery religions with their special revelations, initiatory rites and secret doctrines, and

3. the widespread magico-religious, or Tantric practices of invoking and propitiating the daemons or the Spirits to perform special tasks.

The main enemies of the three religious aspects of Hellenism were the Jews and the Christians whose influence was growing and threatening the very existence of Hellenistic religion and culture.

The point often overlooked is that all the three religious elements of Hellenism had a heavy 'oriental' aspect to them. The Hellenistic culture developed by borrowing liberally from Egypt, Syria, Persia and India, but not apparently much from China. It was always a two-way process. As Greek ideas and culture spread Eastward, the rich culture of the East supplied so much of new insights, so many new ways of doing things, to the Greeks. One can only illustrate here.

Where did Alexander of Macedonia learn empire building in the first place? The Greeks had no such concepts. The Persian wars not only opened up a new world of experience and possibility to the Greeks; it stimulated their resistance to political and cultural domination by foreigners who did not speak their language or behave as was thought proper in their culture. Scholars have been slow in recognizing the enormous role played by the Persian invasions in stimulating Greek culture to great heights of glory and creativity in art, music, literature, poetry, philosophy, politics, rhetoric, historiography, mathematics, geometry and astronomy in the period immediately following the Persian Wars. I have no reason to think otherwise than that post-Enlightenment European scholars generally exhibit a great unwillingness to acknowledge Europe's debts to Asia. They forget what is acknowledged by learned Greeks, that the Greek civilisation owes much to Babylon, Syria and Egypt.

It was the same pattern in India in the wake of the Macedonian's rape of the Indus valley. The Greeks learned much from the Indians, mainly in philosophy and metaphysics, Indians began to be influenced more by Greek art, sculpture and drama than by Greek philosophy as such, which the Indian philosophers acquired some knowledge of, but found little reason to admire profoundly.

Early Greek religion had sages and seers, but no organized hierarchical structure. It had its oracles and soothsayers, but nothing like the Prophet or the Messiah as in the semitic religions. Hellenism developed various rituals and sacrifices; Neoplatonism developed its own theurgy, but most Neoplatonists simply went along with one or other of prevailing cults: the Eleusinian mysteries, the Dionysian Cult, and the more rational Orphic Cult. Plotinus, probably supported the Orphic cult.

Plotinus was a vegetarian. Vegetarianism was part of the Orphic tradition. He went into a seance in the Iseum or Temple of Isis, and a god appeared to him and held converse with him. Unlike us Moderns, Plotinus shared the belief of his fellow Hellenists in the existence of a world of gods.

The points to be emphasized here are two:

1. Insofar as Plotinus is a Hellenist, he is under heavy Oriental influence. This applies to his teacher Ammonius Saccas also. This is particularly evident in Numenius the Neo-Pythagorean of Apamea (2nd century), with whom Plotinus shared many ideas. It is even more evident in the thought and practice of Plotinus' successors in the Neoplatonic tradition.

2. The attempt to make Plotinus totally independent of Oriental influences seems more of an Occidental prejudice than a scholarly proposition based on the evidence. The West cannot lay any such monopoly claims to Plotinus. He belongs to the heritage of the whole of humanity, and he is rejected mainly by dualist Christians

and by devotees of the European Enlightenment's persistent superstition, the exclusive reliance on Critical Philosophy. Plotinus never belonged to the isolated Occident which in fact never existed. European culture developed historically by heavy borrowing from Babylon, India, Syria and Egypt, perhaps also from Iran and Palestine, and Plotinus drank deeply from that composite, creative, cosmopolitan culture of the Mediterranean, which today belongs to the world's common heritage.

It is in this context that many of the participants felt that it was a waste of time to discuss the question about "Oriental" influence on Plotinus. We found it much more useful to examine the affinities and differences between mainstream Indian thought and Plotinus.

I. Plotinus and Indian Thought - Some Primary Divergences and Affinities

1.   The Soul: We became aware that the primary area in which to explore the question of Affinity/Divergence between the Plotinian category structure and that of Indian thought in general was the conceptualisation of the ψυχή[4] or the Soul rather than that of the *One* which after all is strictly nonconceptualisable in both traditions.

The Plotinian Soul (ψυχή) is basically Aristotelian-Platonist, and does not easily fit into the categories in which Indian thought conceived the parallel expression *jivatma*. The First *Ennead*, in Porphyry's arrangement, begins with a discussion of the Soul. It is basically *Form* or εἶδος. It gives form to body but does not receive anything from the body. It is a simple, non-composite substance, as is also the *jivatma* in India. Soul and soulness do not exist independently. To be Soul is to exhibit soulness. Tò ψυχή is identical with τo ψυχῇ εἶναι. The soul cannot thus be described in terms of its composite qualities, since it is simple. The 'procession' or coming forth or origin of the ψυχή is from the *One*, through the *Νοῦς*, born into the world of multiplicity, located in the universe generated by the *World-soul*. This *World-soul* or *Soul of All* is also generated by the *Nous*, as is the human soul, but the latter is not derived from the *World-soul*. It must make the return journey, the ἐπιστροφή, back to the *Νοῦς* and through the *nous* to the *One* (τo ἕν). Professor Mukhopadhyaya argues here that the Samkhya doctrine of the coming forth of multiplicity from the non-conscious *Pradhana*, and of consciousness or *Purusa* from the *One* is a process of Emanation. This can be debated. Nothing like this procession-recession of everything from the *One* and back to the *One*, is conceived in the Indian tradition as far as I know. Pralaya-Vilaya or expansion-contraction, yes, but not exactly proodos-epitrophe, or emanation-return or procession-recession.

The soul of Plotinus is *sui generis*. It is both indivisible and divisible, or μεριστὸς ἀμέριστος, unlike anything else. Indian thought offers no explicit parallel to this conception of the soul or *Jivatma* being *sui generis* or divisible-indivisible; perhaps some aspects of Samkhya imply it.

Nor would it be easy to find something like the Soul as one of the Three Principles of Plotinus in the Indian Tradition. For the Indian tradition the *Javatma* cannot be a distinct hypostasis at all. For Plotinus, it is just three, no less, no more: the *One*, the νοῦς and the ψυχή. In *Ennead* II:9 *Against The Gnostics*, Plotinus attacks the Gnostic multiplicity of principles, and insists that the principles have to be three, no more no less. One does not find such a three-fold or quasi-trinitarian Principle *One*, νοῦς and ψυχή in the Indian tradition; of course there are many three-in-ones in the Indian tradition, but not anything like One-Intellect-Soul.

There are, however, affinities between the Plotinian ψυχή and the Indian concept of the *javatma*. The ψυχή does not suffer; pathè or suffering belongs strictly to the body. Here Plotinus is more Aristotelian than Platonist, yet somewhat original. He makes the distinction between the higher and lower souls. But how can he make that kind of distinction within the ψυχή which is simple? In order to make the distinction, Plotinus conceives, to this end, a new entity called "the living being" or τὸ ζῷον. It is this entity that is composite, constituted of soul and body. The first *Ennead* is about this composite entity, the living being, rather than about the soul as such.

When we come to the later Neoplatonists, we see a slightly more complex pattern of this soul descended into the world of matter, which is no longer the simple ψυχή, but a composite entity of which the ψυχή is one part. The soul as it descends from the hypercosmic realm acquires its own vehicle, the ὄχημα. According to Iamblichus, the ὄχημα is created by the δημιουργὸς. But the ὄχημα is not the physical body; it has a divine origin; it is not something to be cast away. In fact, in Iamblichus at least, the ὄχημα is indestructible and therefore eternal.

This certainly is not the place for an extended discussion of the concept of ὄχημα; but we note that what theurgy does in Iamblichus is to purify the ὄχημα of the soul, permitting its union with a particular god allocated to it. Then the light of the god shines upon the soul in its ὄχημα and begins the process of the soul's elevation to the gods. Ὄχημα has a parallel in the Indian concept of *sukshma sarira* or ethereal body. In both cultures 'out of body travel' occurs through the ὄχημα or *sukshmasarira*. This non-material body is the vehicle of the soul also for experience in the material world. A comparative study of ὄχημα and *sukshmasarira* is likely to show great affinities as well as some differences.

But Plotinus' discussion of the soul in *Ennead* IV: 2 (Armstrong's IV: 1) is one of the most sophisticated such discussions in literature. The Soul is not a body, not a harmony of non-corporeal natures, not an *entelechy* as Aristotle thought it to be; it belongs definitely to the intelligible world, which in the Platonic tradition, is the home of abiding Reality; it shares in the Divine (τῆς νοητῆς φύσεως, καὶ τῆς Θείας Μοίρας, Armstrong IV:1:5-6). There is no attempt to say that the ψυχὴ is identical with the *One* as in the Indian tradition. Plotinus divides Reality into two classes: one group, the sensible world, is composed of the αἰσθητὰ μεριστὰ καὶ σκεδαστά, or the sensibles, the divisibles, and the perishables. The soul does not belong to this class. But neither does it belong to the other class the οὐδαμῇ μερισμὸν δεχομένη, ὁμερής τε καὶ ἀμέριστοσ, or in no way divisible even conceptually, partless and unpartible, unextended (ἀδιάστατος), without spatial location in anything else. The Soul is not in that class either.

The Plotinian Soul does not belong to the class of sensibles, or to the class of purely intelligibles, but belongs to a third class of its own the divisible-indivisible-at-once nature, (ἡ δὲ ὁμοῦ μεριστὴ τε καὶ ἀμέριστος φύσις, ἥν δὴ ψυχὴν εἶναι φαμέν). This is of course an aspect of the Platonic tradition, where according to *Timaeus* 35 A1-14, the Artificer of the Universe "mixed a third form from both, from the indivisible which is always in the same state, and that which becomes divisible in the sphere of bodies". The Plotinian soul is an intermediary, a frontier being, between the intelligible world and the sensible world. Here of course Plotinus is not speaking of the individual human soul as such, but about the single unique entity called the Soul, in which the All-Soul and the Human Soul participate. A parallel conception to this cannot easily be located anywhere in the Indian tradition, as far as I know.

The body, whether it be the human body or other bodies in the Universe, come into being just as the Soul, so to speak, goes out of itself to take or form a body, according to Plotinus. Without the All-Soul, the Universe as such has no existence. Existence is what the Soul gives to the body.[5] Clearly, Plotinus' conception of the soul is partly original, but its roots are strictly in the Platonic tradition, and it seems to have no parallel in Indian thought.

II. General Discussion

In the course of the discussion in the seminar, some other interesting points came up. Here we can only pick up a few highlights of what was indeed a very rich discussion.

1. From the beginning of our discussion it became obvious that it was difficult to define the scope and limits of what is called Indian thought. We have to include Vedic, pre-Vedic, and Avedic thought, the thought of Brahmanas and Sramanas, the Jain tradition which claims to be both avedic and pre-Vedic, the Buddhist tradition which is certainly Avedic, the great Bhakti tradition in its many different forms, Islamic, Sufi and Sikh thought, recent western liberal and western Marxist thought, as well as Christian and Zoroastrian thought, all of which flourished on Indian soil and have not only made rich contributions to Indian culture and thought, but also form an integral part of every Indian's heritage. We are certainly unable to do justice to the vast ocean of Indian thought as it has developed through millennia. When we try to compare Plotinus or other Neoplatonists with Indian thought, it would therefore be wiser to indicate the particular school of Indian thought one has in mind, rather than Indian thought in general.

2. The question came up also about Neoplatonism being both religion and philosophy. In fact classical thought in India as well as in the Mediterranean region, made no distinction between religion and philosophy. Nor did it make religion a compartment of life, as the civilisation of the European Enlightenment often does. In fact the Critical Philosophy of the European Enlightenment writes off any philosophy with the taint of religion as not philosophy at all, since it is dependent on revelation and not exclusively on human reason. For us Easterners, and I think, for many thinking people elsewhere, this appears to be a persistent and pernicious Western prejudice or superstition, without either scientific or philosophical basis.

We must therefore boldly reject this superstition and take into account the whole religious-philosophical matrix of the Eastern Mediterranean (north, east and south, but not west, of the sea), when examining the thought of Plotinus and later Neoplatonists. The thought-world of Parmenides and Heracleitus, of Pythagoras, Socrates, Plato and Aristotle, of the Skeptics and the Stoics, the Epicureans and to a certain extent the Cynics, was always religious and philosophical at the same time. So was that of Plotinus; any non-religious interpretation of Plotinus would be off the mark.

3. The Asian-African (not to use the expression Oriental) thought-world of Alexandria in the third century was one which had fully assimilated the Greek tradition, but was in the process of reformulating it in many different schools, e.g. in Christian (Clement and Origen), Gnostic (the Nag Hammadi documents), neo-Pythagorean (the Therapeutes), Middle Platonist-Aristotelian (Ammonius Saccas, Numenius), and Stoic-materialist frameworks and categories. Plotinus was not only aware of these schools, but often wrote to question and correct some of the views expressed in these schools. But none of the thinkers of this age made the distinction that some moderns make between Oriental and Occidental. Neither was any of the schools exclusively Oriental or Occidental. The same applies to Plotinus. Plotinus heavily influenced many later systems of perceiving reality, especially Jewish, Muslim and Christian medieval and post-medieval philosophy. All these three traditions are Asian or "Oriental" in origin.

4. Plotinus specially targeted three contending forces in Alexandria and the Roman Empire: Stoic Materialism, Gnostic speculation, and Christian soteriology. There was already much tension in the culture among three approaches to salvation: Theoria, $\Theta εωρία$ and $τὰ μυστήρια$. Plotinus definitely emphasized $\Theta εουργία$ or a vision attained by training the mind. $\Theta εωρία$ on the other hand emphasized acts of worshipping God or a god, rather than mental-intellectual contemplation, through which $κάθαρσις$ (spiritual purification), $ἔλλαμψις$ (inner illumination) and $ἕνωσις$ (becoming one with the Divine) were to be achieved. Many who could not scale the ascents of mental discipline, preferred this way of $\Theta εωρία$ in later as well as even in classical Neoplatonist practice. (Iamblichus, Proclus, and so on.)

Plotinus did not wholly approve the growing practice of theurgy in his tradition. For a true Neoplatonist to practice theurgy is similar to a pure Advaita Vedantin practising a Bhakti cult in India. It is often done, but is very difficult to justify philosophically. As far as the neoplatonist use of theurgy is concerned, Plotinus seems to be an exception in the Neoplatonic tradition as a whole, which was heavily theurgic through and through. Plotinus emphasized Θεωρία or mental contemplation, while the Alexandrian tradition as a whole tended to put more faith in θεουργία and τοὶ μυστήρια; even the Gnostics, who seemed to put more emphasis on a secret γνῶσις and thus to be more intellectually oriented, practised some form of theurgy or ritual.

5. It is specifically in relation to θεουργία that there seems to be a major gap between Plotinus and his successors, most of whom were Asians who put more emphasis on acts of worship than on mental or intellectual exercises. Both Porphyry and Iamblichus made θεουργία central. Plotinus probably practiced some form of θεουργία but refused to give it central emphasis, looking upon θεουργία with a measure of disdain, as good only for the mentally incompetent.

Professor Berchman's paper on "Rationality and Ritual in Iamblichus and Proclus", along with his bibliography, is very significant in this connection. Ritual has its own rationality, different from scientific rationality. Theurgy establishes contact with reality at a level different from that of scientific rationality, effects a different entry into the intelligible world and achieves communion with the divine; this is more obvious in his successors than in Plotinus himself.

6. Since Professor Berchman could not attend the seminar, his paper was not discussed in detail. But when we speak of affinities between Neoplatonism and Indian thought, this aspect of Theurgy and its relation to the Tantric and the Vedic-Sacrificial or Purvamimamsa traditions in India should not be overlooked. What the west pejoratively calls 'magic', as Professor Berchman clearly shows, is a highly rational way of operating upon reality. In India both the Tantric tradition and the Purvamimamsa tradition are basically theurgic in nature. This means that in looking for affinities between Neoplatonism and Indian Thought, Theurgy-Tantrism should receive a fuller treatment than it hitherto has. While it may have been true that at one time western scholarship was rather allergic to any notion of Theourgia (e.g. E. R. Dodds, 1947 and H. Lewy, 1946) things seem to be changing.[6] More recently Professor H. J. Blumenthal of Liverpool has made a significant philological contribution to the discussion in his "From

KU-RU-SO-WO-KO to *Theourgos*: Word to Ritual", in the Liverpool Classical Monthly.[7]

7. We sought to compare Plotinus' One (τὸ ἕν) with the Indian concept of *skamadvitiyam*. In both traditions, the limits of the conceptual are recognized. The conceptual cannot by any means lead us to the *One* of Plotinus, or to the *ekam* of the Hindus. In this most Indian traditions would agree with Plotinus that the conceptual cannot attain to the Transcendent Divine, and that the *One* has to be known in a way other than the conceptual. In Sankara Vedanta, we call it *paravidya* or the knowledge that transcends. Modern critical philosophy has no such category, and this seems to be its basic weakness.

8. Both traditions recognize the key epistemological role of self-purification in attaining to the knowledge of the Divine. While the Plotinian tradition refers to this need of κάθαρσις, the Indian tradition goes to great lengths in working out and prescribing the physical and mental exercises which make one capable of receiving the grace of divine illumination and unity. Not only in the Yoga System of Patanjali, but also in the Bhagavadgita, these systems of *nidhidhyasa* are described at length. It would be a useful study to compare the purificatory disciplines in various Indian schools with the Greek disciplines of self-purification. We can also ask the question whether the European Enlightenment tradition of Critical Rationality also has its own *nidhidhyasa* or κάθαρσις, in terms of training the mind for critical rational thinking.

9. It was suggested that the comparative roles of ἔρως and *bhakti* in the ascent of the soul to the divine would be worth careful study. Equally important would be a comparative study of the role of worship, or Indian *aradhana* and Greek θεουργία (related to the concepts of εὐσέβεια and εὐσεβὴς) in self-purification. Indian Tantrism also bears striking resemblances to Neoplatonic θεουργία. These need careful further study.

10. Both traditions acknowledge that the *One* is beyond all predicates. If the *Good* (τὸ ἀγαθόν), the True (τὸ ἀληθινόν) and the beautiful (τὸ καλὸν) are not predicates of the *One*, what are they? According to Plotinus, the Good is only another name for the *One*, but in no way a predicate.[8] If *Brahman* is *Sat-chid-*

ananda, how are *sad, chid* and *ananda* or *Truth, Consciousness* and *Bliss* related to the predicateless and partless Brahman? The Indian answer would be the same as the Plotinian, namely that these are not predicates, but merely different conceptual formulations of the same reality.

11. We came to the conclusion that there were substantial divergences between the Indian tradition and the Neoplatonic tradition in the question of what constitutes True or Transcendental knowledge. In India *paravidya* or Transcendental knowledge demands overcoming the distinction among knower, known and knowledge, or *jnata, jneya,* and *jnana*. In the western tradition however the distinction between subject and object seems to be regarded as essential for all knowledge. Is this true? What then would be the western understanding of the logic of the infinite wherein all distinctions ought to vanish and all things ought to merge into each other as a single entity?

12. Our discussion on the relation between the *One* and the νοῦς-ψυχή needs to be pursued further. The notion of Emanation, if taken literally, would locate the *One* in time and space, which would make it finite. Emanation (πρόοδος) can at best be taken only metaphorically, to denote the relation between the *One* and the νοῦς-ψυχή. Obviously the *One* is not located in one point in space. It is both infinite, omnipresent and invisible. Would the procession or πρόοδος of the κόσμος νοητὸς or the νοῦς be comparable to the Indian *Samkhya* concept of the *vyakta* or manifest universe as coming forth from the unmanifest (*avyakta*)? Neither the concept of πρόοδος nor that of ἐπιστροφὴ or return, seem compatible with the Indian tradition as a whole. In the Sankhya, the relation between the manifest and the Unmanifest is not spelt out so clearly. What is recognized in both traditions is that the Manifest world of our daily experience has come forth from an Unmanifest Reality, upon which it is contingent. But the Plotinian concept of emanation finds no precise parallel in Indian thought. In Plotinus himself the concept of emanation is not philosophically clear, for emanation is undoubtedly a spatial concept, which cannot be applied to the *One* who transcends space. The analogies which Plotinus gives, like a light-source emanating light or a fragrant substance emanating fragrance, imply a source in space from which the emanation spreads around to the contiguous space. In the case of the *One*, the source is not in

space; the concept of emanation does not help the understanding in relation to the *One* and the *Many*.

13. We had an extended discussion on the relation of any proposition to truth. Certainly propositions are not the only form in which human beings linguistically express themselves. There is always literature and poetry, and many other ways of talking. We agreed that propositions do not grasp the truth fully; this is so in Plotinus and in Indian thought. We saw how language can be used metaphorically as well as poetically, to supplement and clarify propositional expressions of truth. But do metaphors and poetry get anywhere closer to reality than propositions? Perhaps metaphors and propositions have their significance in their power to evoke inner experience in a way propositions seldom can. The perception of ultimate reality however always eludes the linguistic medium in every form. This applies also to concepts like emanation, when used as a description of the relation between the three principles of One, νοῦς and ψυχή. Emanation is a metaphor; it can illuminate us only analogically or metaphorically, not prepositionally.

14. Finally, both in Neoplatonism and in Indian thought, the metaphysics is not functionally as important as the praxis of a discipline or *nidhidhyasa* which leads to enlightenment. The metaphysics both prepares for and conditions the experience; metaphysics arises out of experience as an attempt to conceptualise it. We thought it would be healthy to keep this in mind in all serious philosophical discussion. Critical philosophy's major weakness is this overemphasis on the conceptual and the propositional, and the under-emphasis on discipline or *katharsis*.

We concluded that the only option open to us was to begin planning for another Seminar or conference, in India, with wider participation, on The Neoplatonist and Indian Traditions (not just thought, but including praxis or spiritual disciplines, particularly the Yogic and Tantric traditions) in the near future, with special reference to *Theourgia* and Tantrism. Perhaps we should use one of the Himalayan Ashrams as the venue, and also practice some of these disciplines during the Seminar.

Endnotes

1. Cambridge, Massachusetts, Harvard University Press, 1989, front and back flaps.
2. See E R Dodds, *Numenius and Ammonius*, Entretiens Hardt V, See also Schweitzer, *Plotinus* Intro cols 477-81.
3. Armstrong, *Plotinus*. Vol. I. pp Greek text, 56, 58, Eng. 57, 59.
4. Armstrong, vol. I, Gk p. 8 Eng p.9
5. Armstrong, *Plotinus*. IV: 3:9
6. e.g. see R T Wallis, *Neoplatonism*, passim, esp pp 120-123, 153-157.
7. *Liverpool Classical Monthly*, 1993, pp. 75 ff.
8. See *Enneads* II:ix:1 in "Against the Gnostics"

Plato, Neoplatonism and Their Parallel Indian Ideas

D. P. Chattopadhyaya

Fashions and faith change. Languages and ways of doing philosophy are not constant either. But certain fundamental questions of life appear, disappear and reappear in different forms. If one can raise one's vision above the prevailing currents of Analytic Philosophy, Philosophy of Science and Philosophy of Language, or at least if one can see through the issues dealt with in these contemporary areas of philosophy, one can realize the importance of the largely neglected fundamental questions, tackled by great thinkers like Plato, Aristotle, Plotinus, Aquinas and St. Anselm.

How are Essences and Instances related? How is the relation between Good and Evil to be understood? How does One become Many? How are Being and Becoming, Time and Eternity related to each other? It is interesting to recall that none of these questions is peculiar to one particular culture, form of life or system of philosophy. Their trans-cultural or pervasive presence is itself an intriguing philosophical question. How do you account for the fact that in India, Europe and elsewhere, old, new and renewable answers have been and still are being raised in the course of tackling these questions?

What is there in Essence which makes its self-instantiation possible? Is it intensive or extensive or both? Briefly speaking, the Platonist finds an aptitude for, or propensity to, instantiation in the eternal *Ideas*. Sometimes this attitude has been described as an excess of fulfillment or, metaphorically speaking, Divine Envy. All ideas are systematically subordinate to Goodness and Intelligibility. Unity or oneness of Good finds itself as a system of all unities through an eternal Demiurgic vision which articulates itself in all knowing instantial minds. God as Good realizes and reviews Itself in and through all things and beings. Plato sees all Ideas as patterns of Numbers and these patterns are endlessly and hierarchically replicated in all existent patterns, empirical as well as transcendental.

It will not be out of place here to recall that the Unity of Brahman, referred to in the Vedas, expresses itself as *Rta* and *Satya* in the patterned or law-governed multiplicity of the world. This expression is due to the *Ananda-Sakti* or Brahman itself. And this vedic view has a distinct Platonic ring to it. The relation between the One and the Many conceived in the original Samkhya, attributed to Kapila (not Isvarakrsna's *Sankhyakarika*), and the Vedantic theories developed later on are also insightful exercises purporting to explain the relation between the two spheres of reality and often in terms of a mystic theory of Numbers associated with Pythagoreanism.

Aristotle, Plato's disciple and a dissident Platonist, third-century Neoplatonist Plotinus and his fifth-century successor Proclus developed, in the main, Platonism faithfully, and at places interpreted it critically and creatively in such a manner that the influence of Platonism, thanks to their hermeneutic reconstruction, found its way into Jewish, Christian and Islamic theology and philosophy. The ideas of St. Augustine and Aquinas were largely Platonic, though the latter claimed Aristotle as his chief mentor. The Renaissance Platonism of the Florentine Academy, the Platonism of Seventeenth-century Cambridge Platonists, the dualism of Descartes, the Transcendentalism of Kant, and the Dialectical Idealism of Hegel are all different variations on Platonic themes, written and unwritten.

If the European history of philosophical and religious ideas is thus rooted in the Platonic tradition, those who are fairly familiar with the philosophies and religions of India can see that basic European ideas, orthodox as well as heterodox, are seminally found in the Vedas, Upavedas and the Vedangas. These generalizations are not intended in any way to ignore the significant differences between various trends of thought and forms of religion.

Every culture, like every personality, has in it differing, at times even opposite, traits. The complexity of a system of thought, particularly of interactive sub-cultures within it, with the simultaneous presence of distinct types of theories and practices within the same country and in the same age do not negate their underlying affinity or family resemblance. Different ways of thinking and forms of feeling are mutually supportive and influential, positively or negatively. For example, though Jainism and

Buddhism are opposed to the authority of the Vedas in very many ways, the insightful scholars of Indian philosophies and religions have not failed to detect their interconnections. Even Indian Islamic culture which is regarded by some as alien in character, has absorbed much of, and contributed creatively to, what we call the composite culture of India.

II

From general truths of Platonism let me now try to indicate briefly some of its specifics. Both in the tradition of Platonism and that of India, veritable knowledge, as distinguished from unreliable opinion, is said to be due to discernible subsumption of peculiar instances under a truly universal content. In both traditions Intuitive Reason or *nous* is given more cognitive importance than sense-perception as a source of knowledge or validating criterion.

Aristotle, never completely reconciled to the Platonic theory of the relation between the intelligible and the sensible has expressed his questionings and difficulties in his *Metaphysics*. Related to these difficulties is the Aristotelian account of a substantial notion of matter and a quasi-materialistic conception of mind. It seems that Aristotle could not accept Plato's conception of space and the related conceptions of individuation and instantiation. It is in terms of his view of teleology, not by a Demiurgic vision, that Aristotle offers a theory of upgraded individuality of being, which, being downgraded universality, is related to the materiality of matter and to the immaterial Goodness of Prime Idea or Highest Form.

Plotinus, together with some Neoplatonists like Eudorus, Plutarch and Numenius, tried to reconcile the positive elements of the teachings of Plato and Aristotle. Their central thesis rests on three principles of Being:

1. Super-essential, Super-intelligible One or Good;
2. the Timeless Archetypal Mind or Intellect; and
3. the World-Soul, working as a mediatory principle between the ideas and unifying them as perfect patterns and the changeable world of instances or particulars.

Knowledge of the particulars demands of the knowing subjects that these objects have to be viewed under their appropriate patterns or forms. Mind or Nous is said by Plotinus to be a unity of all things together, and yet not altogether, since each has a separate potency of its own. This proposition echoes the spirit of Plato's *Theaetetus* and that of Aristotle's *De Anima*. The World-Soul, informed by the Supreme One, informs everything in space. And this descent of One in Many is claimed to be *logically necessary*. How? Whatever is perceived as actual is stated to be due to its *possibility* and the *possibility* itself is grounded on some *necessity*. Equally important is the Neoplatonic theory of *logical interpenetration*. Everything is simultaneously something primarily and everything else subsidiarily. The elements of this theory of enormous consequence are culled from *Parmenides* and the *Sophist*. The same theory is found in the Upanishadic Principle that every Self is present in every other self; every other self is present in this self: and all selves are identical or One at bottom.

Another variation of this thesis is to be found in the intramonadicity, intermodacity and the monadic unity, *monadus monadum*, of Leibniz. The movements between One and the Many may be viewed in two related ways:

1. vertical ascent-descent, and
2. horizontal expansion and contraction.

Sometimes this truth is metaphorically expressed in terms of mutual mirrorism and according to the laws of continuity and symmetry.

That the insights of Neoplatonism are not exclusive to the non-religious philosophical is evident in Judaism, Christianity and Islam. The God of all these major religions is recognized as infinitely Perfect or Good, lifted above the world of instances, and the latter depending absolutely on God. Such a notion of God is to be understood in terms of *Being* not *having*, of the essential God and Goodness of this instantial world. The transformation of the tribal Jehovah into the Jewish God is illustrative of the above Platonic principle. The transformation of the tribal deities into One Circle of Kaba Masjid of Mecca may also be viewed in a similar way. God is taken as the most generic of *Being* which shapes the world through the Divine Word or Logos.

The Vedic parallel to this Principle is that Ultimate Reality is the Master Sound (*Nadabrahma*) which individuates itself not only in all distinct audibles but also in all distinct sensibilia. The best available systematization of this view is found in the *Sphotavada* of *Bhatrtrhari* and in the *Sabdadvaitavada* of Mandana Misra. Of course the pre-systematic elements of this view are available in many places of the Vedic literature and grammar. Perhaps it is needless to add here that when I speak of doctrinal parallelism between Neoplatonism on the one hand and Indian thought on the other, the same must not be understood literally but only conceptually. At the same time I must add that these and numerous other parallelisms are not merely doctrinal but also argumental in many cases, at least in their intention.

III

Platonic influence on Christianity is clear from Christian philosophers like Clement, Origen, Gregory and Augustine who flourished in the Third and Fourth centuries. They formulate, understandably in different ways, the already referred to three First Principles of Being as the Trinitarian Unity of Goodness as God, Logos and Matter in its two forms, degenerate and regenerate, descent of God in Matter and ascent of Matter towards God.

Even more strongly Platonism is defended by Denis or Dionysus the Pseudo-Areopagite in the fifth-century. He speaks of Transcendent Primal Unity as beyond the realm of Being and Knowledge and as having nothing to do with Truth, Unity, Godhead, Sonship or Fatherhood. Yet curiously enough, this Transcendent Unity is nameable in very many ways as Good, Beautiful, Luminous, Adorable, etc. The nameability of the Primal Unity is to be understood only in relation to its perception by human beings. In the context of Unity-cum-Humanity one can even speak of mutually contradictory names of the Divine such as "Infinitely Great" and also "Infinitely Small".

In the Upanishads of India one comes across parallel conceptions. Philosophers speak of contradictory aspects of the Supreme Reality. It is said to be nameable and yet also nameless, sensible and yet beyond the reach of all senses, greater than the greatest and, also, smaller than the smallest, static and dynamic at the same time, proximate and distant simultaneously, and *vak* (speech) and yet beyond the ken of speech. The seemingly incompatible names and designations of God or Supreme Reality are indicative of its plenitude of Being which makes it unavailable in its fullness under any category, name or speech.

The fullness of the glory or the perfection of God makes it

difficult for us to think that it does *not* exist within the sweep of space, time and causality and in the mosaic of the ephemeral world. Anselm's ontological proof of God's existence, though well-intended, is ill-formulated in the sense that it takes existence in the instantial sense. It is this weakness of his formulation which has been fully exploited by the pro-empiricist Kant when he tries to refute Anselm's argument by pointing out the important distinction between the *idea* of existence and *existence* as such. It is easy to criticize Anselm because of his pro-Platonic dualistic background. But can Kant himself be fully absolved of this charge? What sustains his proclaimed affinity, not full-blooded unity, between the causal Nature on the one hand, and the transcendental Good and Beauty on the other? What is this *telos* which is credited with the capacity to embrace both the empirical and the transcendental?

It is with relative ease that we can criticize Anselm and Kant for their account of the relation between the World of Ideas and the World of Instances of those very ideas and their experiences in us. But called upon to explain this relation to our scientific as well as spiritual satisfaction, we encounter profound difficulties. If perfect God or Supreme Reality is thought to be incapable of self-instantiation, one can think of another superior God or superior Reality to whom or to which this absent ability could be attributed. But this attribution is itself hypothetical. Because we can never be cognitively sure whether this attributed ability or capacity is in the Highest Reality itself or it is due to will or thought, or both, of human beings themselves. Secondly, if God is thought to be incapable of self-instantiation in the realm of existence or experience, the ontological necessity of postulating another God lands us in the logical fallacy of infinite regress.

The logical or critical scrutiny to which the human thought process is subjected is itself a human conceptual contrivance and, what is even more disturbing, the particular logic used is not unique. Unless the human logic of noncontradiction is accepted as the unique articulation of the Logos itself, the logic of grasping Highest Reality and that of grasping the anaemic ontology of the "shadowy" empirical world cannot be claimed to be one and the same. About the unitarian logic itself grave doubts have been expressed by ancient mystic thinkers like Pythagoras, Plato, all the way down to Sri Aurobindo of our own time. Sri Aurobindo is never tired of reminding us that the logic of the Finite is magic in the Infinite. Interestingly enough, neither the so-called mystic nor the so-called rigorous analytic philosophers can totally dispense with some form of logic, whether, two-valued, three-valued or many-valued.

Both Aquinas and much later Leibniz went deeply into the questions raised above. Unlike Anselm, Aquinas does not take his cues from the Aristotelean argument for the Unmoved Mover to prove the existence of God. Without being vulnerable to the logical fallacy of infinite regress in the quest of God (higher than whom there is no other God) as Supreme Reality, Aquinas maintains that God is essentially *simple* through and through. This simplicity is nothing but the complete identity of God's existence with His essence. God knows no difference native to its own nature, distinction between *what* is what it is, and *that* it is. Aquinas's account of the empirical world is offered in terms of *participation*.. Finite and created objects are what they are by virtue of their participation in God's Nature. God's own Nature *is essential*, i.e., has nothing in it requiring it to be instantiated in the world of objects. The world of objects, unlike God's essential Nature, is said to be *accidental*. Yet the realm of Essence and that of Accidents are united and remain so for ever because of God's Goodness bringing about this coincidence between the said two realms, two from the human perspective, but one and the same from the Divine perspective. Strictly speaking, the human perspective, marked by experiential or instantial plurality, is not different from, or external to, God's simple nature.

IV

This line of argument leads one to the view that the Natural World studied in the empirical and experimental sciences has a unity of its own. Natural kinds are not only mutually harmonious but also reciprocally supportive. Bacon takes enormous pains to show that the laws of Nature are there *in* Nature to be discovered by the knowing mind. The reason why our minds are capable of inductive learning and leaping is that there is an orderliness, partly visible and partly invisible, pervading the whole Nature. The reason why laws of Nature form a unity of their own is due to the fact that nature itself is unitarian in its structure. But this structure cannot be easily discovered by the human mind because of its uncritical subjection to some idols or idle dogmas. By contrast, the Divine mind is free from all blemishes or imperfections and informs the whole of Nature.

Critical of the Aristotelian syllogistic, Bacon defends empirical and experimental induction as the *Organon* to be used for delving into the depths of Natural truths. Instances of Natural laws have to be viewed in their mutual relation and not in isolation. Certainly Bacon was not a Platonist in the received sense of the term but his insistence that the existence of orderliness in Nature is to be discovered by inductive exploration and expansion bears the unmistakable stamp of Platonism.

In Leibniz, another scientific philosopher, the influence of Platonism, mediated by Scholasticism, is clear and distinct. In this theory of harmony, simplicity and universality of knowledge, one can easily discern Platonic concerns. First, he tries to resolve by definition every complex term into simple or indefinable terms. Such indefinable terms are represented by mathematical symbols or logical constants. Secondly, he takes pains to show that the distinction between necessary propositions and contingent propositions, truths of reason and truths of fact, is due to the limitations under which human knowledge works, and that from God's point of view this distinction is not there. The Unity of Divine vision comprehends all kinds of truths, scientific, jurisprudential and even theological in a deductive form and which is claimed to be expressible in a universal language, *universal mathesis*. Thirdly, the ideal of harmony is not epistemological in its origin and character. It is monadological or ontological with its moral and theological implications. He speaks not only of the possible union of all Christian *princes* in a future ideal political order, but also of all *beings*, animate and inanimate, as warranted by the Law of Sufficient Reason. Leibniz's theory of "the best of all possible worlds" is developed under the aspect of God's goodness and all-knowing capacity. Even the evil that we come across in our life is said to be compossible with the Leibnizian view of the best of all possible worlds. God is not forced (none to force him from within or without) to create the best or the unique world, but only the best *possible* one, otherwise God's omnipotence and free choice are compromised by implication.

Unlike Newton, Leibniz maintains that space and time are relative, not absolute, and God's *sensorium*, forms of sense-perception of all things in their succession and coexistence. This idea of externality of things to space and time, is borrowed, on his own admission, from the Schoolmen influenced by Plato. Of the phenomenality of space and time he is persuaded. The shadowy or obscure character of inanimate or material things is due to their situatedness within the framework of space and time. His formulation of the relation between the phenomenal world and its transcendental creator is sure to remind one of the Platonic cave and the distorted shadows cast on its walls by external light. It appears that Leibniz did not succeed in satisfactorily clarifying the relation between the subjective and phenomenal forms of space and time. How the subjective forms of space and time and the things in the objective space and time are related and how both stand related under the aspect of Divinity are some of the questions which have been left unexplored by Leibniz.

It fell to Kant, deeply influenced by Newton, to explain the unity of phenomena available in sensibility through its *subjective* forms of space and time and their affiliation to the Supreme Synthetic and Transcendental Principle of Apperceptive Unity. Kant's subjectivist view of space and time is largely due to Leibniz. Also the unity of *sensibilia* in space and time is rooted in our Transcendental Self and as mediated by two other levels of Unity, of Imagination and of Understanding. Without the transcendental rootedness of the Unity of all sensible objects, the inter-subjective and cognitive shareability of the law-governed world of science remains inexplicable. In brief, the Unity of whatever object in space and time, in existence and succession, could not be known alike and by all the knowing beings without postulating the Apperceptive and Synthetic Unity of the Transcendental Self, a functional presence of God in humankind.

Kant's own interpretation of Plato's Idea makes it clear that he, like Plato, concedes the necessity of recognizing a Supreme Transcendental Principle of Unity for both cognitive and ethical purposes. Also for comprehension of change or flux both Plato and Kant maintain that the transcendental approach is absolutely called for. Without a transcendental principle like "I" or "I think" what is meant by such expressions as "I imagine" and "I understand" remain unintelligible. Thus Kant, echoing Platonism, has tried to reconcile the unity of the empirical and the transcendental, the scientific and the metaphysical.

V

In this concluding section I will briefly refer to two Indian types of thought which may appear Platonic or Kantian in their aim and character but were developed independently in India. But, as we know, the fundamental questions of philosophy and their attempted answers in different times and places, are bound to exhibit a striking similarity.

Both in Vedanta and Samkhya, freedom from error and knowledge as freedom are commended as the supreme *purusartha* or end of life. Pain and suffering associated with the principles of materiality of different ascending grades, *bhutadi*, are obstructive of knowledge and freedom unless they are sublated by appropriate spiritual exercises and the resulting identification with Brahman (in Vedanta) and the reflective discernment (in Samkhya). Reflection itself is a freeing process, both conatively and cognitively, and recognizes the dualism between subject and object. But the being of the object is what it is only in reference to the subject. This reference is expressive of an unconscious teleology in Samkhya. The subject or self as body has its two aspects, material and mental. The mental body in its subtle form may survive the dissolution of the material body. Both aspects of the body are informed of an unconscious teleology through *bhava*. The subjective function of referring to what is *bhogya* (the objective) expresses its teleological rootedness.

The teleological character of *buddhi* (intellect), an evolute of *Prakrti*, itself is evident in its twin manifestations, causal and non-causal. The world of experience in its relation to the perceiving body is the content of thought. The world as *bhogya* (enjoyable or sufferable) is the projection of the feeling body, projection due to unmanifest *gunas*. *Buddhi* is causal as manifestation of *Prakrti* and non-causal in relation to its content. Emerging out of causal nature, *mahat* or *buddhi*, according to Samkhya, can assume the dignity of its non-causal or free-creative projection of the world as its content. Interestingly enough, as the confluence of the causal and the non-causal aspects of Nature, our body proves to be a sort of *tertium quid* between the lower nature (*apara prakrti*) and the upper Nature (*para Prakrti*). The causal body unfolds itself, projects itself and creates what is *bhogya*, the ground of pain and joy.

The actions (*karma*) which project their effects in *bhogya* or experienced (Nature) are manifest in real time. But the reals or evolutes of Nature are nodal in character and therefore in a way distinct from one another. Yet our intellect or *mahat* comprehends them as continuity, projective or constructive continuity. This capability of *buddhi* to see unity in the nodally discontinuous reals, i.e. distinct evolutes, shows its relatively free creative character. That subjection to spatiality and temporality does not, rather cannot, take away the continuity of the twenty-five reals or principles (*pancavimsati tattvas*) is further indicative of the self-leaving capacity of *buddhi* from the phenomenal manifestations or sense-capacities and action capacities of the empirical world.

Of this disengagemental capacity of our *prapanca*, or world-projecting *buddhi* from its own bases, somatic sensibility, active and imaginative, has been elaborately argued by Kant in a related context. Like Kant, Samkhya draws a significant distinction between *I*, on the one hand, and *me* and *my* on the other. The body *qua* body has no cognitive capacity of its own. It is only as the body *of* the self, as embodied self, which can be credited with the capacities of knowing, enjoying, or suffering, that cognition is possible.

Again, like the Kantian dualism, Samkhya, especially pre-*Karika* Samkhya, dualism of *Purusa-Prakrti* lends itself to a pro-monistic, non-mechanical or, positively speaking, proteleological interpretation, not to a forced interpretation. For not only *Purusa* is consciousness but *mahat* also is often conceived in terms of intensity, not extensity, relatively free creativity and implicit teleology. The difference between *Purusa* and *Mulaprakrti*, especially the number-based symmetry and orderliness of its evolutes, is not essential. On the contrary, they are affine, or have mutual affinity. That explains, at least partly, why *Yoga* could bring or review them together under God. The *Yoga* interpretation of Samkhya, as I see it, is not forced. It is like Hegel's reformulation of Kant's in the light of the *Third Critique*.

Of the modern philosophers who have shown commendable originality in interpreting Indian philosophical and religious thought two, i.e., Sri Aurobindo (1871-1950) and K. C. Bhattacharya (1875-1949), deserve special mention. Sri Aurobindo in his integral monism, *Purnadvaitavada*, has assimilated in a critico-creative manner the basic insights of Vedanta and Samkhya. He takes his cue from the Gita[1] and from *Svetasvatara Upanisad*.[2] The ultimate Reality is there in beings indivisible and as if divided. *Purusa* and *Prakrti* are both to be taken as eternal without beginning. But Sri Aurobindo recalls the Upanisadic truths that one must know *Maya* as *Prakrti* and the Master of *Maya* as the Lord of All beings, both indivisible and divided. The Lord of Beings is said to be conscious in all conscious beings. But, at the same time, he is also consciousness in all inconscient things. The One...is master and in control of the many that are passive in the hands of Force-Nature (*Prakrti*). He is the Timeless and Time; He is Space and all that is in space; He is Causality and the cause and the effect; He is the thinker and the thought.[3] It is in this way that *Purnadvaitavada* tries to capture the basic insights of Samkhya in pro-Vedantic idioms. Sri Aurobindo opposes the dichotomous Samkhya construal of Purusa and *Prakrti*. I, as *purusa*, am in communion with all other Purusas under the aspect of Divinity. Nature and Self are nothing but the two aspects of the same Absolute. They form a Unity, a dim analogy of which is to be found in the embodied self. The Self in us, embedded in the symmetry of Nature, not only witnesses all that happens in and around us and all that is experienced and performed by us. In principle it is also reflectively capable of grasping that which makes this unitary consciousness possible and all other lesser unities, mental and somatic.

K. C. Bhattacharya is also not inclined to accept the Samkhya concept of *Purusa* as exclusive *of Prakrti*. He makes use of the universality aspects of Purusa when the egoity (*asmita*) lapses. At a higher stage of development the distinguishability of *purusa-samanya* lapses and thus freedom or *mukti* is realized. But, Samkhya maintains, of this *mukti* the individual as individual is not conscious. Vedanta rejects this conception of unconscious individual *mukti*. *Mukti* is associated with deindividualised consciousness. Samkhya points out that deindividualised consciousness can be attained with the lapse of *buddhi*. At this stage any talk of individual consciousness and its *mukti* makes no sense. This position appears to be very close to the Vedantic one. Both Samkhya and Vedanta thus indicate how both the illusoriness and the reality of the objective world, *Prakrti*, and its phenomena, can be accounted for. Also along the same lines is explained the possibility of disengagement of the world-bound *buddhi* and the resulting attainment of liberation.

To modern scientific ears many of the Indian ideas just mentioned may sound metaphysical and speculative in the bad sense. But some scientifically minded philosophers like B. N. Seal[4] and some philosophically minded scientists like P. C. Roy[5] and K. R. Chakravorty[6] have persuasively argued that these seemingly metaphysical ideas are firmly rooted in the scientific findings of earlier ages and that they are, to a certain extent, consistent with the conclusions of contemporary sciences. For lack of time I do not propose to go into these interesting details right now. But interested scholars will be well advised to look into the metaphysical ideas of the past and compare them with modern scientific theories. This will help us understand both philosophy and science in their proper perspective and, what is more, would enable us to realize how true knowledge is basically relevant to the good life, individual, social and even universal.

Endnotes

1. *Bhagavadgita* XIII:17 and 20
2. Svetasvatara IV:10
3. The *Life Divine*, Book One, Pt. I. Ch. 21
4. The *Positive Sciences of the Ancient Hindus*, Motilal Banarsidass, Delhi, 1895
5. *History of Chemistry in Ancient and Medieval India*, Indian Chemical Society, Calcutta, see also his earlier work, *History of Hindu Chemistry*, Calcutta, 19056.
6. *Science Based on Symmetry*, Firma KLM, Calcutta, 1977.

The Omnipresence of Being, The Intellect-Intelligible Identity and the Undescending Part of the Soul
An Essay on the Dispute about Indian Influences on Plotinus

Atsushi Sumi

The majority of leading Plotinus scholars of the twentieth century maintain that Plotinus' thought can sufficiently be characterized as an authentic unfolding of Greek philosophy, especially of Platonism. A nearly well-known exception among them is Émile Bréhier who puts forward the view that Plotinus might have been influenced by Indian thought.[1] Although Bréhier is not the first proponent of the possibility of Indian influences on Plotinus,[2] his view is very often referred to by those who attempt to undermine this possibility.

Let us review Bréhier's argument briefly.[3] Plotinus' notion of Intellect is ambivalent. On the one hand, Intellect is an articulated system of definite notions, which insures the possibility of having a knowledge of the world and the knowability of reality through reason. On the other hand, it is the universal being in which every distinction between subject and object comes to a complete end. This second feature, "the identity of the self with universal being," is unprecedented in Greek philosophy and must derive from elsewhere. Bréhier is thus led to look for the source of Plotinus' doctrine in the religious speculation of India, especially in Upanishads. Strictly speaking, this claim is not a thesis. Bréhier himself regards it as a hypothesis.[4]

One point must be noted. Bréhier quotes several passages from *Ennead* VI 4-5 for the second feature of Plotinus' conception of Intellect. He then holds that these treatises "can easily be read without any reference to Greek philosophy."[5] This observation compels him to say that "the question concerning the origin of these ideas then requires consideration."[6]

Bréhier's hypothesis was not received with favor by Plotinus scholars of this century and several negative responses to it followed. But here arises a question. Can we estimate that his position was totally undermined? Needless to say, his hypothesis cannot be sufficiently refuted by a mere claim that Plotinus' philosophy must be viewed as an authentic unfolding of Greek thought. Only a few critics directly attacked

Bréhier's argument. For instance, Jonathan Scott Lee, in his paper published in 1982, tries to undermine Bréhier's observation that the treatises VI 4-5 can be easily read without any reference to Greek philosophy.[7] In these treatises, according to Lee, Plotinus thematically deals with two problems, the problem raised in *Parm.* 130e4-131c11, concerning a thing's participation in the Form and the problem concerning the causal theory of Forms. Lee thus concludes that the philosophical import of VI 4-5 can only be determined in the context of the metaphysical tradition of Platonism. His attempt can be seen as a methodologically appropriate objection to Bréhier since he directly attacks the vein of Bréhier's argument.

In this paper, I try to make an objection to Bréhier's argument in a way which can be methodologically appropriate. First, the key passages which are referred to in his argument, VI 5,1,25-26, VI 5,12,16-23 and VI 5,7,1-8[8] and the passage quite relevant to the identity of the self with universal being, VI 4,14,16-23, are carefully analyzed. Through the text analysis, the doctrines which support Plotinus' conception of the self as a universal being are identified; they are the doctrines of the intellect-intelligible identity and of the undescending part of the soul. After that, it is clarified that Plotinus, in these doctrines, tackles the problems which are vital to the fundamental theses in Plato's theory of Forms and yet are not fully worked out in his dialogues. In summary, I would like to undermine Bréhier's view by showing that the texts highlighted in his argument must be interpreted in the context of the Platonic metaphysical tradition. Moreover, my discussion will seriously challenge Bréhier's observation of some ambivalence in Plotinus' doctrine of the Intellect, which serves as the starting point of his argument. In addition, I shall also examine whether or not Lee's objection to Bréhier is completely convincing.

I would like to touch briefly upon the scope of my argument. It is not the possibility of Indian influences on Plotinus but Bréhier's argument for that possibility that I examine in this paper. H. F. Müller, in his article published in 1914, is concerned to show the Hellenic authenticity of Plotinus without refuting the suggestion that Plotinus was influenced by Indian thought.[9] Wolters assesses that Müller's arguments do not count against Bréhier's hypothesis, since he does not deal with the possibility of specifically Indian influences on Plotinus.[10] Indeed I also do not deal with that possibility in this paper. From this, however, it does not follow that my argument does not count against Bréhier's hypothesis; for I refute his argument for the hypothesis. Nevertheless the refutation of Bréhier's hypothesis, even if it is successful, does not necessarily eliminate the general possibility of Indian influences on Plotinus.

I. The Omnipresence of Being

It would be unmistakable to say that the great treatise, which originally consisted of two *Ennead* treatises VI 4 and 5, thematically deals with the omnipresence of immaterial being. In VI 4,14,16-16,47, however, Plotinus slightly deviates from the main theme to the distinction between our higher and lower selves and the explanation of the descent and liberation of the soul in terms of that distinction.[11] After this digression, he proclaims the return to the original discussion about the omnipresence of being in 16,47-48.

Thus, in the beginning of VI 5,1 Plotinus resumes his discussion about the omnipresence of the intelligible being by appealing to the general consent of all men that the god within us is one and the same (1,1-8). This one god is the firmest principle of all that is desired by all things (1,8-14). Insofar as that which is one is led to what is really one by its desire for the good or for itself, and belonging to itself and being itself are the good to its nature, the good exists as being proper to that which is one (1,14-21). Hence the good is being and in being so that it is for each individual in himself (1,21-25). Here the passage, to which Bréhier refers, follows:

> We have not, then (ἄρα), departed from being, but are in it, nor has it departed from us: so (ἄρα) all beings are one (1,25-26, tr. A. H. Armstrong, adapted by A. Sumi).

Bréhier takes this passage with 7,4-8 and regards them as Plotinus' expression of an immediate intuition or experience of the unity of being.[12]

Bréhier's reference to the above passage is inappropriate, because it cannot be a textual warrant for the identity of ourselves with the universal being or the intelligible whole. In VI 5,7,4-8, on the one hand, Plotinus focuses on the true self that goes back to real being (7,1), the Form of Man (6,11-12) or pure souls and intellect united with the whole of real being (VI 4,14,19-20). On the other hand, the omission of the subject of ἀπέστημεν and ἐσμέν in VI 5,1,25 would suggest that Plotinus here does not deal with our higher self: the hidden ἡμεῖς in the present text picks up ἡμῶν in 1,3 and is simply editorial. In the present passage, therefore, he neither establishes the identity of ourselves with the noetic world nor describes an experience of that identity.[13]

In the context of the passage above, Plotinus thematically considers the omnipresence of the intelligible whole. The basic features of his doctrine of the omnipresence of being are definitely Platonic. First of all, it is necessary to understand what Plotinus means exactly by the omnipresence of being. In VI 4,2,1-6 he first distinguishes the true All or the intelligible world and its imitation or the sensible world and then ascribes the latter's being situated in the former to the causal dependence of the latter on the former. We are elsewhere told that the problem concerning the omnipresence of one and the same being is tantamount to the problem of how each of many sensible things is not without share in the same being (7,1-3). The omnipresence of being thus primarily represents the causal relation between the intelligible and the sensible worlds. This causal relation is described in two sorts of terminology, participation and paradeigmatism. In the first place, the sensible world is said to participate in the intelligible world (2,18; 8,10-11; 13,5-6).[14] In the second place, the causal relation must properly be compared to the relation between the original and its image as it occurs in pools or mirrors (9,37-10,17). Moreover, Plotinus holds that the causal relation must not compromise the immutability of the intelligible being. The real being is not affected by the participation of material things in it (8,10-12).[15] Also in the beginning of his discussion about the omnipresence of being, Plotinus distinguishes being from becoming, and stresses the unchangeability of being (VI 5,2,12-16; 3,1ff.).

Plotinus' stance in dealing with the omnipresence of being, as shown above, unmistakably conforms to the essential features of Plato's metaphysics. Needless to say, the distinction between constant being and incessant becoming forms the fundamental scheme of Plato's metaphysics in the middle and late periods of his writing.[16] The unchangeability of being or the Form, distinguished from the process of becoming, is hence maintained consistently through the middle and late periods.[17] It must be considered the basic thesis in the theory of Forms,[18] because the denial of the existence of the immutable Forms, according to Plato, results in the destruction of the possibility, not only of philosophy, but of all discourse.[19] Mainly in the middle dialogues, the causal role of the Form is often described as a thing's participation in the Form. For the causal role of the Form and its immutability to be consistent, Plato defines the minimum requirement for the way of participation: "all other beautiful things partake of (μετέχοντα) that Beauty in such a way that, while other things become and perish, that Beauty neither increases nor decreases in the least, nor is acted upon at all (μηδὲ πάσχειν μηδέν)" (*Symp.* 211b2-5).[20] In his discussion about the omipresence of being, Plotinus faithfully abides by this requirement; the causal relation between the intelligibles and the sensibles must not infringe on the immutability or impassibility of the intelligible beings.

Lee maintains that Plotinus' elucidation of the omnipresence of the intelligible being can serve as a solution to the problem, raised in *Parm*. 130e4-131c11, concerning the notion of participation and thereby that the philosophical import of VI 4-5 can only be determined in the context of the Greek metaphysical tradition.[21] We may survey his discussion briefly. In the *Parmenides*, the problem concerning the notion of participation takes the form of a dilemma: either the Form as a whole is in each of many sensible particulars that partake of it, in which case the Form will be separate from itself (131a4-b2), or only a part of the Form is in each of the sensible particulars, in which case the Form will be divisible (131c5-11). The metaphor of the day proposed by Socrates (131b3-6), though not pursued in the *Parmenides*, suggests a way in which the dilemma can be avoided. In the first place, Socrates' suggestion opens up the possibility of an escape from the dilemma, involving the acceptance of the first horn of the dilemma together with a denial of the Form's being separate from itself. In the second place, the metaphor of the day challenges the propriety of a conception of the relation between the Form and sensible particulars as an ordinary relation between a whole and its parts and provides a means by which the Form-sensible relation can be appropriately conceived. In the spirit of Socrates' metaphor, Plotinus replies to the problem in the *Parmenides* by accepting the first horn of the dilemma with the refusal of its consequence that the Form will be separate from itself. Plotinus' discussion slightly diverges from the interlocution in the *Parmenides* since the former concerns the relation between the intelligible world as a whole and the sensible world, and the latter the relation between the individual Forms and sensible particulars. But Lee regards this difference as merely one of emphasis. Plotinus' responses to the problem in the *Parmenides* are found in VI 4,8,2-45, VI 4,13,6-26 and VI 5,3,1-21. Lee focuses on the third passage as the key text. In VI 5,3,1-21, Plotinus gives a detailed account of the nature of the intelligible world. The Form's divisibility entailed in the second horn of the dilemma is inconsistent with the essential character of the intelligible being. The intelligible world must in its nature remain an integral whole and thereby participation requires the existence of the same thing everywhere, that is, the omnipresence of being. The problem in the *Parmenides* thus stems from Parmenides' failure to understand the nature of being. Lee, however, wonders how VI 5,3 serves as an argued response to the problem concerning participation and simply points out that in that passage Plotinus is acting on "the principle that the best defense is attack."

Lee's argument is not cogent enough on several points. It is difficult to think that Plotinus' doctrine of the omnipresence of being serves as a solution to the problem concerning participation in the *Parmenides*.

In the first place, Lee is not aware that the first horn of the dilemma is not valid for Plato's own theory of Forms and therefore that the metaphor of the day does not hint at any real possibility of avoiding the dilemma. Parmenides' objection in the first horn of the dilemma violates Plato's own formula of a thing's participation in the Form. In *Parm*. 130b2-4 Parmenides asks:

> Have you yourself drawn this distinction you speak of and separated apart on the one side forms themselves and on the other the things that share in (μετέχοντα) them? Do you believe that there is such a thing as likeness itself (αὐτὴ ὁμοιότης) apart from likeness that we possess (ἔχομεν)...? (tr. F. M. Cornford).

To this question Socrates replies affirmatively (b6). In the above passage, participation (μετέχειν) is applied to the relation between the Form and the sensible particular, while possession (ἔχειν) is applied to the relation between the particular thing and the immanent character.[22] Once it is seen that εἶναι ἐν (131a8) is a cognate of ἔχειν in Plato's theory of Forms,[23] it turns out that Parmenides' objection in the first horn of the dilemma misinterprets participation in terms of εἶναι ἐν εἶναι ἐπί.[24] This misinterpretation causes the confusion between the separate Form and its immanent character.[25] This confusion further entails the Form's being separate from itself, insofar as it has been established in 130b4 that the Form itself is separate from its immanent character.[26] The consequence of the first horn of the dilemma, that the Form is separate from itself, precisely means that the Form loses its own ontological status as an immutable Form when it is inadvertently and confusedly identified with its immanent character. This entailed identification finally subjects the constant Form to becoming and perishing and so infringes upon the minimum requirement for the way of participation, as stated in *Symp*. 211b2-5, that the sensible particulars participate in the Form while it remains totally unchangeable. As several scholars point out, the first horn of the dilemma rests on the confusion of two idioms, μετέχειν and εἶναι ἐν or the misconstruction of participation as being-in.[27] Insofar as the first horn is itself invalid for Plato's own theory of Forms, neither Socrates in the dialogue nor Plotinus must be forced to accept it. Thus seen, the metaphor of the day does not suggest any possibility of avoiding the dilemma. Also in the metaphor, what is worse, each of the Forms is said to be in all the sensible particulars (ἕκαστον τῶν εἰδῶν..ἐν πᾶσιν..εἴη, 131b5-6). The metaphor is not free from the confusion and misconstruction in the first horn of the dilemma, so that it cannot be a step in the right direction towards the avoidance of the dilemma.[28]

In the second place, Lee confuses omnipresence and immanence. According to him, Plotinus accepts the first horn of the dilemma that the Form as a whole is in each of the sensible particulars that partake of it, with the denial of the consequence that the Form will be separate from itself.[29] Attempting to establish that participation requires the omnipresence of being as an integral whole, Lee refers to VI 5,3,10: "(the real being) is in many things (ἐν πολλοῖς) at once, existing at the same time as one whole with itself."[30] From these points, he seems to take omnipresence as almost synonymous with immanence. But Plotinus himself does not say that the intelligible being is in many sensible things. Let us glance at VI 5,3,7-15, where he develops the immutability of the intelligible being:

> But if real being is going to be in a state of freedom from affection, it will not be in something else (οὐκ ἐν ἄλλῳ). If, therefore, without departing from itself or being divided into parts or itself undergoing any change, it is in many things at once, existing at the same time as one whole with itself, then, being the same everywhere, it will have an existence in many things: but (δέ) this is being on its own and, again, not being on its own. It remains, then (τοίνυν), to say that it is itself in nothing (ἐν οὐδενί), but the other things participate in it, all those which are able to be present to it and insofar as they are able to be present to it. (tr. A. H. Armstrong, adapted by A. Sumi).

Nowhere in the above passage does Plotinus say that real being is in sensible objects. Rather, he holds that real being, in order to be always itself and not to stand apart from itself (lines 3-4), is in nothing.[31] The immanence of the intelligible being in sensible objects is definitely denied. This denial would clearly indicate that Plotinus does not accept the first horn of the dilemma in the *Parmenides*, where the Form as a whole is said to be in each of many sensible particulars that partake of it. Insofar as he does not accept the first horn, VI 5,3 cannot be considered a chapter dealing with his endeavor to escape from the dilemma. Lee appears to overlook the forces of δέ in line 12 and τοίνυν in line 13. Moreover, the omnipresence of real being is not established in the above passage. Lee observes that there, Plotinus replies to Parmenides' objection in *Parm.* 131a4-b2 by showing that the integral omnipresence of being is a logical consequence of the nature of being.[32] This observation rests on Lee's confusion between omnipresence and immanence and his unawareness of the fact that Plotinus in the above passage rejects the immanence of real being in sensible things.[33]

In the third place, Lee does not succeed in explaining how Plotinus' elucidation of the intelligible world as a whole in VI 5,3,1-8 is relevant to the problem in the *Parmenides*. On the one hand, Plotinus' discussion in VI 4-5 concerns the relation between the intelligible world as a whole and the sensible world. On the other hand, Plato's discussion in the *Parmenides* concerns the relation between the individual Form and sensible particulars. Lee is aware of this difference.[34] He regards this difference as "merely one of emphasis" and explains the reason as follows: "the characterization of the participation relation with respect to one *eidos* ought to be applicable to that relation with respect to all *eide* (i.e., to the intelligible world as a whole)."[35]

It is indeed true that the characterization of the participation relation with respect to one Form is applicable to that relation with respect to any other individual Forms. But this fact does not necessarily insure that the characterization of the participation relation with respect to one Form is applicable to that relation with respect to the intelligible world as a whole.[36] Furthermore, Lee points out that Plotinus' claim of the indivisibility of true being in VI 5,3,1-8 dismisses the second horn of the dilemma, in which a thing participates in a part of the Form.[37] He then summarizes Plotinus' claim: "Hence, participation cannot be explained in terms of the apportionment of parts of the intelligible world to sensible particulars."[38] It is indeed correct to say that the Plotinian intelligible world must not be divided and apportioned to sensible particulars. But we cannot apply the same rule to the indivisibility of the single Form and the intelligible world as a complex whole.[39] Nevertheless Lee appears to rest on the assumption that the indivisibility of the intelligible world as a whole is applicable to the problem concerning the indivisibility of the single Form.

Finally, Lee does not succeed in explaining how a clarification of the nature of the intelligible being can be an appropriate response to the problem concerning participation. As already noted, the crux of the problem is how it is possible to conceive the way of the thing's participation in the Form, the way which does not infringe upon the fundamental thesis in the theory of Forms, namely the Forms' immutability. Hence, the reply to the problem by arguing from the nature of real being commits a *petitio principii*. Lee's unawareness of this fact stems from his unawareness that participation is illegitimately interpreted in terms of being-in in the first horn of the dilemma. The problem in the *Parmendies* cannot be sufficiently solved by the acceptance of either horn of the dilemma.[40]

In conclusion, VI 5,1,25-26, to which Bréhier refers, cannot be a textual warrant for Plotinus' expression of an immediate intuition of the unity of being or his identification of the self with the intelligible whole. The passage lies in the context dealing with the omnipresence of real being. Lee tries to reconstruct Plotinus' possible response to the problem concerning participation in the *Parmenides* from his account of the nature of the intelligible being, from which the omnipresence of that being results. But this attempt is not successful. Nevertheless, the omnipresence of true being for Plotinus primarily means the causal dependence of the sensible world upon the intelligible, which forms the basic scheme of Plato's metaphysics. Furthermore, Plotinus defends the fundamental thesis in Plato's theory of Forms, namely the Forms' immutability, by making the notion of omnipresence distinct from immanence.

II. The Identity of Self with the Intelligible Whole

As already mentioned, Bréhier's hypothesis of Indian influence on Plotinus is based on his observation that the view of the identity of the self with universal being is unprecedented in Greek philosophy. Let us see another passage to which Bréhier refers in developing this observation:

> Now it is because you approached the All and did not remain in a part of it, and you did not even say of yourself "I am just so much," but by rejecting the "so much" you have become all yet even before this you were all; but because something else came to you after the "all" you became less by the addition: for the addition did not come from being you will add nothing to that but from non-being (VI 5,12,16-23, tr. A. H. Armstrong).

In this passage, Plotinus explicitly speaks of the identity of the self with the intelligible world. But his explanation is purely descriptive. The reason seems to be that the above passage lies in the context dealing with "a bit of encouragement (τινων καὶ παραμυθίων)" (11,5) for the solution to the problem of how the unspaced can stretch over all the body.[41] The identity of the self with the intelligible world seems to be based on the doctrines of the substantial identity of Intellect and intelligible objects and of the undescending part of the soul. The notion of the self as the intelligible world is satisfactorily established insofar as the self is identified either with Intellect, which comprises the totality of the intelligible objects in itself, or with the undescending part of the soul which is very intimate to such an all-inclusive Intellect. In the subsequent discussion, I shall clarify that these doctrines are both motivated by the problems left unsolved in Plato's philosophy.[42]

A. *The Identity of Intellect and the Intelligible Objects*

In the third passage to which Bréhier refers, Plotinus explicates the identity of ourselves with universal being in terms of "true knowledge":

> For we and what is ours go back to real being and we ascend to that real being and to the first which comes from it, and we think (νοοῦμεν) those beings; we do not have images or imprints of them. But if we do not, we are those beings. If then we have a part in true knowledge (ἀληθινῆς ἐπιστήμης), we are those; we do not apprehend them as distinct within ourselves, but we are within them. For, since the others, and not only ourselves, are those, we are all those. So then, being together with all things, we are those: so then, we are all and one (VI 5,7,1-8, tr. A. H. Armstrong, adapted by A. Sumi).

As Armstrong notes, this passage is the clearest explanation of Plotinus' statement that we are each of us the intelligible universe, as stated in III 4,3,22 and IV 7,10,34-36.[43] Plotinus here does not seem to distinguish fully the intelligible being and the pure soul which always remains in the noetic world (ἐκεῖνο καὶ τὸ πρῶτον ἀπ' ἐκείνου), (line 2). Hence it is adumbrated that νοεῖν (line 3) is applicable to the undescending part of the soul. This point is fully considered in the next section.

In the above passage, "true knowledge," through which we are intelligible beings, means intellection, directed to those beings, which is free from images or imprints of them (line 3). According to Plotinus, an intuitive and immediate knowledge of intelligible beings is insured only by the substantial unity of Intellect and its objects. In fact, "true knowledge" elsewhere signifies the intellect-intelligible identity. In attempting to avoid the tendency to interpret the intellect-intelligible identity in terms of the Middle-Platonic view that the Forms are hypostatized by divine intellection,[44] Plotinus writes as follows:

> But if someone were to say that "in immaterial things knowledge and the thing are the same," one must understand what is said in the sense that it (means)...that the thing itself when it is without matter is object of intellection and intellection, ...intellection in the sense that the thing

itself, being in the intelligible, is nothing else but intellect and knowledge. For the knowledge is not directed to itself, but the thing there makes the knowledge, which does not stay like the knowledge of a thing in matter, to be different: this is true knowledge (ἀληθινὴν ἐπιστήμην): this is not an image of the thing but the thing itself (VI 6,6,19-30, tr. A. H. Armstrong, adapted by A. Sumi).

"True knowledge" represents the unity of Intellect and the intelligible objects. Also in the above passage, "true knowledge" is said to involve no image of the knowable thing. Two passages above cited show that the identity of the self with the intelligible world is based on the substantial unity of Intellect and intelligible objects.

What is the motive for Plotinus' doctrine of the intellect-intelligible identity? What problem does he work out with this doctrine?

In V 5,1, Plotinus devotes the entire chapter to the defense of the intellect-intelligible identity.[45] His argument is a negative one against the claim that the intelligible objects lie outside Intellect.[46] According to Plotinus, the greatest absurdity of this claim is that it inescapably causes Intellect to contemplate images of its objects, but neither the objects themselves nor the truth of them, and thereby to be deceived (lines 50-61). For Intellect's infallibility to be sufficiently defended, therefore, the objects must be placed within Intellect.[47]

"True knowledge," which is said to be free from images of its objects in VI 5,7,1-8, is thus embodied by the intellect-intelligible identity which does not involve any image of object, making Intellect capable of attaining always the truth of its objects.

As several critics remark, the intellect-intelligible identity concerns the exigencies of intellectual knowledge compared with the character of sense knowledge and both the possibility and modality of self-knowledge.[48] But the motive for the conception of the intellect-intelligible unity would not be exhausted by the exigencies that have occurred in Plotinus' own system of philosophy. In concluding his argument in V 5,1, he explicitly mentions the definite position that must be defended by the intellect-intelligible unity:

> But, since one must bring in knowledge and truth and watchfully preserve real beings (τὰ ὄντα) and the knowledge of what each thing is (γνῶσιν τοῦ τί ἕκαστόν ἐστιν) but not the knowledge of what it is like (ποῖόν τι ἕκαστον), since (if we only had that) we should have an image and a trace of real beings, and not possess and live with and be fused with real beings themselves (V 5,2,4-8, tr. A. H. Armstrong, adapted by A. Sumi).

Plotinus here employs Plato's distinction between τὸ ὄν or τὸ τί and τὸ ποῖόν τι (*Epist.* VII 342e7-343a1). This distinction is made among five kinds in such a way that the former corresponds to the Form itself as ὃ δὴ γνωστόν τε καὶ ἀληθῶς ἐστιν ὄν (342b1) and the latter to a name, a definition, an image and a knowledge of that Form. "To preserve real beings and the knowledge of what each thing is" thus means to defend the existence and the complete intelligibility of the Forms. Notice that the incorrigibility of Intellect is inseparable from the complete intelligibility of the Forms. In Plato, as already seen, the denial of the existence of the immutable Forms results in the destruction of the possibility, not only of philosophy, but of all discourse (*Parm.* 135b5-c2), so that the immutability of the Forms must be regarded as the fundamental thesis in his theory of Forms. The possibility of philosophy and other significant discourse, however, cannot be safeguarded solely by the positing of immutable Forms. Plato himself seems to have been aware of this point:

> The result is that the hearer is perplexed and inclined either to question the Forms' existence, or to contend that, even if they do exist, they must certainly be unknowable (ἄγνωστα) by our human nature (*Parm.* 135a3-5, tr. F. M. Cornford, adapted by A. Sumi).

Even if the existence of the immutable Forms is admitted, the denial of their knowability will destroy the possibility of philosophy and other discourse. Hence, the existence of the invariable Forms is the fundamental thesis and their intelligibility the second-fundamental thesis in the theory of Forms. In fact, "the friends of Forms" in the *Sophist* maintain both theses (246b7-8, 248a11-12). But Plato nowhere gives a definite account of how intellect, human or divine, is related to the Forms in the occurrence of intellection. Those philosophers who wish to defend the fundamental position of the theory of Forms cannot avoid drawing a clear picture of the intellect-intelligible relation that not only coheres with the Forms' immutability but insures their complete intelligibility.[49] Hence Plotinus seems to say that we need to maintain the intellect-intelligible unity to preserve not only real beings themselves, but the knowledge of what each of those real beings is.

In summary, Plotinus' notion of the self as the intelligible whole is supported by his doctrine of the intellect-intelligible identity. This doctrine is motivated by his attempt to solve the problem of what relation between Intellect and the Forms coheres with the Forms' constancy and insures their complete knowability. This is the central problem, in Plato's theory of Forms, which has not been fully worked out by Plato himself.[50]

The starting point of Bréhier's argument for Indian influence on Plotinus is his observation of some ambivalence in Plotinus' doctrine of Intellect; on the one hand Intellect is an articulated system of definite notions which can be grasped through reason, on the other hand the subject is indiscriminately identified with all objects on the level of Intellect. But rather, our discussion indicates that Plotinus' doctrine is totally free from such ambivalence, because the knowability of real beings must be based on nothing other than the identity of the noetic subject and the intelligible objects. Therefore it turns out that Bréhier's argument starts from his misunderstanding of the basic features of Plotinus' doctrine of Intellect.

B. The Undescending Part of the Soul and Intellection

As already seen, in VI 5,7,1-8 the systematic connection between the undescending part of the soul, referred to as "the first which comes from real being," and the identity of the self with the intelligible whole is not fully explained, but simply hinted at. How is the undescending part of the soul related to this identity? The following passage, which Bréhier does not adduce, clearly shows the bearing of the conception of the self as the noetic world upon the undescending part of the soul:

> But we who are we? Are we that real being or that which draws near and comes to be in time? No, even before this becoming to arise we were there, men who were different, and some of us even gods, pure souls (ψυχαὶ καθαραί) and intellect united with the whole of real being; we were parts of the intelligible, not marked off or cut off but belonging to the whole; and we are not cut off even now. But now another man, wishing to exist, approached that man (VI 4,14,16-23, tr. A. H. Armstrong, adapted by A. Sumi).

Here, as does in VI 5,12,16-23, Plotinus speaks of the addition of lower self to a higher one. In the above passage, "the first which comes from real being" (VI 5,7,2) is specialized as "pure souls." From the sentence οὐδὲ γὰρ οὐδὲ νῦν ἀποτετμήμεθα in lines 21-22, "pure souls" are identified as the highest part of the soul that does not leave the intelligible world,[51] the part which belongs also to individual souls.[52] While the undescending part of the soul is discussed by many scholars, it is sufficient for the present inquiry to point out that the cognitive activity of this part is non-discursive intellection.[53] In the undescending soul, there are genuine kinds of knowledge (αἲ..ὄντως ἐπιστῆμαι) that are each and all of the intelligible objects and have intellection within themselves (V 9,7,4-8). The undescending part of the soul is very akin to Intellect in its nature and activity.[54] Therefore, taking VI 4,14,16-23 together with VI 5,7,1-8, we can conclude that the identity of the self with the intelligible world is based also on the nature of the undescending part of the soul which exercises intellection and always attains "true knowledge" identical with the intelligible objects.

What bearing does the undescending soul have upon Plato's philosophy? As Blumenthal points out, the undescending soul gives an account of how men can know the Forms.[55] As mentioned repeatedly, the complete intelligibility of the Forms is the second-fundamental thesis in Plato's theory of Forms; the Forms must be knowable precisely "by our human nature" (*Parm.* 135a5). Intellection is one of παθήματα ἐν τῇ ψυχῇ γιγνόμενα (*Rep.* 511d7-8). Again, "the friends of Forms" claim that we have cognitive intercourse with the Forms "by means of the soul through reflection (διὰ λογισμοῦ δὲ ψυχῇ)" (*Soph.* 248a11). Although Plato does not say that the rational part of the soul always remains in the realm of the Forms, the Plotinian undescending soul does not seem to be alien to Plato's philosophy. Plato suggests the possibility of the soul in her purity to be in perpetual contact with real being (ἀεὶ μετ' ἐκείνου τε γίγνεται, *Phd.* 79d3).[56] In sum, Plotinus' theory of the undescending part of the soul certainly concerns the knowability of the Forms, the second-fundamental thesis in Plato's theory of Forms.

Lee attacks Bréhier also with regard to the weight of Plotinus' treatment of the universal soul in the treatises VI 4-5.[57] Lee points out a misdirection of emphasis in Bréhier's view of the main task of VI 4-5; Bréhier regards it as the elucidation of Plotinus' doctrine concerning "the relations of the individual soul to the universal Soul."[58] Lee notices that the doctrine of the universal soul he calls it the doctrine of monopsychism plays an especially significant role in VI 4,14-15. But he estimates that the doctrine comes up in Plotinus' analysis of eidetic causation and supposes, by referring to VI 5,9,1-13, that the doctrine is devoted to the explanation of the intersubjective accessibility of the sensible world. Lee's view, however, is not tenable. In the first place, he overlooks the context of VI 4,14. As the query in VI 4,14,16-17 indicates, the previously considered passage, VI 4,14,16-23, primarily concerns the inquiry into the true self of the human person, but does not come up in the elucidation of eidetic causation.[59] Again, the final sentence of the treatise (16,48) marks the divergence of Plotinus' preceding discussion from the main theme of the treatise, namely the omnipresence of real being which denotes the causal dependence of the sensible world upon the intelligible. In the second place, it is apparently difficult to read the intersubjective accessibility of the sensible world into VI 5,9,1-13. This passage simply deals with the unity of the productive cause of the sensible realm. In light of the force of τοίνυν in line 13, the sentence καὶ πᾶσαι αἱ ψυχαὶ τοίνυν μία (lines 12-13) merely points to the unity of life on which the sensible world depends (lines 10-12) and thereby does not imply such a unity of souls that insures the intersubjective accessibility of the sensible world. In addition, Plotinus' account of the true self of the human person in VI 4,14,16-23 is not strictly monopsychic; the undescending soul is mentioned in plural (ψυχαὶ καθαραὶ, line 19). Lee points out Bréhier's failure to place the problem of monopsychism within the scope of the problem of eidetic causation and participation. As shown above, however, his argument against Bréhier is not convincing enough.

III. Conclusion

We have critically examined Bréhier's argument for his hypothesis of Indian influence on Plotinus through the careful analysis of Plotinus' texts referred to in his argument. It has been pointed out that Plotinus' conception of the self as the intelligible whole, which Bréhier attempted to explain in terms of Indian influence on him, is supported by the doctrines that are definitely motivated by the problems concerning the basic theses in Plato's theory of Forms. We now conclude our inquiry by saying as follows.

In the first place, the passage VI 5,1,25-26, referred to by Bréhier, does not deal with the identity of the self with the intelligible world. The passage is in the section where Plotinus thematically considers the omnipresence of true being. Although Lee, arguing against Bréhier, emphasizes the Hellenic purity of Plotinus by claiming that the omnipresence of real being suggests Plotinus' response to the problem concerning participation in Plato's *Parmenides*, his attempt is not fully successful. Nevertheless the omnipresence of true being denotes the causal dependence of the sensible world upon the intelligible, which delineates the basic scheme of Plato's metaphysics. Insofar as this causal relation presupposes the separateness of the intelligible beings from the realm of becoming, which confirms the constancy of the intelligible Forms, the omnipresence of real being is inseparably linked with the fundamental thesis in Plato's theory of Forms, the immutability of the Forms.

In the second place, the identity of the self with the intelligible universe is supported by the doctrine of the intellect-intelligible identity.

The doctrine represents Plotinus' reply to the problem raised and yet unsolved in Plato's philosophy, that is, what relation between Intellect and the Forms can insure the latter's complete intelligibility. This problem precisely concerns the second fundamental thesis in Plato's theory of Forms, the complete knowability of the Forms.

Finally, the identity of the self with the intelligible cosmos is also supported by the doctrine of the undescending part of the soul which is very intimate to Intellect. The doctrine provides an explanation of how men can know the Forms and thereby safeguards the second-fundamental thesis in Plato's theory of Forms, the Forms' knowability *to us*.

Although our argument results in the disclosure of Plotinus' serious endeavor to defend the basic theses of Plato's theory of Forms, this result does not count against the general possibility of Indian influences on Plotinus. Wolters rightly remarks:

> There is overwhelming evidence that Plotinus lived and moved in the horizon of the Greek philosophical tradition, but there is no evidence that he was a prisoner of it.[60]

The complete intelligibility of being, which Plotinus' doctrine of the intellect-intelligible identity puts forward, urges us to understand thoroughly the complete fact of our world by abandoning dogmatic attitude towards foreign traditions of culture and religion and then continuing untiringly our intellectual and ethical inquiry in the universal horizon. If Plotinus were to be confined in the self-closed world of Greek philosophy, the vital force of his philosophy would remain dormant. One of the remarkable features of Plotinus' philosophy as the basis of a viable *Weltanschauung* seems to me to reside in its potential openness to various cultural and religious traditions.

Endnotes

1. É.Bréhier. *The Philosophy of Plotinus*, translated by J. Thomas (Chicago: The University of Chicago Press, 1958), pp.106-131.
2. The possibility of Indian influences on Plotinus was entertained by several scholars of the nineteenth century. See A. M. Wolters, "A Survey of Modern Scholarly Opinion on Plotinus and Indian Thought," in *Neoplatonism and Indian Thought*, ed. R. B. Harris (Albany: State University of New York Press, 1982), pp.294-295.
3. For a rough sketch of Bréhier's argument, I refer to Wolters' summary of his view. See A. M. Wolters, *op.cit.*, p.298.
4. É. Bréhier. *Op.cit.*, p.118.
5. É. Bréhier. *Op.cit.*, p.111.
6. *Ibid.*
7. J. S. Lee. "Omnipresence, Participation, and Eidetic Causation in Plotinus," in *The Structure of Being: A Neoplatonic Approach*, ed. R. B. Harris (Albany: State University of New York Press, 1982), pp.90-103.
8. These passages are cited in É. Bréhier, *op.cit.*, p.110.
9. H. F. Müller. "Plotinische Studien II: Orientalisches bei Plotinos?" *Hermes* 49 (1914):70-89.
10. A. M. Wolters. *Op.cit.*, p.298.
11. Plotinus' argument in VI 4,14,16-16,47 does not totally diverge from the central problem of the treatise. As seen in 14,1-2, the omnipresence of the indivisible life naturally raises the problem of the particularization of the soul and the difference in the soul's disposition.
12. É. Bréhier. *Op.cit.*, p.110. Bales finds Plotinus' denial of the meontological character of the One in 1,21-26. See E. F. Bales, "Plotinus' Theory of the One," in *The Structure of Being: A Neoplatonic Approach*, ed. R. B. Harris (Albany: State University of New York Press, 1982), pp.43-44. This interpretation is evidently untenable, because τὸ ἀγαθόν (line 20) indicated by αὐτό (line 21) does not mean the transcendent Good.
13. Bréhier observes that we are dealing with an experience, but not a rational explanation, in the present passage. Is this observation accurate? The repeated occurrence of ἄρα in 1,25-26 would rather adumbrate that a rational argument is developed in 1,24-26. The argument in 1,24-26 is elaborated on as follows:

    (a) The good is being and in being (1,24).

    (b) Belonging-to-itself and being-itself are the good to the nature of one being (1,18-19).

    (c) Then the good is for each individual in himself (1,24-25) (by (a) and (b)).

    (d) Therefore (ἄρα) we have not departed from being, but are in it, nor

has it departed from us (1,25-26) (by (a) and (c)).
(e) (b) means being-one (1,20).
(f) Therefore (ἄρα) all beings in ourselves are one (1,26) (by (c), (d) and (e)).
The above explanation shows that the passage under discussion just concerns the rational argument for the unity of being.

The objection may be made that the occurrence of ἑαυτῷ in 1,24 implies that "we," the subject of ἀπέστημεν and ἐσμέν is our higher self, that is, either pure soul or intellect. But this objection is not convincing enough. As already pointed out, the subject of two verbs is omitted. It would be reasonable to think that our higher self enters the scene with τὸ ἡμέτερον καὶ ἡμεῖς in 7,1.
14. See also VI 5,3,14. As we shall see, this use of terminogy lacks rigidity in terms of the original use of the idiom in Plato.
15. With Henry-Schwyzer, Harder, Cilento and Armstrong, Gollwitzer's emendation πάσχοντος is read for the MSS παντὸς in 8,11. The emendation is justified by the force of γάρ in 8,12.
16. *Rep.* 525b5-6, c4-6, 526e6-7, 534a2-3; *Soph.* 248b6-c2; *Tim.* 27d5-28a4, 29c3. See also *Phd.* 79c2-d7, 80b1-5; *Symp.* 211a1. With several critics, we take "the friends of Forms" of the *Sophist* as representing Plato's own theory in the middle period. See F. M. Cornford, *Plato's Theory of Knowledge* (London: Routledge & Kegan Paul, 1935; reprint ed., Indianapolis: Bobbs-Merrill, 1957), pp.243-244; W. D. Ross, *Plato's Theory of Ideas* (Oxford: Clarendon Press, 1951; reprint ed., Westport, Conn.: Greenwood Press, 1976), p.107; P. Seligman, *Being and Non-Being: An Introduction to Plato's Sophist* (The Hague: Martinus Nijhoff, 1974), p.34; R. S. Bluck, *Plato's Sophist*, ed. G. C. Neal (Manchester: Manchester University Press, 1975), p.94. For the list of various views and their proponents, see W. D. Ross, *op.cit.*, pp.105-106; G. Martin, *Platons Ideenlehre* (Berlin: Walter de Gruyter 1973), p.153. For more detailed discussion for identifying "the friends of Forms," see my dissertation "The One's Knowledge in Plotinus" (Ph.D. dissertation, Loyola University of Chicago, 1993), pp.28-29.
17. The immutability of the Forms is emphatically asserted by "the friends of Forms" in the *Sophist* (248a12). This section is regarded as the reminiscence of *Phd.* 79d5 and 80b2-3. See F. M. Cornford, *op.cit.*, p.244, note 1; H. -E. Pester, *Platons Bewegte Usia* (Wiesbaden: Otto Harrassowitz, 1971), p.42. The Forms' immutability has never been abandoned up to the *Seventh Letter* (342c2-4).
18. A systematized theory of Forms is nowhere found in Plato's dialogues. By "the theory of Forms" we temporarily mean a form of insight based on the single hypothesis positing constant Forms. The fundamental hypothesis is that "there is a beautiful alone by itself (τι καλὸν αὐτὸ καθ' αὑτὸ) and a good, and a great, and so with the rest of them" (*Phd.* 100b5-7). As ἐκεῖνα τὰ πολυθρύλητα in b4-5 refers back to the Forms mentioned in the recollection argument and the

kinship argument, the location τι καλὸν αὐτὸ καθ' αὐτὸ quite certainly implies the unchangeability of that hypothetical entity. Hence the immutability of the Forms constitutes the fundamental hypothesis, rather than a thesis, of Plato's theory of Forms.

19. *Parm.* 135b5-c2. Cornford observes that Parmenides here accepts "the fundamental thesis of Plato's theory" (*Plato and Parmenides* [London: Routledge & Kegan Paul, 1937], p.100).

20. For the impassibility of the Forms, see also *Epist.* VII 342c3. Apelt correctly associates *Symp.* 211b4-5 with the refusal, by "the friends of Forms" in *Soph.* 248d10-e4, to consider intellectual knowledge in terms of acting and being acted upon. See *Platonis Sophista* recensuit Prolegomenis et Commentariis instruxit O. Apelt (Leipzig: B. G. Teubner, 1897; reprint ed., New York: Garland, 1979), pp.151-152.

21. The following sketch of Lee's argument is based on his "Omnipresence, Participation, and Eidetic Causation in Plotinus," in R. B. Harris, *The Structure of Being: A Neoplatonic Approach*, pp.90-95.

22. In the hypothesis argument of the *Phaedo*, a perfect consistency is seen in the usage of these two idioms. See N. Fujisawa, "Ἔχειν, Μετέχειν, and Idioms of 'Paradeigmatism' in Plato's Theory of Forms," *Phronesis* 19 (1974):45. Also in *Parm.* 130e5-6, participation is understood as applying to the thing-Form relation. Some may observe that Plato inadvertently applies ἔχειν to the thing-Form relation in 130d9. But this observation is not accurate because 130d8-9 ἃ νυνδὴ ἐλέγομεν εἴδη ἔχειν simply refers to 130d4 εἶδος...τι αὐτῶν οἰθῆναι εἶναι.

23. For the cognate idioms of ἔχειν, see N. Fujisawa, *op.cit.*: 40; W. D. Ross, *op.cit.*, p.228. See also Aristotle, *Met.* 1023a23-25.

24. εἶναι ἐν, 131a8, b1-2; εἶναι ἐπί, 131b9, c3.

25. Supposing that in the present passage Parmenides takes the locution accompanied with εἶναι ἐν and εἶναι ἐπί in the most materialistic sense, Allen points out his confusion between a physical relation and a metaphysical relation. (*Plato's Parmenides* [Minneapolis: University of Minnesota Press, 1983], p.120). For the physical sense of εἶναι ἐν, see G. Vlastos, "The Third Man Argument in the *Parmenides*," in *Studies in Plato's Metaphysics*, ed. R. E. Allen (London: Routledge & Kegan Paul, 1965), p.256, note 1. But what Allen means by the "metaphysical relation" is not fully clear. If the metaphysical relation in question implies a transcendence, it will be totally absurd to express the metaphysical relation by εἶναι ἐν since this idiom properly implies an immanence (see W. D. Ross, *op.cit.*, p.228; N. Fujisawa, *op.cit.*: 40). The confusion between the physical relation and the metaphysical relation is only discernible as the confusion between ἔχειν or εἶναι ἐν and μετέχειν. Several critics are inclined to treat μετέχειν and its cognates as describing the Form's immanence. See W. D. Ross, *op.cit.*, pp.228-230; P. Natorp, *Platons Ideenlehre:*

Eine Einführung in den Idealismus (Leipzig: Dürr, 1903; reprint ed., Hamburg: Felix Meiner, 1961), pp.88, 155, 409. But, since these idioms express the relation between the sensible particular and the separate Form, we may regard them as implying the Form's transcendence. See N. Fujisawa, *op.cit.*: 40.

26. We should note that χωρίς occurs five times in 130b-d, but does not always concern the separateness between the Form and the thing partaking of it. Whereas χωρίς in 130b2, b3, c1 and d1 concerns the separateness between the Form and the thing, χωρίς in 130b4 alone concerns the separateness between the Form and its immanent character.

For the rejection of the immanence of the Forms, see *Symp.* 211a8-b1 and *Tim.* 52a3. See also R. Hackforth, *Plato's Phaedo*, translated with an Introduction and Commentary (Cambridge: Cambridge University Press, 1955), pp.143-144.

27. N. Fujisawa. *Op.cit.*:34; H. Teloh, *The Development of Plato's Metaphysics* (University Park, London: The Pennsylvania State University Press, 1981), p.155; idem, "Parmenides and Plato's *Parmenides* 131a-132c," *Journal of the History of Philosophy* 14 (1976):128. See also F. M. Cornford, *Plato and Parmenides*, pp.86-87.

28. For an attempt to show that the metaphor of the day cannot save Plato's theory of participation in the middle period, see S. Panagiotou, "The Day and Sail Analogies in Plato's *Parmenides"*, *Phoenix* 41 (1987):10-24.

29. J. S. Lee. *Op.cit.*, p.92.

30. J. S. Lee. *Op.cit.*, p.94.

31. See also VI 4,2,2-3.

32. J. S. Lee. *Op.cit.*, p.94.

33. As already mentioned, the omnipresence of real being for Plotinus primarily denotes the causal dependence of the sensible world upon the intelligible. In this causal relation, that which comes after the true All is in the really existent All (VI 4,2,3-4). Again, we are told that the visible universe is, in a way, based on and resting on true All (2,10). Plotinus' position is precisely that the sensible world is in the intelligible rather than that the intelligible world is in the sensible. But VI 4,3,17-19 appears to run counter this. The passage reads:

"There is nothing, therefore, surprising in the true All's being in all things (ἐν πᾶσιν εἶναι) in this way, because it is in none of them (ἐν οὐδενί ἐστιν) in such a way as to belong to them" (tr. A. H. Armstrong, adapted by A. Sumi).

Plotinus here does not say that the intelligible world is literally immanent in the sensibles. As οὕτως in line 18 indicates, he explains a way in which the intelligible world is present to the sensible in the preceding passage. But the text in lines 15-16 is corrupt, so that we cannot accurately know his explanation. Nevertheless it is evident that the true All is not possessed by any sensible (οὐ γενόμενον ἐκείνου, line 16). As already seen, ἔχειν is a cognate of εἶναι ἐν in

Plato. But since Plotinus rejects the possession of the true All by the sensible object, the locution ἐν πᾶσιν εἶναι in line 18 must be distinct from such locutions like ἐν πολλοῖς..οὖσιν..ἐνέσται in *Par.*, 131b1-2 and ἐν πᾶσιν..εἴη in b5-6. We must not be misled by this locution. Plotinus explicitly states in line 12 that the true All itself is present to the sensible, being all the same separate. Therefore the above cited passage does not establish the immanence of the intelligible world in the sensible.

Lee's confusion between omnipresence and immanence is not without cause. In the metaphor of the day itself, omnipresence and immanence are not fully distinct from each other:

"[The Form would not be separate from itself] if it were like one and the same day, which is everywhere (πολλαχοῦ) at the same time and nevertheless is not separate from itself. Suppose each Form is also in all things (ἐν πᾶσιν..εἴη) at the same time as one and the same in this way (οὕτω)" (*Parm.* 131b3-6, tr. F. M. Cornford, adapted by A. Sumi).

In the metaphor of the day, omnipresence is not fully distinct from immanence. Lee might possibly be misguided by this ambiguity. Hence we can conclude that Plotinus in VI 4-5 does not faithfully follow the spirit of the metaphor of the day, but makes omnipresence distinct from immanence.

34. J. S. Lee. *Op.cit.*, p.92.
35. *Ibid.*
36. Lee refers to VI 5,3,13-14, where the things are said to participate in real being as a whole (τὰ δ' ἄλλα ἐκείνου μεταλαμβάνειν), in his reconstruction of Plotinus' response to the problem in the *Parmenides* (*op.cit.*, p.94). If the characterization of the participation relation with respect to one Form is precisely applicable to that relation with respect to the intelligible world as a whole, the things which participate in real being ought to have an immanent character of the intelligible world as a whole. But this is obviously unreasonable. Hence the use of μεταλαμβάνειν in VI 5,3,14 must be clearly distinguished from the normal use of the participation idioms in the passages where Plato deals with the Forms. Moreover, the principle of the causal theory of Forms, τῷ καλῷ τὰ καλὰ καλά (*Phd.* 100e2-3), on which the participation relation with respect to one Form is based, is not applicable to that relation with respect to the intelligible world as a whole.
37. J.S. Lee. *Op.cit.*, p.93.
38. *Ibid.*
39. The indivisibility of the intelligible world must be distinguished from that of the individual Form, because the former means that the intelligible world consists of many Forms and yet is indivisible (II 4,4,14-15).
40. For another attempt to reconstruct Plotinus' reply to the *Parmenides* problem concerning participation, see J. Fielder, "Plotinus' Reply to the Arguments of *Parmenides* 130a-131d," *Ape.ron* 12 (1978):1-5. As does Lee, Fielder holds that

the clarification of the nature of immaterial entity leads to the solution to the problem. I do not maintain that no solution to the problem is suggested in VI 4-5. My own position is that Plotinus' possible response can be reconstructed from VI 5,8. I will leave the full explanation of my reconstruction and the examination of Fielder's view for another occasion.

41. In VI 7,40,2-5, παραμυθία, coupled with πειθώ, is contrasted with logical necessity (ἀνάγκη).

42. Bréhier takes VI 5,12,16-23 as an expression of the disappearance of an individual consciousness (*op.cit.*, p.110). Bussanich contrasts the present passage, V 8,7,32-35 and V 3,4,9-13 with III 8,11,32-38 and maintains the disappearance of human individuality and individual consciousness on the intelligible level (*The One and Its Relation to Intellect in Plotinus*, A Commentary on Selected Texts [Leiden: E. J. Brill, 1988], pp.128-129). For the opposing view, see M. Atkinson, *Plotinus: Ennead* V.1, A Commentary with Translation (Oxford: Oxford University Press, 1983), pp.104-105; G. M. Gurtler, *Plotinus: The Experience of Unity* (New York: Peter Lang, 1988), pp.63-64. But Arnou tries to reconcile the present passage with VI 4,14,17ff., where Plotinus says that we exist as particulars in the noetic world (*Le Désir de Dieu dans la Philosophie de Plotin*, 2nd ed., [Rome: Presse de l'Université Grégorienne, 1967], pp.204-208). See also H. J. Blumenthal, *Plotinus' Psychology: His Doctrines of the Embodied Soul* (The Hague: Martinus Nijhoff, 1971), pp.123-125. In this essay, I do not go into the problem concerning our status in the intelligible world, which is linked with the grand problem of whether or nor Plotinus believes in Ideas of individuals.

According to Lee, in VI 5,12,19-22 Plotinus claims that the soul, which was identical with the intelligible world, becomes more of a non-entity through the addition of the self to the objects of her contemplation (*op.cit.,* p.99). I cannot see how such an interpretation is possible. The addition of "something else" (line 20) is said to be from non-being (line 22), namely sensible matter. The passage in question does not warrant the negativity of self-consciousness.

43. *Plotinus*. Text with an English Translation by A. H. Armstrong, 7 vols. (Cambridge, Mass.: Harvard University Press, 1966-88; London: William Heinemann, 1966-88), 6:340-341, note 1.

44. For a detailed discussion about Plotinus' attempt to draw the line between his own doctrine of the intellect-intelligible identity and the Middle-Platonic conception of the Form as God's νόημα, see A. Sumi, *op.cit.*, pp.124-126

45. For the full analysis of Plotinus' argument in V 5,1, see A. Sumi, *op.cit.*, pp.103-107.

46. See M. R. Alfino, "Plotinus and the Possibility of Non-Propositional Thought," *Ancient Philosophy* 8 (1988):278.

47. This argument is prefigured in III 9,1,6-9 and reappears in V 3,5,21-26.

48. See J. Pepin, "Élements pour une Histoire de la Relation entre l'Intelligence et l'Intelligible chez Platon et dans le Néoplatonisme," *Revue Philosophique de la France et de l'Etranger* 146 (1956):48-49; J. Bussanich, *op.cit.*, pp.91-92.
49. See A. H. Armstrong, "The Background of the Doctrine 'That the Intelligibles are not outside the Intellect,'" in *Les Sources de Plotin* (Geneva, Vandoevres: Fondation Hardt, 1957), p.401:
> "Plotinus in formulating his doctrine that the Intelligibles are in Intellect seems to me to be concerned with a question of a different sort 'What is the *relationship* of eternal intuitive thought to its object (or objects) and how is that object to be conceived?'" (Italics mine).

I do not go into details about how the intellect-intelligible unity coheres with the Forms' immutability here. For my discussion about this problem, see A. Sumi, *op.cit.*, pp.113-118, 127-128.
50. Needless to say, Plotinus' doctrine of the intellect-intelligible unity historically goes back to Aristotle' doctrine of divine Intellect. Aristotle's psychological formula of the identity of mind in activity with the object of thought, which is applied to his analysis of the internal structure of divine intellection in *Met.* 1072b14-28, has philosophical merits of insuring the infallibility of divine intellect and safeguarding its immutability. Exploiting these merits fully, Plotinus tackles the problems which remained unsolved in Plato. For the connection of Plotinus' doctrine with Aristotle, see A. Sumi, *op.cit.*, pp.73-74, 78-80.

We may briefly touch upon the philological source of Plotinus' expression ἀληθινὴ ἐπιστήμη. This expression seems to go back to the *Phaedrus* myth, which, according to his own exegesis, implicitly suggests the intellect-intelligible unity. He writes:
> " . . . but about the knowledge there which Plato observed and said 'that which is not a knowledge different from that in which it is (οὐδ' ἥτις ἐστὶν ἄλλην ἐν ἄλλῳ),' but how is so, he left us to investigate and discover" (V 8,4,52-54, tr. A. H. Armstrong).

It is evident that οὐδ᾽ ἥτις ἐστιν ἄλλην ἐν ἄλλῳ is a paraphrase of ἐπιστήμην..οὐδ᾽ ἥ ἐστίν που ἑτέρα ἐν ἑτέρῳ οὖσα ὧν ἡμεῖς νῦν ὄντων καλοῦμεν (*Phdr.* 247d7-e1). Notice that ἑτέρα ἐν ἑτέρῳ (d7-e1) explains ᾗ γένεσις πρόσεστιν (d7) and is contrasted with ἐν τῷ ὅ ἐστιν ὄν (e1-2) which characterises Knowledge itself or τὸ τῆς ἀληθοῦς ἐπιστήμης γένος (c8). (Hackforth's translation of d7-e1 "knowledge that...varies with the various objects" overlooks the first ἐν in e1). Whereas there is some confrontation and heterogeneity between sense knowledge and becoming, Knowledge itself is totally harmonious with real being. In the *Phaedrus* myth, the expression τὴν ἐν τῷ ὅ ἐστιν ὄν ὄντως ἐπιστήμην indicates at most the homogeneity and concord between Knowledge itself and real being, but not the presence of the Forms in Knowledge; for true Knowledge is simply about (περί) real being. Plotinus further reads the unity of Knowledge or Wisdom and real being (V 8,4,47-48; 5,15-16) into the phrase οὐδ'..ἑτέρα ἐν ἑτέρῳ. In 4,3-4, moreover, he contrasts ἐπιστήμην, οὐχ ᾗ γένεσις πρόσεστιν with ὁρῶσι τὰ πάντα..οἷς οὐσία, καὶ ἑαυτοὺς ἐν ἄλλοις. Here he takes οὐδ'..ἑτέρα ἐν ἑτέρῳ or οὐδ'..ἄλλην ἐν ἄλλῳ as suggesting ἑαυτοὺς ἐν ἄλλοις.

As III 9,1,14-15 insinuates, Plotinus believes that the doctrine of the intellect-intelligible unity is entertained by Plato himself. For more detailed discussion about the *locus classicus* in Plato's dialogues for Plotinus' doctrine, see A. Sumi, "Plotinus on *Phaedrus* 247D7-E1: The Platonic Locus Classicus of the Identity of Intellect with the Intelligible Objects," *American Catholic Philosophical Quarterly* 71 (1997): 404-420.

51. For the undescending part of the soul, see II 9,2,4-5; III 8,5,10-11; IV 8,8,1ff.; V 1,10,21-24. In V 3,9, "the most divine part of the soul" (line 1) is called "pure" (lines 18-19).

52. See IV 8,8,2-3; 8,16-18.

53. See IV 8,8,6; 8,15; V 3,9,28-29, See also IV 3,30,11-12. For intellection as the proper activity of soul, see G. M. Gurtler, *op.cit.*, pp.195-196. On the other hand, the undescending part of the soul is called τὸ λογιστικόν in III 8,5,10 and διάνοια is attributed to "the pure part of the soul" in V 3,3,11-12 (see also V 1,7,42-43 τὸ διανοούμενον). Hence Atkinson is inclined to think of the undescending soul as, in some way, a part of διάνοια (*op.cit.*, pp.61-64). Here we do not go into detail about the status of the undescending soul.

The rational soul is sometimes called "ourselves." In V 3,3,35-36, λογίζεσθαι and διάνοια are attributed to "ourselves." In I 1,7,21-22, the true man is identified with the rational soul (τῇ λογικῇ ψυχῇ). Here διάνοιαι, δόξαι and νοήσεις are ascribed together to the rational soul or ourselves (lines 14-17). For the kinship between V 3,3 and I 1,7, see G. M. Gurtler, *op.cit.*, p.233.

Rist points out the difficulty in Plato's tripartite division of the soul; though the infallible νόησις and the fallible διάνοια must be clearly distinguished, they are together attributed to τὸ λογιστικόν, the highest part of the soul ("Integration and the Undescended Soul in Plotinus," *American Journal of Philology* 88 (1967): 413-414). He explains how the Plotinian undescending soul is related to the Platonic λογιστικόν as follows:

"If there were a tripartite division of the soul in Plotinus, therefore, with τὸ λογιστικόν at the top, it would be below the level of the upper soul which is eternally in contact with νοῦς in contemplation" (*op.cit.*:416).

This view is not accurate. First, the Plotinian undescending soul is endowed with the intellective function of the Platonic λογιστικόν. Second, Rist's observation of the Plotinian λογισστικόν is not fully accurate. In light of V 3,3,23ff., he regards the middle part of the soul in II 9,2,5-6 as τὸ λογιστικόν whose proper activity is διάνοια (*op.cit.*: 416). But τὸ λογιστικόν in V 3,3 is also denominated "the pure part of the soul" (lines 11-12). Rist does not consider the fact that Plotinus sometimes calls the undescending soul τὸ λογιστικόν. Although it is true, as Rist points out, that the Platohic tripartition of the soul does not fit well with Plotinus' psychology, we should not overlook the noetic feature that the Plotinian undescending soul has inherited from the highest element of the Platonic soul.

54. This point entails the difficulty in demarcating the undescending soul from Intellect. See H. J. Blumenthal, "Nous and Soul in Plotinus: Some Problems of Demarcation," in *Plotino e il Neoplatonismo in Oriente e in Occidente* (Rome: Academia Nazionale dei Lincei, 1974), pp.203-219.

55. H. J. Blumenthal, "Soul, World-Soul, and Individual Soul in Plotinus," in *Le Néoplatonisme* (Paris: Centre National de la Recherche Scientifique, 1971), p.62, note 1.

56. In the recollection argument, Plato characterizes the Forms as "what was formerly ours" (*Phd.* 76e1-2), implying that they were known by us before our birth. From this characterization, however, we cannot conclude that the soul's prenatal knowledge of the Forms attains her identity with them, because the characterization seems to be simply contrasted with the soul's loss of her prenatal knowledge in the present life.

57. The following sketch of Lee's view is based on J. S. Lee, *op.cit.*, pp.102-103.

58. É. Bréhier. *Op.cit.,* p.117.

59. By "eidetic causation" Lee means "a theory of the way in which the *eide* that make up the intelligible world of Being are the causes of sensible particulars" (*op.cit.,* p.96). He explains the intermittent character of eidetic causation in terms of the discursive nature of the soul's contemplative activity (*op.cit.,* pp.95-101). Although the intermittent character of eidetic causation, as Lee points out (*op.cit.*, p.101), is mentioned in VI 4-5, it would be impossible to explain it by the cognitive activity of the undescending soul, which is characterized as primarily non-discursive in VI 4-5.

60. A. M. Wolters. *Op.cit.,* p.305.

The Oriental Influences Upon Plotinus' Thought: An Assessment of the Controversy Between Bréhier and Rist on the Soul's Relation to the One

Roman T. Ciapalo

The question of whether or not the thought of Plotinus owes any debt to what might be called the Oriental (or perhaps more precisely, Indian) intellectual tradition has been widely and fervently debated for many decades. Although it is possible, and indeed perhaps even likely, that no conclusive resolution to this controversy will ever be reached, at least in the absence of some dramatically new body of evidence-namely, the discovery of the Neoplatonic equivalent of the Dead Sea scrolls-it would nevertheless be worthwhile to revisit briefly the various arguments, pro and con, which have been put forth in order to determine their individual and collective merits.

Accordingly, in this paper I propose to do three things. I shall, first, briefly review the essential literature of this subject. Second, I shall summarize the argument between Emile Bréhier and John Rist over whether or not Plotinus was influenced by Indian thought. Finally, I shall offer my own assessment of the merits of the Bréhier-Rist argument in particular, and of the issue of Plotinus' "Orientalism" in general.

The general question before us would seem to be this: Are the apparent similarities between elements in Plotinus' thought and in various Oriental views, notably Indian thought, just that, mere *per accidens* similarities, or are they evidence of a stronger sort of relationship, namely, as Albert Wolters has articulated in his very illuminating article on this topic, "an 'influence', 'source', or 'determinative factor' on Plotinus"?[1]

That there appear to be points of similarity is largely not disputed, although A. H. Armstrong in his now venerable article ("Plotinus and India") denies that there is any sort of convincing *evidence* of Indian influences on Plotinus.[2] Likewise, John Rist, in his own way, disputes Bréhier's thesis.[3] Still others, like Willy Theiler, Philip Merlan, Cornelia De Vogel, and H. J. Kramer, belong, in one way or another, to the "anti-

Bréhier" ranks.[4] The question, of course, is what ought to be made of this phenomenon of similarity and what sort of importance to assign to it.

How might we classify the various perspectives on this issue? Perhaps in the following twofold way. Some might be counted as supporters of the milder position: what might be termed the "mere *per accidens* similarity" thesis. Others might be listed as supporters of the stronger position: the "direct causal influence" thesis. For our purposes, it might be convenient to appoint Rist as the representative of the former thesis, and Bréhier of the latter.

Let us now look more carefully at the positions of Bréhier and Rist. For Bréhier, there are good reasons to believe that Plotinus was influenced in a direct and causal way by Indian thought. In chapter seven of his very informative book, *The Philosophy of Plotinus*, his primary argument revolves around what he takes to be the double aspects of Plotinus' understanding of *Nous*. There, Bréhier notes. . .

> that on the one hand, Intelligence is an articulated system of definite notions. On the other hand, it is the universal being in whose bosom every difference is absorbed, in which every distinction between subject and object comes to a complete end. In the first respect, it expresses the rationalist thesis that it is possible to have a knowledge of the world and that reality can be grasped through reason. In the second respect, it involves the mystical ideal of the complete unification of beings in the Godhead, with the feeling of intuitive evidence which accompanies it.[5]

Although Bréhier admits that the former view is the result of Plotinus' exegesis of Plato, Aristotle, and the Stoics, he argues that the latter cannot be so explained.

Furthermore, and more to the heart of the matter, the chief Plotinian problem, according to Bréhier, has to do with. . .

> the relation of the particular being, of whose existence we are conscious, to the universal being. How did the conscious self, with its characteristics, its union with a fixed body, its faculties of memory and reasoning, emerge from the universal being and form itself in a distinct center? What is the relation of individual souls to the universal Soul? In general, how is the universal being present in its entirety in all things without ceasing meanwhile to be universal?[6]

For Bréhier, the soul's union with the One is ultimately not something to be explained in rational terms, but rather something to be experienced in a mystical way.

Later in the same chapter, he argues that. . .

> the common and rather monotonous theme of all the Upanishads is that of a knowledge which assures the one possessing it peace and unfailing happiness. This knowledge is the consciousness of the identity of the self with the universal being.[7]

And in order to emphasize this point further, he notes that. . .

> the philosophy of the Upanishads, in fact, does not go beyond the self. This is its characteristic trait. But it holds as certain that this self is without limits and that it is all things. It utilizes two fundamental concepts-that of Brahman, the universal being, the unfathomable principle of all forms of reality, and that of Atman, which is the principle in so far as it exists in the human soul, the pure self, independent of all particular functions of the soul, for example, as the nutritive or cognitive. The main thesis is that Brahman is identical with Atman, that is to say. . the force which creates and preserves the world is identical with what we discover in ourselves as our true self when we disregard all the activities related to definite objects.[8]

Bréhier claims to have found in the doctrine of the Upanishads the very same question that concerns Plotinus. . .

> it consists in inquiring in what sense the self, in concentrating upon itself, finds within itself the very principle of the universe.[9]

Accordingly, this mystical element in his thought is to be explicated in extra-Hellenic terms. Thus, Bréhier argues. . .

> we find at the very center of Plotinus' thought a foreign element which defies classification. The theory of Intelligence as universal being derives neither from Greek rationalism nor from the piety diffused throughout the religious circles of his day.[10]

In addition to this sort of internal evidence, Bréhier addresses various essentially historical facts to make his point, which, however, I shall not treat explicitly here. Suffice it to say that, for a variety of doctrinal and historical reasons, Bréhier concludes that...

> one must seek the source of the philosophy of Plotinus beyond the Orient close to Greece [whose cults maintained a variety of convictions and practices abhorrent to Plotinus, among them the idea of a mediator or savior destined to bring man into relation with God, ritual prayer, thanksgiving, and outpouring of religious feeling], in the religious speculations of India, which by the time of Plotinus had been founded for centuries on the Upanishads and had retained their vitality.[11]

To summarize, what relates Plotinus to Indian thought is...

> his decided preference for contemplation, from which he derives the only true reality, his scorn for the practical moral life, and finally, the egoistic and universal character of the spiritual life as he conceived it. Indeed, in its highest stage, the spiritual life consists in the relationship in which the soul is 'alone' with the universal principle.[12]

Now, what of Rist's objections to this thesis? Rist's fundamental argument relies on R. C. Zaehner's four-fold division of mysticism—pantheistic or natural, ascetic, monistic, and theistic.[13] But, even though Zaehner himself did not locate Plotinus within his scheme, Rist argues confidently that the mysticism of Plotinus is of the *theistic* sort, "where the isolated soul attains to union and is 'oned' with a transcendent God, though *a fortiori* it is not itself identical with that God."[14] For him, accordingly, the mysticism of Plotinus is not monistic, "where the individual soul is declared to be completely identical with the power behind the universe—Atman is Brahman, as the Indian monists would put it,"[15] whereas, according to Rist and his unnamed "experts," the mysticism of the Upanishads is fundamentally monistic. Rist notes that...

> it is precisely this monistic strand that Bréhier tries to find in the *Enneads*. There then in simple terms lies the difference between the two systems. And if the doctrines are unlike, derivation or significant influence can be forgotten.[16]

The crux of Rist's argument here seems to be that the human soul, since it consists of higher and lower parts, does not completely lose itself in its union with the One. Accordingly, he writes as follows:

When therefore the higher soul is enjoying the vision of the One, its lower counterparts do not strictly speaking cease to exist, but become irrelevant to the concentrated personality. Not that the union with the One is a 'self-conscious' union, for self-consciousness as normally understood only blunts the activities with which it is concerned, and in the mystical union the self is transcended or rather 'filled with God.'[17]

The soul, then, since it has a natural kinship with the Primal Reality can and does return to its source and becomes "united" with it. According to Rist...

> such a return, as Plotinus tells us again and again, is a rest after our labours and a perfect stillness. But this rest is not a rest in nothingness, nor a blankness like dreamless sleep. True it is attained by a kind of 'confusion and annihilation' of *Nous*, but it cannot be attained without *Nous*, and should be viewed as the fulfillment rather than the negation of the level of existence. It is not blankness, but rapture, delight and perfect happiness. It is not nothingness...but everything, in the sense that the One is everything. He who understands the One understands the soul when it is 'oned'.[18]

At this juncture, how might one approach the evaluation of the controversy between Bréhier and Rist on the issue of the soul's relation to the One and, ultimately, on the question of the Oriental influences upon Plotinus' philosophy? Let me begin by reviewing what I take to be the first principles of Plotinus' philosophy. My struggles with the *Enneads* over the years have left me with the following three convictions. The first of these is fundamental to all Plotinian thought, namely, that to be real is to be one. As Leo Sweeney has noted...

> Any item is real because of its unity and a fall into multiplicity is likewise a fall into unreality. So true is this that the more unified something is, the more real it is, with the result that what is totally simple is also the Primal Reality - namely, The One, the absolutely first and highest hypostasis.[19]

The second of these essential principles is as follows:

> Whatever is one is good, since that which is one is not only real, but also is perfect and powerful.

This second principle inserts a dynamic aspect into Plotinus' universe, since it is bound up with the position that whatever is genuinely real must by that very fact cause subsequent realities, which turn back to their source because of dependency upon it and desire for it. This principle, then, issues into Plotinus' doctrines of procession and reversion (*prohodos* and *epistrophe*).[20]

The One-Good, then, has a dual status. It is both the source of all subsequent realities (by causing them through its overflow) and the object of their desire and love (by being that upon which they depend for their ultimate perfection and fulfillment).

Finally, because whatever is one is also good-"good *to* others by producing them automatically and necessarily, good *for* others as the object of their seeking,"[21] it follows that the third essential principle is that "whatever is prior is of greater reality than that which is subsequent".[22] In other words, "the relationship of prior/subsequent is simultaneously a relationship of higher/lower in actual values."[23]

Thus, the third principle illuminates the essential nature of the relationship between the One and its overflow. Generally speaking, what is prior is of greater worth, importance, and reality than what is posterior. All levels of reality below the One, then, are thereby less real than the One, precisely because they are less unified than the Primal Reality. As such, these lower levels of reality are *logoi* of the One: they are the One, but as found on a lower, less unified level.

Now, armed with these three Plotinian principles, I wish to argue that Plotinus' account of the final stage of the soul's ascent to and unification with the One may be seen as the conclusion of a long and careful deductive argument whose major premise is that first principle mentioned earlier-to be real is to be one. The existential status of both the human soul's *ascent* to the One and its actual *union* with the Primal Reality is, to be sure, a mystical one. For surely at that supreme level of achievement, the soul's relation to the One involves no duality of whatever sort and is no longer rational in nature, but rather is supra-rational, and, hence, mystical (or to paraphrase Zaehner, monastically mystical). Accordingly, on this point I find Bréhier's position more appealing than Rist's. As attractive and forcefully articulated as the latter's arguments are, they force us to abandon, or at least weaken, what is central to Plotinus' thought-his consistent monism. And this I cannot bring myself to do.

What is most interesting about this area of his thought however, is that he is thoroughly Greek in his approach to philosophical problems. Namely, he is eminently rational. Yet he is led by the relentless application of his logic to eventually draw conclusions that themselves defy complete penetration by human reason, because ultimately they are in their content supra-rational, or, in other words, mystical.

It appears to me that at various junctures of his speculation he notices that the power of human thought, or human rationality itself, if you will, is inadequate to the ultimate task before it, namely, the understanding in a discursive way and the eventual articulation in human language of the individual human soul's relationship to the Primal Reality. He comes closer than other Greek thinkers have in explicating the nature of this union, however inadequate even his articulation may be. In the final analysis, then, it is Plotinus' essentially monistic viewpoint, coupled with the virtual ruthlessness of his logic, that leads him to draw conclusions that seem to defy rational penetration and thus appear to be mystical in nature, but which nevertheless are the necessary implications of his line of reasoning, whose starting point is the trio of fundamental principles enumerated earlier. Among these conclusions, I believe, is the view that the human soul does indeed lose its identity in its ultimate unification with the One.

Now, what has all of this to do with the question of Plotinus' Orientalism? Although several studies have already considered this issue in a most admirable fashion, among them the studies of Staal, Schlette, and, more recently, Tripathi and Wolters being worthy of special mention,[24] let me conclude this presentation with a few remarks of my own on this matter.

First, although it is entirely *possible* that the thought of Plotinus on the question of the soul's relation to God, and perhaps on other issues as well, was influenced in some direct and causal way by the Orient, I cannot, on the basis of my analysis, go beyond the available evidence, which is essentially oblique and circumstantial. Hence, I believe Bréhier goes too far in asserting that Plotinus indeed was indebted to Indian sources. In other words, I am uncomfortable with anything more than a "*per accidens*" explanation of the apparent similarities. Certainly, there seems to be little if any justification for the stronger "direct causal influence" thesis.

Second, there would not seem to be much, if any, merit to the adoption of a fundamentally agnostic stance on this question as long as new, relevant, and conclusive evidence is not brought to light. Frankly, I do not look upon such an eventuality with any great degree of optimism. That is why I am led to the following conclusion. It would not be inappropriate, I think, to seek a kind of middle ground on this issue, midway between what perhaps may be termed the two extreme positions of Bréhier and Rist. Such an intermediary stance would affirm the following three points:

> 1. There seems to be a striking affinity between relevant elements in Indian thought and in Plotinus, particularly in the description of the soul's striving toward union with God and of the nature of that union. One need only compare the description of the human soul's ultimate and complete union with the One found in the *Enneads* with the identification of Atman with Brahman found in Indian thought. 2. There is no need, however, from an exegetical point of view, to argue for the necessity of Oriental influences upon Plotinus. Why? Because he arrives at his conclusions by means of the consistent application of his logic to his three principal insights, particularly, the first-to be real is to be one. There is an internal consistency within his position such that all of his conclusions flow naturally from those fundamental insights.
>
> 3. It is possible that the affinities between Plotinus and the Orient constitute evidence of the existence of something which currently does not enjoy much popularity, but which nevertheless may be of value for our present purpose, namely, the concept of a perennial philosophy, defined here as a philosophy which is both permanent and significant, precisely because its features transcend historical and cultural changes.

In the final analysis, this last point may constitute the most satisfactory answer to the problem at hand. It is not so much a question of chronology or causal influence, I believe, but a matter of concomitant or parallel insights, independently reached. There is too little evidence to suggest anything more than this. And, as Wallis has argued...

> the tendency of the mystical experience to express itself in similar ways at all times and in all civilizations must also be taken into account.[25]

In this way, perhaps one can say that there is a measure of Orientalism in Plotinus and not at the same time impugn his philosophical originality, intellectual gifts, or Greek heritage.

I favor this "perennial philosophy" thesis, then, primarily because it offers the possibility of a profoundly constructive solution to the problem of adjudicating cross-cultural influences, whether philosophical or otherwise. This thesis represents a positive approach to the solution to the problem and is not fraught with the divisive and counter-productive elements of the alternatives. It affirms, I believe, what we all suspect, or at least hope, is the case, namely, that human experience is fundamentally universal. Perhaps, then, what I have been discussing is but one instance of the affirmation, in both Eastern and Western voices, of the common elements of human experience. Perhaps, for our purposes, it might be possible to speak of Plotinian Hinduism, or of Hindu Neoplatonism. In this way, the thought of Plotinus might function as one of the intellectual bridges across that great chasm that has divided East and West for so long.

Endnotes

1. Albert M. Wolters, "A Survey of Modern Scholarly Opinion on Plotinus and Indian Thought," in *Neoplatonism and Indian Thought*, ed. by R. Baine Harris, (Albany: State University of New York Press, 1982), p. 294. Hereafter, Wolters, *Survey*.
2. A. H. Armstrong, "Plotinus and India," *The Classical Quarterly* XXX (1936), 22-28. Hereafter, Armstrong, "India."
3. John Rist, *Plotinus: The Road to Reality*, (Cambridge: University Press, 1967), pp. 213-230. Hereafter, Rist, *Road to Reality*.
4. Willy Theiler, *Die Vorbereitung des Neuplatonismus*, (Berlin, 1940); Philip Merlan, *From Platonism to Neoplatonism* (The Hague, 1953); Cornelia de Vogel, "On the Neoplatonic Character of Platonism and the Platonic Character of Neoplatonism," *Mind* (1953), 43-64; H. J. Kramer, *Der Ursprung der Geistmetaphysik*. (Amsterdam, 1964).
5. Emile Bréhier, *The Philosophy of Plotinus*, transl. by Joseph Thomas (Chicago: The University of Chicago Press, 1958), p. 106. Hereafter, Bréhier, *Plotinus*.
6. *Ibid.* p. 109
7. *Ibid.* p. 123.
8. *Ibid.* p. 125
9. *Ibid.* p. 125.
10. *Ibid.* p. 116.
11. *Ibid.* p. 117.
12. *Ibid.* pp. 132-33.
13. R.C. Zaehner, *Mysticism, Sacred and Profane*, (Oxford, 1957).
14. Rist, *Road to Reality*, p. 214.
15. *Ibid.* p. 214.
16. *Ibid.* p. 229.
17. *Ibid.* p. 230.
18. *Ibid.* p. 230.
19. Leo Sweeney, S. J., "Basic Principles in Plotinus' Philosophy," *Gregorianum* (1961), p. 511.
20. *Ibid.* p. 511.
21. *Ibid.* p. 512.
22. *Ibid.* p. 512.
23. *Ibid.* p. 512.
24. J. F. Staal, "The Problem of Indian Influence on Neoplatonism," in *Advaita and Neoplatonism, A Critical Study in Comparative Philosophy* (Madras, 1961); H. R. Schlette, "Indisches bei Plotin," in *Apgrie und Glaube* (Munich, 1970), pp. 125-51; C.L. Tripathi, "The Influence of Indian Philosophy on Neoplatonism," pp. 273-292 and Albert M. Wolters, "A Survey of Modern Scholarly Opinion on

Plotinus and Indian Thought," in *Neoplatonism and Indian Thought*, ed, by R. Baine Harris, State University of New York Press, 1982).
25. R.T. Wallis, *Neoplatonism* (London: Gerald Duckworth & Co., Ltd., 1972), p. 15.

Plotinus and Interior Space

Frederic M. Schroeder

A.H. Armstrong entitled his pioneering book *The Architecture of the Intelligible Universe in the Philosophy of Plotinus.*[1] This title has entered and informed the language of Plotinian scholarship.[2] It is the purpose of the present paper to explore an aspect of "intelligible architecture" which, I would suggest, has been largely neglected. The architectural metaphor suggests a verticality, hierarchy, and externality that Plotinus counterbalances with another architecture, that of interior space.

H. P. L'Orange, in his *Art Forms and Civic Life in the Late Roman Empire,* speaks of the dissolution of the classical building structure in late antiquity with an abandonment of emphasis upon the external appearance of the building. However, he observes,

> A positive side of this transformation is a new experience of space, a new feeling for the interior itself, which is an expression of the new spirit of the time. An appreciation of this positive side makes it possible for us to meet with a better understanding the peculiarly abstract as it were, the distant glance which we have continually encountered in Late Antiquity... Architecture becomes introspective. The building structure is reduced to a mere shell surrounding what is encompassed. It becomes no more than the enclosure of space.[3]

and further:

> Above all, light is the space-creating element and models in its various intensities the different parts of the interior.[4]

He also remarks:

> A completely new aesthetic was developed during the third century: beauty does not reside in the proportions of the body, but in the soul which penetrates and illumines it, that is, in expression (the Enneads of Plotinus). Beauty is a function of the inner being (τὸ ἔνδον εἶδος).[5]

L'Orange does not remark, however, on the possibility that Plotinus may ground the sculpting of inner space in the architecture of late antiquity.

Let us examine some passages that use interior space in figurative language describing the intelligible world. We may turn now to an example of interior space in Plotinus that illustrates these principles with reference to the soul's vision of the One (6.9 [9].11.17-23):

> Like a man who enters into the sanctuary and leaves behind the statues in the outer shrine; these become again the first things he looks at when he comes out of the sanctuary, after his contemplation within and intercourse there, not with a statue or image but with the Divine itself (οὐκ ἄγαλμα οὐδὲ εἰκόνα, ἀλλὰ αὐτό); they are secondary objects of contemplation. But that other, perhaps, was not an object of vision, but another kind of seeing (οὐ θέαμα, ἀλλὰ ἄλλος τρόπος τοῦ ἰδεῖν).[6]

The god in the inmost sanctuary is "not an object of vision" (θέαμα), but "another kind of seeing" (ἄλλος τρόπος τοῦ ἰδεῖν).

Trouillard says of the vision of the One that what is required is, not a different object of regard, but a change in our way of looking:

> Il est clair qu'il ne s'agit pas de renoncer à tel ou tel objet, mais à une optique, à un système de valeurs: "changer son regard" (1.6.8.25), "chasser les croyances imposées du dehors" (III.6.5.17) "s'éveiller des représentations absurdes" (III.6.5.24) "non plus une contemplation, mais une autre façon de regarder" (οὐ θέαμα, ἀλλὰ ἄλλος τρόπος τοῦ ἰδεῖν) (VI.9.11.2 2). Et cet abandon n'est possible que sous l'influence d'une illumination antérieure.[7]

Of the passages cited, only one (1.6 [1].8.25-26) offers a linguistic parallel to the crux at 6.9 [9].9.11.22-23 (οὐ θέαμα, ἀλλὰ ἄλλος τρόπος τοῦ ἰδεῖν) in its requirement to "change to another way of seeing" (ὄψιν ἄλλην ἀλλάξασθαι). This phrase, however, clearly refers to a change in *our* way of vision, whereas in 6.9 [9].11.22-23 the One is described as another way of seeing. Trouillard's interpretation requires a metonymous transference of the seeing in question from the One to ourselves. The discipline of strict construction (which I shall argue is the most fruitful approach) demands that we insist that, in some sense, the One is itself "another way of seeing."

Bréhier translates, "un mode de vision tout différent." This translation appears to require, as does Armstrong's (which I use here) and Trouillard's interpretation, that the vision in question be our vision, a vision that is transformed. Yet it is the One that is described as (another) way of seeing. However, Bréhier comments, "C'est la vision unitive dont il était question tout à l'heure."[8]

What Bréhier has in mind with this comment may be illustrated by Arnou's intepretation of the phrase as:

> Une contemplation où s'est effacé la distinction entre le sujet et l'objet, où il ne faut plus parler de θέαμα, (VI.9.10; VI.9.11), ni de θεατής, (V.8.10).[9]

In the same vein, Rist argues that Plotinus, who really prefers the language of union, employs the language of sight in deference to Plato who uses it of the experience of the ultimate principle in the *Symposium* (Beauty) and in the *Republic* (the Good).[10]

The claim that the phrase "another way of seeing" refers, not to a transformation in *our* way of seeing, but to a suspension of the subject-object distinction in the act of vision, still requires an evasion of the Plotinian ascription of this phrase to the One itself. Plotinus could have said that vision of the One demands such a suspension, but he does not say this. He says rather that the One is "another way of seeing." Implicit in the metonymous interpretations of this phrase that we have examined must be the notion that such a strict construction is to be avoided simply on the grounds that it makes no sense. Plotinian scholars disagree on the question of whether the One has any form of consciousness, even of itself.[11] Such a consciousness, however, would surely never be described by the language of vision which obviously carries the subject-object disctinction with it and would thus violate Eleatic principle.

We may now turn to similar language in another passage. Plotinus describes the progress of the human soul from the vision of the Platonic Forms in Intellect to the vision of the One (6.7 [38].35.7-16):

> It is as if someone went into a house richly decorated and so beautiful, and within it contemplated each and every one of the decorations and admired them before seeing the master of the house, but when he sees that master with delight, who is not of the nature of the images [in the house], but worthy of genuine contemplation, he dismisses those other things and thereafter looks at him alone, and then, as he looks and does not take his eyes away, by the continuity of his contemplation he no longer sees a sight, but mingles his seeing with what he contemplates, so that what was seen before has now become sight in him, and he forgets all other objects of contemplation (ὥστε ἐν αὐτῷ ἤδη τὸ ὁρατὸν πρότερον ὄψιν γεγονέναι, τῶν δ' ἄλλων πάντων ἐπιλάθοιτο θεαμάτων).

Even as the god in 6.9 [9].11.22-23 is described, not as an object of vision, but as another way of seeing (ἄλλος τρόπος τοῦ ἰδεῖν), so here it is said that in him (ἐν αὐτῷ) [sc. the master] that which was an object of vision has become vision (ὄψις). Again, we might be tempted to a metonymous transference of vision from the object of vision to ourselves, or construe this language in such a way that it would simply explicate the union of vision with its object. However, a strict construction would again demand that we understand the ostensible referent (in this case the master) as indeed in some sense (yet to be defined) as "vision."

To understand the sense in which the One may be "another way of seeing" or "vision," we must digress to the subject of Plotinian optics. Plotinus polemicizes against the view that sense-perception results from the imprinting of a sense-impression upon the soul (4.6 [41].1.14-21):

> It is clear presumably in every case that when we have a perception of anything through the sense of sight, we look there where it is and direct our gaze where the visible object is situated in a straight line from us; obviously it is there that the apprehension takes place and the soul looks outwards, since, I think, no impression has been or is being imprinted on it, nor has it yet received a seal-stamp, like the mark of a seal-ring on wax.

Plotinus examines the question of why it is that distant objects appear small (2.8 [35].1). When things are far removed from us, we do not see them in their detail. It is by measuring from the several objects in a landscape in relationship to each other that we arrive at the size of the whole (33-36):

> What happens to them [sc. colours and sizes] becomes clearer in things of many and varied parts, for instance, hills with many houses on them and a quantity of trees and a great many other things, of which each individual one, if it is seen, enables us to measure the whole from the individual parts which we observe.

Plotinus comments further (47-51):

> And things far off appear near because the real extent of the distance appears in its true extent, from the same causes; but the sight cannot go through the far part of the distance and see its forms as they really are, and so it is not able to say how great in magnitude it really is.

The art historian André Grabar argues that the optical theory set forth in these passages grounds the aesthetics of space in late antique and early medieval plastic art. There the perspective or angle of vision belongs, not to the spectator of the work of art, but to the central figure. Thus the perspective may be inverted, so that everything is seen from the point of view of the central figure. Also, the other objects radiate from the central figure to the same effect. The result is that the spectator enters into the perspective of the central figure. Thus the apprehension has its locus, not in the percipient (the spectator), but in the perceived (the central figure in the work of art) and the whole is measured from the central figure.[12] One could surely say that the central figure is, in this sense, "another way of looking," or "vision."

Art historians distinguish two theories of perspective, the *perspectiva naturalis*, or natural perspective, and the *perspectiva artificialis*, or artificial perspective. The artificial perspective is the perspective familiar to us from the painters of the Renaissance, such as Raphael (we may think of his *School of Athens*). In this perspective, the eye is regarded as immobile and the scene is static. Everything is measured from the angle of vision of the ideal spectator. Space is organized with respect to this orientation (it is in Panofsky's terms a *Systemordnung*).[13] In the natural perspective, which belongs to classical art, the ray from the object is projected on the internal surface of the extremity of a visual sphere, the retina. Our field of vision is spherical and the image we have of an object is projected onto a concave surface. Only the ray which is rigorously perpendicular to the retina will suffer no deformation (vertically, horzontally, and longitudinally), but the others will in proportion as they are removed from that central ray. The size of objects is given, not by their distance from the eye, but by the measure of the angle of vision. The evaluation of the size of an object is expressed in degrees of angles or arcs and not in simple sizes.[14] The size of the object varies, not with distance, but with the angle of vision.[15]

In the artificial perspective, the artist imposes a geometrical order proper to plane surfaces upon empty space. In the natural perspective, the space is not empty, but is a function of the things seen. Their inclusion is additive, rather than belonging to a systematic organization of empty space. In Panofsky's language, this is not a *Systemordnung*, but an *Aggregtraum*.[16]

The artificial perspective would more readily direct our attention to the central figure than would the aggregate inclusion of objects about a central figure as in the natural perspective. In the former the systematic organization of space is designed precisely for that indicative purpose.

Plotinus argues against the theory that the relative size of perceived objects is governed by our angle of vision, preferring the theory that we have examined above.[17] It is clear that his perspective inclines toward the natural, rather than toward the artificial pespective. We should for this reason expect that it views a scene in terms of additive inclusion, rather than of sytematic organization of space. Of course, such a scene may also be controlled by a central figure (around which, of course, the scene is organized according to its persepctive, rather than the perspective of the ideal spectator).[18]

Plotinus presents a phenomenology of illumination. We see all things by means of light. Light, so long as it is merely an instrument of vision, is among the intentional objects of consciousness. It is "seen together with" with them (συνορώμενον). Yet it may also become the theme and focal object of consciousness, so that all is seen as light or a function of light. Plotinus develops this investigation of light in describing how Intellect experiences the dawning vision of the One. Yet it is applicable to all illumination, including the manifestation of light in the sensible world.[19] Notice that this transformation of our vision requires no conversion in the sense of turning away from one thing and looking at another as in the illuminationist passage concerning the Sun and Cave in Plato's *Republic*.[20] The light and the illumined objects are beheld conspectively.

Let us now return to the passage describing the experience of the great man and his splendid house.[21] We need not think that the separation between our admiration of the appointments of the house and our vision of the great man is merely temporal, so that now we see the objects of the house, and then the great man. Certainly we do not need to turn around in order to see the great man. The interior of the house and its appointments may be seen conspectively even as the light is experienced conspectively with the objects that it illumines. It is rather that the great man is the central object that provides the angle of vision from which we may measure and evaluate the other objects in the scene. In a sense, the great man is the light by which they are illumined. It is his taste and his mind that is reflected in the interior space. As we come to this realization, the great man is thematized as the focal object of consciousness.

An optical theory that grounds an aesthetic belonging properly to painting on plane surfaces (or relief sculpture) is adapted to architectural uses. In the interior of the great house, of course, the mobility of our vision is more actual than is the fictive illusion of that mobility in the painting. Indeed the great man is, not merely an object of vision, but vision (ὄψις), as he informs and interprets the entire scene.[22] Again, the natural perspective lends itself more to the kind of gradual and dawning apprehension of the primary figure than would the artificial perspective that so abruptly guides the eye to the central point.

Although in the previous passage there is no mention of illumination, Plotinian illuminationist theory is helpful toward its interpretation. The point about the central object of the piece being a source of illumination to other objects becomes explicit in the following passage in which the soul's vision of the One as light is described (5.3 [49].17.30-37):

> We must think that he is present when, like another god whom someone called to his house, he comes and brings light to us: for if he had not come, he would not have brought the light. So the unenlightened soul does not have him as god; but when it is enlightened it has what it sought, and this is its true end, to touch that light and see by itself, not by another light, but by the light which is also its means of seeing. It must see that light by which it is enlightened: for we do not see the sun by another light than his own.

Above we examined the passage concerning the man who enters the sanctuary and leaves behind the statues in the outer shrine to see, not a statue, but the god himself within who is not an object of vision, but another way of looking.[23] In that passage, unlike the passage about the great man in his house,[24] the vision of the first things seen and the primary figure is not conspective, but successive. Yet we may still say that the perspective with which the statues outside the sanctuary is seen upon the departure from it belongs to the primary figure in that the contemplative sees the other statues now, not from his own, but from its perspective. Both passages treat of interiors, but in the first, the progress into inwardness involves a spatial progress within not demanded by the second.

As I suggested above, the real tendency of the figurative use of interior space in Plotinus is to qualify the spatial metaphor of conversion, of turning as from one thing as to another thing. It is not simply the substitution of one spatial metaphor (inwardness and depth) for another (verticality and ascent).

Plotinus asks how we may see the ultimate Beauty of Plato's *Symposium* (1.6 [1].8.1-6):

> But how shall we find the way? What method can we devise? How can one see the "inconceivable beauty" which stays within in the holy sanctuary (οἷον ἔνδον ἐν ἁγίοις ἱεροῖς μένον) and does not come out

where the profane may see it? Let him who can, follow and come within, and leave outside the sight of his eyes and not turn back to the bodily splendours which he saw before.

The passage concludes (lines 21-27):

> Our country from which we came is there, our Father is there. How shall we travel to it, where is our way of escape? We cannot get there on foot; for our feet only carry us everywhere in this world, from one country to another. You must not get ready a carriage, either, or a boat. Let all these things go, and do not look. Shut your eyes, and change to another way of seeing (ὄψιν ἄλλην ἀλλάξασθαι), which everyone has but few use.

Notice here again the "other way of seeing" which is common to such descriptions.

The only appropriate conversion (ἐπιστροφή) is that of the aspatial, atemporal, and non-dualistic turning of the One toward itself (5.1 [10].6.12-19):

> The contemplator, then, since God exists by himself as if inside the temple, abiding quiet beyond all things (μένοντος ἡσύχου ἐπέκεινα ἁπάντων), must contemplate what correspond to the images already standing outside the temple, or rather that one image which appeared first; and this is the way in which it appeared: everything which is moved must have some end to which it moves. The One has no such end, so we must not consider that it moves. If anything comes into being after it, we must think that it necessarily does so while the One remains continually turned toward itself (ἐπιστραφέντος ἀεὶ ἐκείνου πρὸς αὐτό).[25]

The words "beyond all things" (ἐπέκεινα ἁπάντων) here recall the Platonic description of the Good as "beyond essence" (ἐπέκεινα τῆς οὐσίας) in the *Republic* 509b9. In light of the topography of the Sun and the Cave, we may wish to see in Plato a transcendence appropriate to a vertical structure of intelligible architecture. Here, the One or the Good is beyond by being within.

Notice here the language of "abiding in silence" (ἡσύχου μένοντος).[26] The verb "abide" (μένειν) is used in other contexts of the production of what is below the One in undiminished giving. The source abides in its native and intransitive acitivity and there proceeds from that activity, with no deliberation or external movement on the part of the

One, a transitive activity, as warmth from a flame or light from a luminous source.[27]

Such effortless production is expressed by the language of abiding (μένειν) and silence (ἡσυχία, σιωπή).[28] I have argued elsewhere that this model of effortless and unmediated production counterbalances that of the Demiurge conceived as an agent external to the pattern and the copy who mediates between them and exercises deliberative thought. The demiurgic model implies a vertical space between the pattern and the copy, a space that must be bridged by demiurgic intervention. The present passage suggests that the silent abiding of the One is located in the context of inwardness. Plotinus also counsels that our manner of returning to the One, our source, is to practise its quietness and abiding.[29]

The Soul's effortless production of the sensible world is described in terms of the relation of an architect to a house he has created, but in such a way that he builds without effort and from within his own spirit (4.3 [27].9.29-44):

> There came into being something like a beautiful and richly various house which was not cut off from its builder, but he did not give it a share in himself either; he considered it all, everywhere, worth a care which conduces to its very being and excellence (as far as it can participate in being) but does him no harm in his presiding over it, for he rules it while abiding (μένων) above. It is in this sort of way that it is ensouled; it has a soul which does not belong to it, but is present to it; it is mastered, not the master, possessed, not possessor. The universe lies in soul which bears it up, and nothing is without a share of soul. It is as if a net immersed in the waters was alive, but unable to make its own that in which it is. The sea is already spread out and the net spreads with it, as far as it can; for no one of its parts can be anywhere else than where it lies. And soul's nature is great, just because it has no size, as to contain the whole of body in one and the same grasp; wherever body extends, there soul is.

How is it that the world is in the Soul, or the house, as it were, in the divine architect, rather than *vice versa*? The Greek verb "to be" contains an inherent locative value. This fact is evidenced in the sophistic conundrum that, if place is, it must be in place, and so forth to infinite regress.[30] This locative value is in Homer very often inseparable from the existential value of the verb.[31]

It is doubtless because of the inherent locative value of the verb "to be" that Plato feels constrained to locate the Forms somewhere. In the *Phaedrus* they are in a "place above the heavens"[32] and in the *Republic* (with greater subtlety) in an "intelligible place."[33]

Aristotle defines place as the inner limit of the containing body.[34] From this definition he draws the important corollary that the universe as a whole is not in place since it has no containing body.[35] In general, the ancients had, not a concept of space as a discontinuous and homogeneous medium to be filled with things, but place as a function of each thing that is.[36]

Aristotle rejects the notion that there can be an actually infinite.[37] Plotinus reasons that that principle that confers limit need not itself be limited. Thus, while Intellect is, in its relation to the One, limited, the One, which confers limit upon it, is unlimited.[38] Thus, although he agrees with Aristotle that the corporeal universe cannot be contained by the inner limit of a further containing body, the Soul, that is (in relation to the corporeal world) unlimited, contains the world in the sense that the unlimited principle that confers limit contains the limited as the greater contains the lesser.[39] Each hypostasis contains its inferior in this manner, as each is unlimited with respect to its inferior and limited with respect to its superior.[40] We may conclude that for Plotinus the spiritual pleroma is the place or container of the corporeal world.

At the moment of the epiphany, the interior that is designed to contain the divine presence is itself embraced by the god. To this inversion of location there corresponds an inversion of perspective. We, the spectators, are located within the angle of vision belonging to the god (even though we cannot be the *intentum* of his consciousness). In "another way of looking," we are introduced to an agreeable awe and sense of our own place in the scheme of things as we discover that the epiphany is not altogether our project (even though it cannot belong to demiurgic deliberation on the part of the god). It is indeed true that the effect of this phrase is to ovecome a subject-object distinction. Yet that effect results, not so much from our effort to see, as from the way which the thing seen imposes itself upon our vision. The One retains its sovereignty in our experience of it. While the One may be the Good for us, it is so by being the Good in and of itself.

The imagery of interior space occurs in Plotinus as an illustration of metaphysical and spiritual truths. Thus Plotinus does not show a direct interest in the aesthetics of interior space for its own sake. Indeed it is difficult and typical of this author that one is hard put to test his interest in the sensible world, for everything in it seems but an explication of what is enfolded in the intelligible world. Yet this very fact tells us much about the imagery of interior space. That which constitutes the internal space is intelligible form as its interior and formative principle. The object of the metaphor *is* the very principle of architecture and spatial organization. It is not so much that the god appears in space as that, by appearing, he creates place. Indeed he is the place in which the objects that occupy the interior appear in numinous transparency.

Endnotes

[1] Cambridge: Cambridge University Press, 1940; reprinted Amsterdam: Hakkert, 1967.
[2] E.g. A. Charles-Saget, *L'Architecture du divin: Mathématique et philosophie chez Plotin et Proclus* (Paris: Société d' édition "Les Belles Lettres, " 1982).
[3] *Art Forms and Civic Life in the Late Roman Empire* (Princeton: Princeton University Press, 1965), 19.
[4] *Ibid.*, 21.
[5] *Ibid.*, 27-28.
[6] This and other translations of Plotinus are from A. H. Armstrong, *Plotinus*, 7 vols. (London and Cambridge, Mass.: Heinemann. 1966-88). The edition of Plotinus consulted is the *editio minor*, P. Henry and H. R. Schwyzer. *Plotini Opera*. 3 vols. (Oxford: Oxford University Press, 1964-1982).
[7] J. Trouillard. *La Purification Plotinienne* (Paris: Presses Universitaires de France, 1955), 139.
[8] E. Bréhier, Plotin, *Ennéades* VI (Paris: Société d' édition "Les Belles Lettres." 1963) 187n.1.
[9] R. Arnou, *Le Désir de Dieu dans la Philosophie de Plotin* (Rome: Presses de l'Université Grégorienne, 1967), 237.
[10] J. M. Rist, *The Road to Reality* (Cambridge: Cambridge University Press, 1967), 197-98. Rist cites 6.9 [9].10.11-12: ὄψεται, μαλλον δὲ ...συνέσται and 6.9[9].11.6: μὴ ἑωράμενον, ἀλλ' ἡνωμένον.
[11] Cf. my "*Synousia, Synaisthêsis* and *Synesis:* Presence and Dependence in the Plotinian Philosophy of Consciousness," *Aufstieg und Niedergang der Römischen Welt,*, 2.36.1, ed. W. Haase, 677-99 (Berlin and New York: Walter de Gruyter,1987) 691-92 and my *Form and Transformation. A Study in the Philosophy of Consciousness* (Montreal and Kingston, London, Buffalo: McGill-Queen's University Press, 1992), 110 and n. 81.
[12] A. Grabar, *L'Art de la fin de l'antiquité et du moyen âge* 3 vols., I: 15-29 (Paris: Collège de France, 1968), 17-20; 23; cf. now G. M. Gurtler, "Plotinus and Byzantine Aesthetics," *The Modern Schoolman,* 66 (1988-89), 275-84 at 277-79 and Plotinus 4.5 [29].3.32-38 which offers a better example of the thesis that Grabar wishes to advance than do Grabar's texts.
[13] Cf. E. Panofsky, "Die Perspektive als 'symbolische Form,' " in *Vorträge der Bibliothek Warburg* 1924-1925 (Leipzig and Berlin: Teubner, 1927), 258-330; reprinted in *Aufsätze zu Grundfragen der Kunstwissenschaft*, ed. H. Oberer and E. Verheyn (Berlin: B. Hessling, 1974), 99-167. The distinction is between *Systemordnung* and *Aggregatraum*, 109; 122-123.

[14] Cf. the lucid account of the two versions of perspective in L. Brion-Gierry, "L'espace et les perspectives," *Annales d'Esthétique. The Hellenic Society for Aesthetics. Athens* 13-14 (1974-1975) 18-44 at p. 27; for the account of the curvilinear character of natural perpective, cf. Panofsky, 101-108.
[15] Cf. Panofsky, 104-108.
[16] Cf. note 13 above. Indian art favours the natural perspective, cf. Brion - Gierry, 22-23. Dr. Basu, whom I had the pleasure of meeting at our 1992-1993 conference on Neoplatonism and Indian Thought, assures me that the natural perspective in Indian art is, as in Plotinus, metaphysically grounded.
[17] 2.8 [35].1.
[18] Gian Paolo Lomazzo, in Chapter XXVI, "Del modo di conoscere e constituire le proporzioni secondo la bellezza," of his treatise *Idea del Tempio della Pittura* in *Scritti sulle Arti* ed. R. P. Ciardi, vol. 1 (Florence: Marchi and Bertolli, 1973), 311, following Ficino's account of beauty in his commentary on Plato's *Symposium*, argues that order does not consist in quantity, but in the relation of the parts or members of the composition to each other. Measure is not itself a part or member of the composition, but resides in all the parts or members. Measure is not material, because measure is the limit of quantity and consists in lines and points that have no depth and thus cannot be corporeal. Thus Lomazzo offers a Renaissance and Neoplatonic argument for natural, and against artificial, perspective. I thank Dr. Paulos Mar Gregorios for this reference.
[19] Cf. 5.5 [32].7 and my *Form and Transformation*, 47-54; for συνορώμενον see 5.5 [32].7.5-6.
[20] 515c7-8; d3-4; 518c4-d1.
[21] 6.7 [38].35.7-16.
[22] The Greek word for "master" that describes the lord of the house in question is δεσπότης (6.7 [38].35.10). This word would translate the Latin *princeps* or *dominus* , cf. H. J. Mason, *Greek Terms for Roman Institutions* (Toronto: Hakkert, 1974), 34 (for the Greek); 195 (for the Latin). Thus the term could certainly describe the Roman emperor. Perhaps Plotinus has in mind the emperor Gallienus with whom Porphyry says that Plotinus had a close relationship in *Vita Plotini* 12. I thank my colleague A. J. Marshall for the reference to Mason.
[23] 6.9 [9].11.17-23.
[24] 6.7 [38].35.7-16.
[25] I have here slightly altered the Armstrong translation.
[26] We may compare the beauty "which stays (μένον) within the holy sanctuary" in 1.6 [1].8.2 cited above.
[27] Cf. 4.5 [29].7.33-49; 5.4 [7].2.22-37; 6.4 [22].9-10 and my *Form and Transformation*, 24-32.
[28] Cf. 1.7 [54].1.13-19; 3.2 [47].2.10-16; 3.8 [30].4.5-10; 6.9 [9].9.18-19; and my *Form and Transformation*, 43-44.
[29] 5.5 [32].8.1-16 and my *Form and Transformation*, 45-46.

[30] Cf. Gorgias DK B53, vol.1,280.26 (=Sextus Empiricus, *Adversus Mathematicos* VII.70); cf. also Zeno, DK A 24, vol.1,253 esp. Aristotle, *Physics* 1.209a23.

[31] Cf. Homer *Iliad* 6.152; 11.722-23; *Odyssey* 19.172; on the locative and existential values of the Greek verb "to be," cf. C. H. Kahn, "The Greek Verb 'To be' and the Concept of Being," *Foundations of Language* 2 (1966) 245-65.

[32] 247c3; cf. 247a8-b1.

[33] 508c1; 517b5.

[34] *Physics* 4.212a6.

[35] *Ibid.* 212b8-10.

[36] Cf. Panofsky, 110-111.

[37] *Physics* 4.208a5-23.

[38] 5.5 [32].6.1-7.

[39] 6.4 [22].2.

[40] 5.5 [32].9; the One acts as a limit to Intellect (6.7 [38].17.14-16); Intellect to Soul (3.9 [13].5; 5.1 [10].7.36-42); and Soul to the sensible world (6.5 [23].11.11-14). For a fuller discussion of this subject, see my *The Doctrine of Presence in the Philosophy of Plotinus* (Diss. University of Toronto 1969 [microfilm]), 100-109 (Summary: *Dissertation Abstracts* 32 (1971) 491A). We should now accept that the One is infinite, not by extrinsic, but by intrinsic denomination, cf. my *Form and Transformation* 63 and n. 65 and H. Blumenthal, "Plotinus in the Light of Twenty Years' Scholarship, 1951-1971" I n *Aufstieg und Niedergang der Römischen Welt*, 2.36.1, edited by W. Haase, 528-70 (Berlin and New York: Walter de Gruyter, 1987), 551. I would like to thank the Advisory Research Committee of Queen's University for their support of my participation in the conference that gave rise to this volume.

Unity and Multiplicity: Reflections on Emanationism as a Philosophical Theme in the Context of Neoplatonism

P. K. Mukhopadhyaya

I

I wish to discuss here the theme of Emanation in the context of Neoplatonism and Indian Philosophy. I argue that Emanationism can be conceived as (and it was perhaps so conceived originally) a powerful alternative to what is called "creationism", an alternative which has within its scope both empirical selves or *jivas* and the created inanimate world; but as the doctrine has been developed, discussed and criticized many other considerations have been allowed to become mixed with it. Perhaps this is as it should be; nothing wrong or unusual. But for proper appreciation of the theme and also to avoid unmerited criticism or undeserving praise we should be very clear as to which tenets of the Neoplatonist philosophy of Emanationism are logically related and which are logically independent.

The problem is less acute when we consider the two Indian schools of philosophy, which advocate two versions of *Satkaryavada* or Emanationism-II. Within none of these schools there is much internal difference. But interschool difference is quite clear even though one version of *Satkaryavada* is advocated by both the schools. On the other hand considered as a single school internally distinguished into four sub-schools, Neoplatonism or Emanationism-I exhibits major internal differences in respect of the conception of emanation and other matters of philosophy and religion. But the four forms of Emanationism-I are not so clearly distinguished as the two versions of Emanationism-II.

My choice of this theme for discussion here is not without reason. In the first place I think that it is neither impossible nor so unnatural to view the theme of Emanation as essentially the philosophical theme of the One and the Many. When so viewed one can find in this theme a counter-example to some familiar misconceptions (to which I refer below) about ancient philosophy in general and classical Indian philosophy in particular. My second reason is that an Indian philosopher is in a better position than scholars belonging to many other cultures to appreciate and respond to the Neoplatonist doctrine of emanation. For Emanationism-I as well as Emanationism-II emerged in non-Christian pagan culture. Even if we ignore the attitude of indifference or opposition to Christianity of many Neoplatonist emanationists yet so far as Emanationism distinguishes itself from Creationism it is anti-Christian in spirit. Perhaps this partly explains how a scholar who is otherwise universally known for his objective and unbiased approach misunderstood the Neoplatonic doctrine of emanation in the following passage, if of course it is, as I think it is, an actual case of misunderstanding:

> ". . they (the Neoplatonists) failed to see the unsatisfactory character of their attempt to steer a middle way between a true creation and monism, and that their theory of "emanation", given their denial of creation out of nothing on the one hand and their denial of the self-diremption of God on the other hand, could possess no intelligible significance, but remained a mere metaphor. It was left for Christian philosophy to assert the true solution of *creatio ex nihilo, sui et subiecti*"

Emanation is a topic around which there is a prospect of meaningful dialogue taking off among scholars of different cultures. Such a dialogue in the context of varying cultures can enrich the concerned doctrines through exchange of insights and arguments. Standard expositions and criticisms of the different versions of emanationism are rigorously analytical and the respective philosophies to which these versions belong are highly developed. Even if elements of metaphor or mysticism mark the theory of emanationism in some or all the schools of Neoplatonism, it does not follow that the theory admits no rigorous rational formulation.

One of the misconceptions to which I referred above may not always be publicly proclaimed, or even explicitly or consciously affirmed, in so many words, but it seems present behind the back of the mind of many. Philosophy had no distinctive subject matter before the birth of modern European science. In the Middle Ages of Europe, either there was no philosophy or the philosophy that was there did not have any distinctive matter. This is thought to be true as much about India as about the medieval West. Any attempt to say that there was philosophy is considered to be a sure case of equivocation with the word "philosophy". Any substantive subject which received serious attention of thinkers in those ages would immediately be set aside as religious at bottom. This betrays a firm conviction that so called philosophy in the Middle Ages had no distinctive subject matter; it was religion or theology.

A very wide spread view about Indian philosophy in general is that it is a thing of the past. The Modern scientific revolution did not take place in India or in any Asian country. Whatever may be the reason for that, Indian philosophy could not, according to this view, have or have had, then or now, the proper subject matter of philosophy as has developed in modern times; it remained confined to its medieval setting. Any philosophy that may develop in modern India must be therefore on themes taken over from the Modern scientific West. Many scholars in modern India think that what goes in the name of philosophy in modern India is not strictly speaking Indian, and the type of literature of medieval India, now-a-days referred to as philosophy, is not really that if we keep to the more or less precise and technical sense the term philosophy has in the land of its origin.

Philosophy, according to some, is nothing if it is not epistemology or analysis themes and subjects forced on us by developing science. If one tries to argue that even in ancient times very great importance was given to analytical rigor and precision of expression, one is likely to be told that that was all scholasticism an attitude wherein this emphasis on method ensues mostly in the absence of substance or failure to tackle substantive issues. It is a type of scholarship which evaded completely any commitment to real life and its concerns; it is full of artificialities. In the absence of a serious and sincere effort at analysis informed by the new discoveries of science and necessitated by the impact of such discoveries on the developing conception of science, all we have in the middle ages, according to these, is idle logic-chopping. If one tries to argue on the other hand that there had been much discussion on such substantive and serious problems as unity, universals etc. more often than not one will be told to probe deeper and discover for oneself that both the nature of the problem and the motivation behind taking it up for discussion were religious.

The problem of Emanation as discussed in Neoplatonism and its near analogue *Satkāryavāda* in India was not necessarily regarded as a strictly religious theme. It had been originally and prominently discussed by non-Christian pagan scholars. But just as in India many non-theist philosophers contributed to this problem so also among the Neoplatonists some at least could clearly keep their discussion of the problem free from whatever religious commitment they had. The idea of emanation in which we are particularly interested here has a history much older than Christianity. The idea was brought to Christianity from Neoplatonism and the Neoplatonists are mostly not only not Christian; but some of them were fighting against Christianity.

In India though the history of the analogous doctrine, Emanationism-II, a term we shall use here to refer to the theories of *Satkáryaváda*, cannot be claimed to be older than the *Vaidika* culture; yet the *Vaidika* culture cannot be equated with Hinduism in the popular, narrow and Indologist/Orientalist sense of a mere form of religion. Thus both Emanationism-I and analogue-emanationism or Emanationism-II as we shall call it here, are in a sense neutral to either paganism or to any form of religion. But Neoplatonism of the West on the one hand and the *Sámkhya* and *Advaita Vedanta* systems of thought, which advocate the two familiar and major forms of emanationism in India on the other, have certain similarities. Soteriological concern, emphasis on spiritualism, asceticism and to some extent an attitude of other-worldliness are quite visible in both.

One word about the terminology adopted here may be in point before we proceed any further. In most of the standard expositions of *Sámkhya* thought in English the expositors use the expressions evolution and evolutionism where I have been and will be using the words emanation and emanationism. Emanationism is a process which according to the Neoplatonists provides a better description of the way the multiplicity or the many came to be there from the first single principle or the "first cause". The term used for the analogous process by the *Sámkhya Satkáryavádins* is *parináma*. And the process of *parináma* agrees with the process of emanation in some of those essential features in which emanation is commonly contrasted with evolution. Evolutionism advocates a certain actual and temporal process of change and transformation which is, at the same time, a process of development and progress in some specifiable sense of the term.

But in the first place it is at least doubtful if the advocates of emanationism or of *parináma* doctrine believe their process to be temporal or developmental. It may also be noted that there is another process, let us say, of reverse transformation which many of the emanationists and *parināmavādins* admit. Whether a belief in it is strictly consistent with the philosophy of emanationism as distinct from evolutionism is a different issue. But the doctrine of evolution does not normally permit a process of reverse evolution.

These and some other similar considerations suggest strongly that evolution and evolutionism may not be the most suitable expressions for the exposition of *Sāmkhya* thought. This explains our preference for coining a new expression Emanationism-II to refer to the Indian version of emanationism. In spite of its difference from the emanationism-I of the Neoplatonists, the *Sāmkhya* doctrine of *satkārya* and *parināma* are closer to emanationism than to evolutionism.

II

The striking similarities between Emanationism-I and Emanationism-II will be apparent to the reader if he cares to look into any standard account of these doctrines. It would be helpful if I could present here, side by side, some of the comparable theses of these doctrines. I may attempt that at the end of the paper if space permits.

What I want to do at this stage is develop some basic themes of the philosophy of Emanationism and make specific reference to the views of both Emanationists-I and Emanationists-II as and when necessary. To begin with there are two questions which may naturally be expected to be raised. The first is, "How could such a philosophy of Emanationism ever suggest itself to the thinkers of any particular culture or at any particular period in history?" It may be thought that it is not a proper question to ask a philosopher of Emanationism; neither is a philosopher particularly obliged to answer such questions. It is a question for the historians and historians of philosophy. Without disputing that this may be generally true, the reason why I ask this question will become clear soon. The second question is why in the theory of Emanationism the One or the first principle, cause, or hypostasis, starts emanating at all? Why must the One start multiplying itself?

In the system of Plotinus, from the One comes by way of emanation the *nous*, which is variously rendered as Intelligence, Spirit, Mind and so on. From Intelligence emanates *Psyche* or Soul. These are said to correspond to the three realms of the ideas, the mathematicals and the sensibles which, according to Aristotle, Plato admitted.

In one of the two schools of Emanationism-II, viz., the *Sámkhya* school, the first cause or principle is called both *Pradhána* and *Prakrti*. The etymology of these two words tells us clearly that it is the source of everything other than itself and that it is the First and hence it comes from nothing else. So both the One of Emanationism-I and the *Prakrti* of Emanationism-II are eternal and uncaused. From *Prakrti* emanates all the rest. The total number of items which emanate from *prakrti* at least from the point of view of the general *Sámkhya* philosophical account is twenty three. These are *Mahat* (1), *Ahamkára* (1), *Indriyás* (5+5+1), *Tanmátrás* (5) plus *Mahábhútas* (5).

According to the highly general picture of the *Sámkhya* school of Indian philosophy and Emanationism-II, the world consists thus of twenty four items. These fall into two groups. In the first group there is only one item, *Pradhána*, from which everything else emanates but which itself does not emanate at all. In the second group belong twenty three items which emanate from the First cause; yet there are only some five stages in the entire course of the 'process' of emanation from the first to the last item. This may suggest that in the account of the *Sámkhya* emanationists both vertical and horizontal emanations were admitted from the beginning. In some schools of Neoplatonism the need was felt to add a horizontal emanation to the original and generally accepted vertical emanation.

Though this parallelism is there, it seems that there are some differences of detail. What corresponds in *Sámkhya* philosophy to the horizontal emanation of the Athenian school of Neoplatonism or in the system of Proclus is better described as simultaneous emanation or concurrent emanation.

The answer to the question why Emanation begins at all depends on the very nature of that process. One characteristic answer to that question, which states: "... nor is any justification of why the One had to become multiple, necessary", bears reference to and is based on, the generally accepted view that Emanation is an involuntary, unconscious and natural process. It seems the implication is that no further explanation is available; things are the way they are, and that is the end of the story.

Let us reformulate the question: What in the nature of the One makes it thus overflow? Or perhaps, What is it in the nature of the One or of *Prakrti*, in virtue of which entities can emanate from it or out of it? What causes the first ever cause to be activated at all?

Emanation is an explanation of, or accounting for, the fact that the First Principle yields the universe. But it does not really tell us why. In Neoplatonism the One is ambiguously described as utterly undetermined, so much so that nothing whatever can be said about it. We cannot even predicate Being to the One. It is ineffable. The One is absolutely undifferentiated, and all multiplicity falls outside of it. In this sense it is simple.

If these are indeed the characteristics of the One, how can it overflow at all? We will return to this question after we hear what the Emanationists have to say in answer to the second question. Then we shall consider the *Sámkhya* Emanationist-II answer to the same questions.

Certainly neither Emanationism nor the doctrine of the One arose in a vacuum. There was a historical discussion and development that led to these answers. Plotinus certainly knew the Stoic emphasis on unity and the Epicurean emphasis on plurality. He knew the Pre-socratic and Neo-Pythagorean teachings on these issues. The problem of the One and the Many dominates the entire gamut of Greek philosophy. Emanationism as one possible way of reconciling the One and the Many is certainly better than Creationism, in any case.

The Neoplatonist would find the excessive transcendentalism of the Christian doctrine of Creationism its most objectionable feature. The *Sámkhya* or Emanationist-II objection is somewhat different. They probably never knew of the Christian doctrine of Creation. In the *Vaidika* or *Vedic* tradition, creationism is seldom advocated. The principal objection to all *Árambhavada*, the Indian equivalent of Creationism, is its doctrine of causality. *Parinámavada* conceives the One as transforming itself into the Many which is not what Creationism holds. The *Satkáryavada* of *Sámkhya* Emanationism-II insists on the whole that the effect is somehow already in the cause. This should be acceptable to Neoplatonism as well. All schools of Neoplatonism seek to steer a middle course between absolute transcendence and total immanence in the relation between the One and the Many.

There are a number of other parallel points between the Emanationism of *Sámkhya* and that of most Neoplatonist schools. They both agree that the Many has to come from the One. The One must, however, yield the many without suffering any loss, remaining undiminished. They also agree that the notion of causation or emanation must remain an involuntary process, not needing any particular form of willing or action at any given time, either at the beginning, or at any subsequent stage of the process, on the part of the One.

Let us now come back to our second question: "What in the nature of the One makes it emanate into the Many?". The *Sāmkhya* Emanationist-II answer to that question seems more clear and straightforward. If the process by which the Many comes forth from the One is to be understood in a way that is not totally mystical, there is no alternative to avoid admitting that there is some first principle which transforms itself into the Many.

Sāmkhya holds that non-conscious material entities alone can undergo transformation. Conversely, if an entity is not subject to change in principle, it cannot be material. Thus it is in the very nature of material entities to undergo change and transformation, though matter itself, when regarded as pure matter as such, would be simple and therefore unchanging. This is corroborated by our daily experience. A physical entity, be it mountain or mustard seed, a living organism like the human body or some inorganic substance, undergoes slow or fast, perceptible or imperceptible change. This is not so with Consciousness. Mental states do change in us; that means only that one mental state is replaced by another. But no given conscious state changes or transforms itself into another.

So if the One is to change itself in order to become the Many, then the One would have to be regarded as material or non-conscious. The *Sāmkhya* philosophers say not only that the process of Emanation-II is non-conscious, but also that the emanating principle, the *Pradhāna*, is itself non-conscious. They go on to say that the reason why consciousness cannot change is that it is essentially simple, indivisible and without parts. On the other hand, material entities are not simple, they are complex and therefore essentially subject to change.

The logical consequence of all this is that the *Sāmkhya* One or *Pradhāna* must always be in a state of transformation. The process of emanation must have neither beginning nor end. That process will be as eternal as the *Pradhāna*. *Sāmkhya* accepts this logical consequence.

Does the acceptance of this consequence cause anomalies and inconsistencies in the *Sāmkhya* system? Here is the point at which *Sāmkhya* Emanationism-II and Neoplatonist Emanationism-I disagree with each other. Perhaps it is a point for dialogue between the two cultures and their differing conceptions of Emanation. Such a dialogue may turn out to be of mutual benefit.

A related question is: If both the Primordial Stuff and the Principle of Emanation are thus non-conscious, and nothing more is needed to account for the multiplicity, why bring in the Conscious Principle at all? If the argument so far is correct, then the First Principle cannot be Consciousness, for Consciousness cannot transform itself, and multiplicity cannot be derived from it.

No conscious principle is necessary to activate the Unconcious First Cause to yield the things in the world of multiplicity. Why do *Sāmkhya* Emanationists as well as Neoplatonist Emanationists insist that the principle of emanation should be non-conscious? One argument discussed already is that if it is not in the very nature of the primordial stuff to emanate, then the existence of this world would be a matter of mere 'accident'. On the other hand, if the very nature of the *Pradhāna* or the One is to transform, then Emanationism II is simply another name for this natural process of the One or *Pradhāna* transforming itself continuously, uninterruptedly and without interference from or intervention by an Other.

This elimination of consciousness, or any conscious principle, does not arise from any prior commitment or from any reductionist zeal. It is simply that there is no need for introducing consciousness as an explanatory principle for the multiplicity that exists. This is an important point to note. Emanationism-II is neither materialistic nor spiritualistic. And for that reason there may be place in it for consciousness.

As a matter of fact, both Emanationism-I and Emanationism-II do admit consciousness. One reason given by Emanationism-II is that the world of ordinary experience does contain both material things and consciousness. This fact has to be recognized and accepted. It is not possible for Consciousness to emanate or arise at a later stage from the *Pradhāna*. For unlike Evolution, the principle of Emanation is that it cannot give rise to anything that is not already there in the One or the First Cause. Otherwise the One would not be full; it would be less than the multiplicity. Both schools of Emanationism admit that the One is, and must remain, full and undiminished.

The *Sāmkhya* philosophers find here an argument to abandon Monism. They argue that, there must exist, side by side with the one eternal, material and transforming principle the First Cause or

Pradhána another Principle of Consciousness. This principle they call *Purusa*. This must also be eternal; for it cannot come from *Pradhána*, and there is no other source from which anything can come.

Consciousness is what it is by nature; its nature, however, is the opposite of *Pradhána*. Because it is nonmaterial, its nature is not to change. Therefore it is outside the process of emanation, which is after all a process of change and transformation. The *Pradhána* and the *Purusa* are distinct realities; neither of them originates in or emanates from the other. Neither needs, or is dependent on, the other. Thus in *Sámkhya* there are two irreducible and eternal principles. One of them, the *Pradhána*, is eternal, but changing or emanating, non-conscious. The other, *Purusa*, is also eternal, but conscious, non-emanating, unchanging, and the very Principle of Consciousness.

Why then should such a principle be introduced at all? The *Sámkhya* answer is that there is no other way to account for the experienced fact of consciousness and mental states. Without that principle we could not even account for the existence of the *Jíva* or the experiencing soul; they are not only there as given, they are the very ones who raise and discuss these philosophical questions. If these empirical selves were just material, we could have accounted for them as arising from the *Pradhána*, which is capable of giving birth to everything that is material. The *jívas* are embodied souls, whose bodies alone could be accounted for as arising from the *Pradhána*. But they are consciousness as well.

But even *Purusa* cannot, it may be said, explain the existence of the experiencing self. For the *Purusa* cannot cause anything. So *Sámkhya* Emanationism-II posits yet another principle: that of the Witness. *Purusa* is above all the witnessing principle; it is this witness which enables us to posit the One or the Many which emanate from It. For all that emanates from the *Pradhána* is material and unconscious. Further, *Purusa* has the capacity of being reflected in suitable matter, like, for example, the sun being reflected in water or in a mirror. In this case the reflecting medium for the *Purusa* is the very first item or hypostasis that emanates from the *Pradhána*: the *Ahamkára* or ego-consciousness, which is generically different from consciousness as such which knows no desire, change or transformation. The ego is thus not strictly speaking consciousness, but only a mirror for the true consciousness of the *purusa* who remains non-composite, therefore unchanging, inactive.

Being and Knowing in Plotinus

Lloyd P. Gerson

The *fons et origo* of the ancient Greek philosophical association of being and knowing is a fragment of Parmenides' poem preserved for us by Clement of Alexandria and Plotinus:

...τὸ γὰρ αὐτὸ νοεῖν ἔστιν τε καὶ εἶναι[1]

The interpretation of this fragment is of course exceedingly contentious.[2] If, as seems reasonable, we must seek to be guided in our interpretation of it by an attempt to locate its context in Parmenides' poem, then the best guess is that it is a continuation of fragment 2 whose last line is relatively unproblematic in meaning and can be translated "For you could not know that which is not (τὸ μὴ ἐόν) (because that is not possible) nor could you express it." Then, fragment 3 would naturally be translated, "... because the same thing is there for thinking and for being," which would be an explanation of why it is not possible to know that which is not. We cannot know that which is not because we cannot think about it. No reason is given for *this* claim. Perhaps the reason underlying the interpretation expressed in the translation is that thinking is a relation between a thinker and (a) being and without one term of the relation, the relation itself cannot exist. But this certainly cannot have been Parmenides' reason, for in his account of being there can be nothing outside of being that stand in relation to it. This fact raises the serious question whether any authentically Parmenidean reason could be given for a claim interpreted to indicate a separation of thinking and being. And if there is no such reason, then fragment 3, even as a continuation of fragment 2, should perhaps not be such that it makes a claim that is insupportable on Parmenidean principles.

Outside the Eleatic school, Plato was the first philosopher to grasp the importance of the arguments of father Parmenides. He was evidently impressed both with Parmenides' account of being in general and also with the implication of that account for thinking. He seems to reject that account taken in the strongest sense in the first hypothesis of the second part of the *Parmenides*. On a radically monistic interpretation of being, being cannot be known or thought about at all (142a). The rejection of radical monism is confirmed in the *Sophist* (244b-245e). For my purposes, however, I propose to emphasize the positive lessons Plato learned from Parmenides rather than what he rejected. These lessons are incorporated into the middle and later dialogues with considerable subtlety.

The principal lessons are three: First, Eleatic monism can be shown to be false when one realizes that τὸ ὄν is complex. That is, whatever exists is really distinct from the existence it has.[3] This realization has two consequences: we can now legitimately talk about that which exists imperfectly, namely, the world of γένεσις, and we have to distinguish an ἀρχή of οὐσία from complex οὐσία itself, for if οὐσία is complex it cannot be the self-explaining source of being for everything else. Complexity presupposes simplicity, hence the ἀρχή of all must be beyond οὐσία, as Plato tells us in the *Republic* (509b6-10).

The second lesson regards the relation of being thus conceived to knowing. The ἀρχή of οὐσία is also the ἀρχή of knowability (τὸ γιγνώσκεσθαι) for that which is knowable, namely, οὐσία itself or the Forms.[4] Why should this be so? Why should the knowable as such *require* an ἀρχή that is "beyond οὐσία," as Plato says? Is it not enough that there be an ἀρχή of οὐσία and οὐσία itself be the ἀρχή of knowability? One might have supposed that the principle of knowability is finite structure or order or arrangement of parts and that is precisely what οὐσία represents. I would suggest, however, that just because to be knowable is to be complex in this way, the knowable requires a simple ἀρχή beyond it.

Consider a simple example illustrating this point. If a triangle is a three-sided plane figure, then knowing triangularity is a case of knowing that $A = B + C$. $A = B + C$, or more generally, $A = D$, is a representation or, in Platonic language, an image of perfect identity, that is, $A = A$. An image is relationally dependent upon its model. And this is what the ἀρχή of knowability is, the Form of the Good. Aristotle, and the entire Platonic tradition had no difficulty in surmising that Plato meant to identify the Good with the One. In this, Plato will have transformed what for Parmenides is the name of being into the ἀρχή of being.

The third lesson takes us back to the fragment of Parmenides' poem with which I began this paper and to Plato's interpretation of it. For Plato, a reasoned empirical judgment of the form "x is f" depends upon knowing what "f" is. I take it that this is the central point of Socratic questioning in the early dialogues. Knowing what "f" is or just knowing "f" is the paradigm of cognition. If the object of knowing is a finite structure or οὐσία, then there are two general alternatives for describing the state of mind of the knower. Either the mind is in a state representative of that structure or it is characterized by that structure itself, that is it is identified with it. It is clear enough that if these alternatives are mutually exclusive, then the first alternative cannot describe knowing for Plato. For if the representation of the finite structure is other than it, as for example, in a symbolic representation, then knowing would not occur unless one already knew the object of the symbolic representation. Either the knower symbolically represents what he already knows, or all he knows is that the object of knowledge is symbolically represented by someone in some way. But then what is known is not that which is for Plato what is truly knowable. If, then, representation is excluded as the mode of knowing, which is intrinsically a plausible hypothesis for any pre-Lockean philosopher, then knowing is something like an identification of the knower with the structure known.

Plato does not of course give us an account of knowing that consciously contradicts representationalism. What he does do in a number of places is stress that a knower must be the same sort of thing as that which is known. In the so called affinity argument of the *Phaedo* (79a6-7), for instance, knowledge depends upon the soul being akin to that which is known. In *the Sophist* (24836-9a2) τὸ παντελῶς ὄν is said to include νοῦς and hence soul and life.[5] That is, νοῦς possesses the same character as that which is really real. If at the time of writing either of these works Plato supposed that knowing could be representational, then these claims would be unnecessary. For if all that is wanted is a representation of a finite structure, then anything in the sensible world will do as a medium of representation. A body can represent beauty, say, or words or images can represent a truth. The reason why the soul must be made of the same sort of stuff as that which is known is that knowing a truth is not representing it. As Plato puts it in *the Philebus* (65d2-3), "νοῦς is either the same thing as truth or the most like it and the truest thing there is."[6]

If Plato means to make knowing οὐσία something that only that which has true being can do because knowing is some sort of identification of knower and known, then a Platonic interpretation of Parmenides' fragment suggests the translation: "thinking and being are the same thing."[7] This certainly has the virtue of being a literal translation of the Greek. Unfortunately, even if literalism were our only option, which it of course is not, I doubt that the interpretation suggested by this translation accurately represents Parmenides' thought. I also doubt that Plato thought it did. For the qualified identity of thinking and being, which the Platonic tradition infers to be Plato's doctrine on the basis of the dialogues, is inconsistent with monism. I do think, though, that Plato believed that Parmenides "made better," as in the dialogues *Parmenides and Sophist,* was in possession of a valuable insight. That insight is that the highest form of cognition, namely, knowing, is a state or activity that is properly also called the highest form of being. This is a much stronger claim than saying that "only that which is really real can know that which is really real" or something similar. It is a claim that was to resonate down through the history of Greek philosophy.

Viewed from the Eleatic perspective, it is indeed strange that Aristotle should endorse the identification of being and knowing. That he does so on the basis of explicitly anti-Platonic principles indicates the strength of the claim. The manner in which he approaches their identification is instructive. For in the Book Lambda of the *Metaphysics* Aristotle identifies "the best οὐσία" with the highest form of cognition, νόησις, via ἐνέργεια (cf 7.1072b8; 9.1074b2O; 9.1074b34). The unmoved mover, putatively being in the primary sense, is identical with a pure activity which is nothing but νόησις. But because thinking by the best is always of the best, the unmoved mover is thinking of itself (1074b33-4). Thus, primary being is identified with self-reflexive thinking.

According to this claim, and Aristotle's doctrine of πρὸς ἕν equivocity, οὐσία in everything besides the unmoved mover is derived from it. But if to be in the primary sense is to think self-reflexively, then must not everything that has derived being also have derived self-reflexive thinking? It would seem so. One must not suppose that this conclusion can be avoided by saying that thinking is a property of primary being and so that what is derived to everything else is being but not the property of thinking. For if thinking were a property of primary being, then primary being would be in potency to its thinking. But it is the principal burden of the ninth chapter of the twelfth book of the *Metaphysics* to expunge every vestige of potency from being. That is why the unmoved mover cannot even be said to be a νοῦς as opposed to being νόησις, for if it were, it would be in potency to its thinking.

Nor of course can the conclusion be avoided by saying that thinking is just what perfect ἐνέργεια is, and so since nothing but the unmoved mover is perfect ἐνέργεια, nothing else can think! It is true that human thinking is imperfect, but it is also true that an animate nonsensate substance like a tree possesses ἐνέργεια imperfectly.

I do not think that Aristotle's position is hopeless, even on his own expressed principles. For he could interpret thinking in such a way that what the unmoved mover is said to do paradigmatically, even trees could be said to do derivatively. In other words, thinking is just an unimaginable ἐνέργεια in its perfect manifestation, as it is unimaginable in substances inferior to us. Of course, Aristotle represents the thinking of the unmoved mover as pleasurable and as the sort of activity in which we can share sporadically (7.1072b14-18). But these claims seem to be an extra-metaphysical excrescence on the main line of the argument. I mean that Aristotle need not have identified the unmoved mover with a thinker whose activity we can sporadically share in.

In support of this proposed refinement of Aristotle's position, the perfect self-reflexivity of the unmoved mover's thinking might seem to be that which ordinary thinking only approaches asymptotically. For there is no intentionality in it. There is no complexity in it sufficient to differentiate a thinker and an object of thought. Nevertheless, as Plotinus will argue, the conclusion that we should draw from this is not that perfect thinking is perfect ἐνέργεια but that since perfect thinking is essentially intentional, the unmoved mover, if it is a νοῦς or even it is just νόησις cannot be perfect ἐνέργεια.

Apart from the travails of the unmoved mover, Aristotle in *De Anima* explicitly endorses the anti-representationalism implicit in Plato's account of knowledge of Forms: "For in the case of objects without matter, that which thinks and that which is being thought are the same"[8] As it stands, this claim is ambiguous. It can either be interpreted to reject intentionality, as in the case of the unmoved mover, or to affirm it. In the former case, our thinking would be perfectly self-reflexive. But there is no reason for Aristotle to say this, and much evidence to indicate that he believed otherwise. In the *Metaphysics* (12.9.1074b34-5) he tells us that all forms of cognition are intentional, that is, "of something else" (ἄλλου) and only incidentally of themselves. If this is so, how are that which thinks and the object of thought the same?

Perhaps the argument is as follows. If thinking is identification with an intentional object, then in thinking about one's thinking about that intentional object, the thinker has himself indirectly as an object of thought. This might mean that he comes to know that he is a thinker, the sort of thing that can identify with an intentional object.[9] It is reasonable enough that in thinking, the thinker should come to recognize that it is capable of doing just the sort of thing it is doing. But it is difficult to see how this interpretation explains the identity of the thinker with an intentional object other than it. It would seem that if one thinks of oneself indirectly in thinking of the intentional object, then one is precisely not identical with that direct intentional object.

Evidently, Aristotle's solution to this problem is to apply his account of perception to thought and to say that the intentional object and the thinking of it are one in ἐνέργεια but differ in essence.[10] This is a special case of the more general principle that in efficient causality the ἐνέργεια of the agent and the patient are one but not in essence.[11] Thus, for example, an act of teaching and an act of learning are the same ἐνέργεια, but the formula of each is different. Aristotle is apparently led by this analysis to infer that that which is one in ἐνέργεια but two in formula is an imperfect version of that which is both one in ἐνέργεια and one in formula, namely, the thinking that is the unmoved mover and putative primary being. But if it turns out that that thinking is essentially intentional, then primary ἐνέργεια cannot be thinking. And if explaining the relation between thinking and being means explaining it in its most perfect form, then we do not as yet have a proper account of being and thinking. One could say, for example, that thinking is intentional, but that this tells us nothing about the nature of being.

I turn now to Plotinus whose critical appreciation of Aristotle is practically unmatched in the history of philosophy. In his account of νοῦς and οὐσία, Plotinus aims to build a defense of Plato with Aristotelian material. He concurs with Aristotle in rejecting a representational theory of knowledge. He has Epicurus particularly in mind, but the gist of his argument is a general *reductio ad absurdum* of all versions of representationalism. If the intentional object of νόησις is other than the Forms themselves, then νοῦς will have to be able to compare the representation of the Forms in order to know that they are accurate. If it can compare them, it does not need the representation in the first place. If it cannot, then eternal truth is not guaranteed. For the eternal judgments in νοῦς will be judgments whose contents are other than eternal being.[12] Plotinus is here arguing for the claim that truth is not something possessed, where possession is understood as a representational state. So long as truth is agreed to be being in relation to intellect, the only alternative to representationalism of any sort is identity.[13]

Plotinus' claim that eternal truth implies an eternal νοῦς actually has enormous anti-Aristotelian implications. First, it implies that the primary ἀρχή of all is not a knower, for that ἀρχή in its perfect simplicity cannot possess the complexity that knowing requires. Second, as we shall see, the identification of νοῦς with οὐσία is refined in the light of the limitless existence of the One. Third, representationalism is resurrected in order to account for modes of cognition inferior to that of eternal νοῦς. Even the highest form of cognition in an incarnate νοῦς is only an image of the cognitive life of its discarnate paradigm. These anti-Aristotelian implications need to be stressed for it is sometimes supposed even by those sympathetic to Plotinus that his metaphysics is but an embellishment or continuation of its Aristotelian antecedent.

In the remainder of this paper I should like to focus on the second point, Plotinus' reconstruction of the account of being in the light of the account of eternal truth and its subordination to the first principle of all, the One.

Eternal truth is supposed to entail the existence of eternal νοῦς. The entailment is supposed to hold because eternal truth is complex, whereas the One is simple, and the complexity of cannot be grounded in a mere multitude of unconnected beings or Forms. Even eternal existential truths express a connection among Forms. Thus, eternal truth is being for an intellect. But this is construed, on Aristotelian grounds, as the being *of* an intellect. To have νοῦς "looking in at Forms from the outside" would be to concede that νοῦς is irrelevant to the existence of eternal truth. It is not enough, though, to "internalize" the Forms in νοῦς. Plotinus cannot allow that knowing is different parts of a complex whole related to each other.[14] For what would be in the knowing part would be different from what the other part is. Thus, the requirement that eternal νοῦς exist in order to ground truth leads to the requirement of a particular conception of thinking or knowing. According to this, self-knowing is knowing in the proper sense. But this self-knowing is somewhat more problematic than it is in Aristotle's paradigm case, for intentional complexity is not removed from it.

How is this self-knowing then to be understood as knowing Forms? It is to be understood as the claim that there is no conceptual distinction between knowing and knowing that one is knowing.[15] Thus, sKp and sKsKp are mutually implicative, where "s" is νοῦς or a νοῦς, "K" is the activity of knowing (νοεῖν), and "p" is not a proposition but οὐσία or the complex whole containing all the Forms. One difficulty here would seem to be that if in sKp "p" is not to be construed as a proposition, in sKsKp "sKp" must be so construed. That this is not so follows from the fact that if "sKp" is different in content from "p", then self-knowing is regressive rather than reflexive as it must be if knowing (Forms) is self-knowing. For if sKp entails sKsKp but "p" is an intentional object different from sKp, then knowing "p" is different from knowing sKp, and the identity of subject and object of knowing would involve a vicious expansion of the object of knowing.

Many philosophers from widely different backgrounds believe that sKp and sKsKp are mutually implicative. Many fewer interpret this implication as a characterization of self-evidence such that for s, sKsKp is sufficient evidence for p. Thus, knowing would entail certainty or infallibility. Knowing requires sufficient evidence. The only sufficient evidence for "p" that "s" could adduce without initiating an endless regress would be the claim that sKsKp. "s" knows "p" if and only if "p" is self-evident to s. Plotinus is among the philosophers who believe that knowing thus implies certainty.[16] But few philosophers accept the further implication that the self-reflexivity of self-evidence is only possible if intellect is an immaterial entity.[17] For Plotinus, we might say that since νοῦς is immaterial, it naturally follows that knowing is essentially self-knowing. For knowing implies certainty and certainty can only obtain when there is self-reflexivity. More precisely, there is certainty about what is known non-inferentially only when there is self-reflexivity.

It would seem that owing to the condition that knowing is not representational but an identification of knower and known, knowing cannot be essentially inferential. For inference requires a representational element of a logical connective and a judgment that A is so because of B. So, if the intellect is immaterial and if knowing in the primary sense is non-representational and non-inferential and certain, these conditions are accurately albeit elliptically contained in the claim that knowing is self-knowing. I think it is important to mention here in passing a point that we shall return to later. Plotinus' characterization of νοῦς does not depend on an appeal to our own experience, for we are not aware of the ἐνέργεια of separate νοῦς, neither our own nor that of the demiurge. He is not arguing that, say, infallible judgments about our own sense-experience indicate the immateriality of νοῦς or self-reflexivity as its essential property. For sense-experience is not an activity of νοῦς. And yet all forms of cognition inferior to that of νοῦς are potentially illuminated by their paradigm.[18]

From the identity of νοῦς and Forms and the mutual implication of sKp and sKsKp, Plotinus draws a conclusion that is unfortunately easy to misunderstand. He says that Forms themselves possess life.[19] This has been taken to mean that each Form, for example, the Form of Beauty, is itself a νοῦς. So Armstrong translates Plotinus' words καὶ ὅλος μὲν ὁ νοῦς τὰ πάντα εἴδη, ἕκαστον δὲ εἶδος νοῦς ἕκαστος, "And Intellect as a whole is all the Forms, and each individual Form is an individual Intellect."[20] This translation is inaccurate. The last clause is better rendered "and each form is each νοῦς" This text thus rendered only affirms the cognitive identity of each νοῦς with all Forms. It does not obliterate the distinction between νοῦς and Forms or that between the activity of thinking and its intentional objects. The supposed interpretation of the above text is not supported by the identity of νοῦς, νόησις, and τὸ νοητόν.[21] For as Plotinus says elsewhere, it is false to say that Forms are νοήσεις, if this is taken to mean that Forms are not prior to thinking of them or to mean that the Form is just the thinking.[22] On the contrary, we only need to take Plotinus as affirming Aristotle's point that νοῦς is intelligible in the sense that it is identical with intelligible cognitively, from which it follows that what is intelligible, i.e., each Form, is identical with every νοῦς.[23]

The identity of νοῦς with its objects requires the complexity of intentionality. Therefore, νοῦς and οὐσία are subordinated to the ἀρχή of all, which is what Plato explicitly holds in the *Republic* and Aristotle explicitly denies. Therefore, strictly speaking, we should not say that νοῦς is identical with being but that it is identical with what οὐσία actually stands for, namely, essence. The cognitive identity of νοῦς with οὐσία is not the paradigm of being, but the paradigm of complex unity, which everything else "below' νοῦς partakes of insofar as it is one and has an essence. The ἐνέργεια of νοῦς, which is self-reflexive identification with its intentional objects is indeed the paradigm for all cognition. But we are not thereby forced to say that a molecule of water is thinking because it instantiates a Form. For the molecule partakes of νοῦς only insofar as it partakes of its eternal intentional objects. Since thinking is essentially intentional or bipolar, it need not be otherwise. Something does not have to be cognitive in some obscure way in order to be an image of a Form, even though all Forms are eternally identical with a mind.

When in V. 1.8 Plotinus quotes Fragment 3 of Parmenides and endorses what he takes to be Plato's interpretation of it, he says that Parmenides erred in believing that being is one, whereas in fact it is many. As the subsequent reference to Plato's dialogue *Parmenides* shows, Plotinus is not making the point that a plurality of things exists. Rather, he means that finite being or οὐσία is complex. This does not gainsay the unqualified unity of the paradigm of being, the One.

The identity of νοῦς and οὐσία also does not obliterate the logical priority of being to knowing.[24] Neither νοῦς nor the One produce οὐσία if its production is taken to imply logically the possibility that it should not be produced. The eternal dependence of οὐσία on the One and its eternal identity with νοῦς precludes mind-dependent idealism where this is contrasted with realism.[25]

Aristotle's hypothesis in the *Metaphysics* that being is οὐσία is disconfirmed when he identifies οὐσία with the ἐνέργεια of νοῦς (7.1072b26-7). For the ἐνέργεια of νοῦς cannot be perfect ἐνέργεια. It cannot be so because it is essentially intentional and therefore complex. A complex ἐνέργεια cannot be what being is itself because that which is complex has as its own ἀρχή that which is simple. If being were itself complex, consider what we would say about the simples of which it is composed. This last point is an authentic Eleatic insight that Plotinus rescues from the wreckage of extreme monism.

Once being is understood not to be οὐσία, the connection between οὐσία and νοῦς can be reconstructed. The identity of νοῦς and οὐσία need not be taken to imply that to be is to be a thought or a thinker. In this regard, Plotinian epistemological realism is what Aristotelian epistemological realism should have been. If we ask the Aristotelian question "what is being?" the Plotinian answer is being = ἐνέργεια instead of being = οὐσία.[26] Nothing in Plotinus more dramatically shows how he uses Aristotle to rehabilitate Plato than this answer, for the concept of ἐνέργεια does not even appear in Plato.

Once this move is made, an independent line of investigation is opened regarding the question of the *eternal* identity of νοῦς and οὐσία. There is no longer a need to posit an eternal νοῦς to account for eternal motion. The Plotinian approach is rather to argue that eternal truth exists, but that it could not exist without eternal νοῦς. Those who agree that eternal truth exists, but deny that an eternal νοῦς exists which is cognitively identical with Forms must say either that eternal truth can exist without such identification or that these truths are in fact identical with the One, which is beyond νοῦς.

Plotinus' response to both possibilities amount to the same thing. Since the One is the cause of the being of everything, it follows that the One is virtually all things, that is, it has the power to cause all things to be, including Forms.[27] But it does not follow from this that the One is *eminently* all things, that is, among other things, the perfect instance of eternal truths. Plotinus cannot say this because that would compromise the simplicity of the One.

Let us recognize that Plotinus does actually say that the One has all Forms m it "indistinctly" (μὴ διακεκριμένα).[28] In fact, the reason given for the One's having the ability to give existence to everything is just that it has everything in it "beforehand." But this claim must be balanced by another sort, according to which "there is no necessity for something to have what it gives" and "the Form is in that which is shaped (νοῦς), but the shaper was shapeless."[29] If the indistinctness of the Forms in the One were intended to represent a state prior to a temporal creation, then Plotinus would I think have to say that the One is eminently as well as virtually all the Forms, in which case his position would not be substantially different from that of, say, Aquinas. But since νοῦς is eternally caused to be by the One, its having the Forms "indistinctly" should not be understood in this way.[30] Rather, as Plotinus tells us, to say that the One is none of the Forms means that they are "later (ὕστερα)" than it, but to say that the One is all of them means that they "come from it (ἐξ αὐτοῦ)."[31] The Forms are later in the sense that they are an effect of which the One is the cause, though *what* they are is uncaused.[32] The phrase "come from it" is difficult, but it cannot indicate a process of emptying where the result is that something is *outside* the One, for there is no such thing. I would suggest that the phrase "come from it" indicates the result of νοῦς's contemplation of the One under the aspect of the Good. That is, when νοῦς achieves the Good it does so by contemplating all the Forms.[33] So the indistinct existence of Forms in the One does not indicate another mode of being for Forms, much less a superior mode of being.[34] It indicates that the eternal achievement of goodness for νοῦς requires that it go beyond itself to the Good itself, but that this amounts to identification with all the Forms in contemplating.[35]

Another reason why the One cannot be eminently all the Forms is that a paradigm is really related to its images. As Plato tells us in the *Parmenides* (132d), we can consider a Form and its image "insofar as they are like" and this surely indicates a real relation. But Plotinus says that the One is related to nothing. Hence, it cannot be a paradigm, which it must be if it is eminently all Forms.

The only way that the One can be virtually all the Forms but not eminently all the Forms as well is by positing eternal νοῦς. For it is νοῦς's relation to the One under its aspect of the Good that is the instrument of the creation of eternal truth.[36] Why should it not have been the case that the diffusion of the infinite goodness of the One results in eternal Forms but not eternal νοῦς? Why is it necessary, as Plotinus puts it, that νοῦς is generated from the One?[37]

This is an unusually difficult question to answer. It is not satisfactorily answered by saying, as Plotinus does, that νοῦς is "closest" to the One, so that when the One produces it produces νοῦς. "Closest" here means that the complexity of νοῦς is least removed from the simplicity of the One. That is, νοῦς is closest to being one that a complex thing can be. Thus, νοῦς is called ἕν πολλά.[38] But I think there is a hint here of a more profound answer.

Consider the putative eternal truths "three is odd" or "fire is hot." The Platonist must explain these truths as grounded in Forms. But how are, say, the Forms of three and odd related eternally? The history of Platonic answers to this question is part of the history of the doctrine that Forms are ideas in the divine mind. Plotinus is too good of a philosopher to be satisfied with the typical naive interpretation of this claim. He sees that Forms must be distinct yet somehow identified.[39] Distinctness and identification are not here contradictories. The identification of Forms is a cognitive activity, as is the "separating" of them. In fact, Plotinus distinguishes two kinds of νοῦς, ὁ μερίζων νοῦς and ὁ ἀμέριστος νοῦς, engaged in such activity.[40] The judgment made by dividing νοῦς that "three is odd" involves concepts and is in time. It is a representation of what "undivided νοῦς" does. "Three is odd" could not be an eternal truth unless there existed an eternal mind making the identification.[41]

Perhaps I can make this clearer in the following way. Eternal truths for Plotinus are of the form A = B, not of the form A = A. This is sometimes obscured by uncritical characterizations of the ἐνέργεια of νοῦς as non-propositional. The formula A = B cannot stand for anything real, if by "real" we mean extra-mental or non-cognitive. For the real world tells us, as Bishop Butler said, that "a thing is what it is and not another thing." One who identifies eternal truth with a simple ἀρχή is content with this. Plotinus is not because he does not. Complex eternal truth could only be *for* a mind that is making the identification of A and B eternally. Add to this claim the Aristotelian claim that mind is cognitively identical with what it knows and we arrive at the Plotinian conclusion: μία μὲν οὖν φύσις τό τε ὄν ὅ τε νοῦς.[42] Without νοῦς there could be Forms, but there could be no truth.

Endnotes

1. This is usually given as fragment 3, indicating a continuation of line 8 of fragment 2. Clement of Alexandria, *Stromata* U.440.12 and Plotinus, *Enneads* V.1.8.17, 1.4.10.6, and IR.8.8.8 preserve the fragment but do not suggest its relative location in the rest of the poem.
2. For discussion of the problems and possibilities see L. Taran, *Parmenides* (Princeton University Press: 1965),41-44; D. Gallop, *Parmenides of Elea* (University of Toronto Press: 1984), 8.
3. Cf. *Sophist* 245d4-6: ὥστε οὔτε οὐσίαν οὔτε γένεσιν ὡς οὖσαν δεῖ προσαγορεύειν [τὸ ἓν ἢ] τὸ ὅλον ἐν τοῖς οὖσι μὴ τιθέντα. The wholeness referred to here is the complexity of that which is, whether it be οὐσία or γένεσις.. The second hypothesis of the *Parmenides* makes the same point at 142b6-8: ἆρα οἷόν τε αὐτὸ εἶναι μέν, οὐσίας δὲ μὴ μετέχειε; —Οὐχ οἷον τε.— Οὐκοῦν καὶ ἡ οὐσία τοῦ ἑνὸς εἴη ἂν οὐ ταὐτὸν οὖσα τῷ ἑνὶ οὐ γάρ ἂν ἐκείνη ἦν ἐκείνου οὐσία. The words οὐ ταὐτὸν referring to "one" and οὐσία indicate the real distinction.
4. It is evident from 510a9 that τοῖς γιγνωσκομένοις of 509b6 refers at least to that which is νοητόν (cf. 509d4), which I take it is primarily the Forms.
5. *Republic* 510b is also relevant in its insistence that the mode of cognition that is the highest part of the divided line must proceed "without images."
6. There is another somewhat more indirect piece of evidence for this interpretation from the *Timaeus*. At 30d1-2 the demiurge is said to make the world according to the "noblest among the things which are intelligible" and at 37a1-2 the demiurge itself is said to be "the best of the eternal intelligible." The clear implication is that there is some sort of identity between demiurge and Forms.
7. It is clear from the passage in which Plotinus cites the fragment (V.1.8.15-17) that he interprets Parmenides in this way and that he believed Plato held the same view, that is, he believed that Plato interpreted Parmenides thus and that Plato thought that the claim thus interpreted is true.
8. *De Anima* 3.4.430a3-4. Cf. 7.431b17.
9. So R.D. Hicks, *Aristotle's De Anima* (Cambridge: Cambridge University Press. 1907), 485, and 429b9 where Aristotle says that only when an intellect becomes an intelligible object is it capable of thinking itself.
10. Cf. *De Anima* 2.2.425b26-7: ἡ δὲ τοῦ αἰσθητοῦ ἐνέργεια καὶ τῆς αἰσθήσεως ἡ αὐτὴ μεν ἐστι καὶ μία, τὸ δ' εἶναι οὐ τὸ αὐτὸ αὐταῖς. By contrast, Plotinus, V.1.8.8, will say that thinking and object of thought are one ἐν οὐσίᾳ.
11. *Physics* 3.3.202a20.
12. Cf. V.5.1.19-21. In this passage, Plotinus uses the Epicurean term τύποι for the putative impressions or representations in νοῦς. I take it the argument is

generalizable whatever the exact of the representations, so long as they are distinct from Forms. At line 55 he uses the more general term εἴδωλα.

13. Cf. III.5.7.50-3; III.9.1.6-10; V.3.5.21-9; 13,12-14; V.4-2-44--6; V.5.1.19-23; V.9.5.7-8; VI.6.7.8-10; VI.7.41.12-13. At V.5.2.8 Plotinus characterizes the identification as a kind of "fusing" (συγκραθέντας) with Forms. This indicates well the real identity of that which is nevertheless distinct.

14. Cf. V.3.5.17-23; V.5. 1. Cf. J. Pepin, "Elements pour une histoire de la relation entre l'intelligence et l'intelligible chez Plato et dans le neoplatonisme," *Revue Philosophique de Louvain* 53 (1956): 54-5 and R.T. Wallis, "Scepticism and Neoplatonism," in W. Haase and H. Temporini (eds.), *Aufsteig und Nedergang der Romischen Welt Teil* 11: Bd. 36.2 New York. Walter De Gruyter (1987): 922-5 on the skeptical background of this argument Sextus Empiricus, *Against the Logicians* 1.310-312, states the dilemma faced by those who hold that cognition is an identification: "For if the mind apprehends itself, either it as a whole will apprehend itself, or it will do so not as a whole but employing for the purpose a part of itself. Now it will not be able as a whole to apprehend itself. For if as a whole it apprehends itself, it will be as a whole apprehension and apprehending, and, the apprehending object will no longer be anything; but it is a thing most irrational that the apprehending subject should exist while the object of the apprehension does not exist. Nor, in fact, can the mind employ for this purpose a part of itself. For how does the part itself apprehend itself? If as a whole, the object sought will be nothing; while if with a part, how will that part in turn discern itself?"

15. This is most clear at 11.9.1.36-9; 46-54. CL V.3.1.15-28. The passage at II.9.1.53-4 ends: τὶς χώρα τῇ ἐπινοίᾳ τῇ χωριζούσῃ τὸ νοεῖν ἀπὸ τοῦ νοεῖν ὅτι νοεῖ; this would seem to indicate an absence even of conceptual distinctness between knowing something and knowing that one is knowing something. But if this is so, then the only way we can preserve distinct knowers is to say that "p" as known by "s" has some different quality from the way "p" is known by "r". Thus, "s" knows "p" in a unique manner or from a unique perspective. This fact does not, however, entail an obliteration of the distinction between subject and object. If it did, there would be no reason for denying Aristotle's claim that νοῦς is unqualifiedly actual. Cf. J. Hintikka, *Knowledge and Belief* (Ithaca, N.Y. Cornell University Press, 1962), 103-25, for a useful survey of various versions of the claim that knowing "p" and knowing one knows "p" are mutually implicative.

16. V.5.1.1-2: Τὸν νοῦν, τὸν ἀληθῆ νοῦν καὶ ὄντως, ἆρ' ἄν τις φαίη ψεύσεσθαὶ ποτε καὶ μὴ τὰ ὄντα δοξάσειν; cf. VI2.8.2-5 where the infallibility of νοῦς is explained by saying that the being of the object of thinking is just its being thought. With this passage should be read V.6.6.24-7 where Plotinus distinguishes "man" and "thought of man," "horse" and "thought of horse," etc. We can reconcile these two passages if we say that "man" and "thought of man" are

distinct according to a real minor distinction in the latter passage, though in substance they are identical. Cf. Pepin (1956:49-50).
17. Proclus, *The Elements of Theology, prop.* 15 in (Dodds, ed. Oxford: Oxford University Press, 1963), states this with utmost clarity. Since a material entity has parts outside of parts, them could never be literal self-reflexivity (πρὸς ἑαυτὸ ἐπιστρέφειν) in it. Cf. the commentary of Dodds (202-3) on this passage with references.
18. V-3.4.1-4 seems to contradict this when it says that we are in accord with νοῦς in two ways: "either by having something like its writing written in us like laws, or by being as if filled with it and able to see it and be aware of it as present." The "laws" are evidently concepts. I think that the second way we are in accord with it need only mean that we are aware that νοῦς exists and is active, without our actually engaging in that activity. For how could we engage in that activity while in time and without being aware of all the Forms at once? There is no conceptual space in Plotinus' system for incomplete identification with οὐσία.
19. For Plotinus the most important association of life with Forms is of course to be found in Plato's *Sophist* 248e. Cf. IV.7.9.24; V.4.2.43; V.5.1.33ff; V.9.8.1-8; VI.2-20. Cf. Hadot (1960:108-9). That each Form is an intellect means that the world of Forms is in fact also a community of distinct intellects. Cf. IV.3.5.6-8: ἐπεὶ κἀκεῖ οἱ νόες οὐκ ἀπολοῦνται, ὅτι μὴ σωματικῶς μεμερισμένοι, εἰς ἕν ἀλλὰ μένει ἕκαστον ἐν ἑτερότητι ἔχον τὸ αὐτὸ ὅ ἐστιν εἶναι. W. Himmerich, *Eudamonia, Die Lehre des Plotin von der Selbstverwirklichung des Menschen* (Wurzburg, K. Trilische, 1959), 50 cites III.2.16.17-20 where Plotinus says that πᾶσα δὲ ζωὴ ἐνέργεια. In connection with this statement Himmerich argues, Plotinus employs Aristotle's principle that actuality precedes potency to conclude that primary life has primary ἐνέργεια. This is not strictly true because the One is primary ἐνέργεια. Cf VI.8.20.9-16. Also, III-8-8.8; V.1.8.17; V.3.5.26; V.6.6.21; V.9.5.29; VI.6.2.9; VI.7.40.15 on the identification of thinking and object thought As H.R. Schwyzer, *Plotinos in Pauly-Wissowa RE-Sonderausgabe* (Munich: 1978), 553-4, points out, Plato nowhere implicitly identifies νοῦς and οὐσία but this is a natural inference from *Republic* 507b, 509b, and 509b.
20. V.9.8.3-4. Cilento's translation is not so misleading, "E, precisamente, nel suo complesso lo Spirito é il complesso delle forme; ma la forma nella sua singolaritá é lo Sprito preso come singolo." Similarly, but more literally Bréhier, "L'intelligence complète est faite de toutes les idées, et chacune des idées, c'est chacune des intelligence" and Harder-Theiler, 'Und zwar ist der Geist als Gesamtheit alle Ideen, die einzelne Idee aber ist der Geist als einzelnes . . ."
21. V.3.5.44-5.
22. V.9.7.14-17: ὅθεν καὶ τὸ λέγειν νοήσεις τὰ εἴδη, εἰ οὕτω λέγεται ὡς, ἐπειδὴ ἐνόησε τόδε ἐγένετο ἤ ἔτι τόδε, οὐκ ὀρθῶς ταύτης γὰρ τῆς νοήσεως πρότερον δεῖ τὸ νοούμενον εἶναι. D.Roloff, Plotin *Die Grosschrift* III8-v8-v5-II.9 (Berlin, Walter de Groyter, 1970, 18 commenting on III.8, where Plotinus

explains how thinking and being are identical and νους is true life, says: "Der Geist ist als Subject zugleich das intentionale Objekt, wie dieses umgekehrt zugleich Object denkende-Subject ist." Cf. 51. Against this view, I hold that the Forms are intentional objects of νοῦς and that self-reflexivity means the subject thinking the subject thinking the intentional object, thereby maintaining the distinction between subject and intentional object. For at VI.2.8.4-5 Plotinus says ἃ δ' ἔστιν ἄυλα, εἰ νενόηται, τοῦτ' ἔστιν αὐτοῖς τὸ εἶναι.

23. Cf *De Anima* 3.4.430a1-2. G. Huber, *Das Sein und das Absolute. Studien zur Geschichte der ontologischen Problematik in der spätantiken Philosophie* (Basel: Verlag für Recht und Gesellschaft argues that in the "Spiritualisierung des Eidos" Plotinus develops an idea beyond anything explicit in Plato or Aristotle. I think this is true only in that Plato is not explicit on the cognitive identity of νοῦς and Forms and for Aristotle, cognitive identity of νοῦς and its objects is not identity with Plato's Forms.

24. Cf. VI.6.6.5-10, 31-3; οὐ γάρ, ὅτι ἐνόησε τί ποτ' ἐστὶ δικαιοσύνη, δικαιοσύνη ἐγένετο, οὐδ' ὅτι ἐνόησε τι ποτ' ἐστὶ κίνησις, κίνησις ὑπέστη (8-10). Cf. also V.9.7.11-12; VI.2.8.14-16; VI.2.19.18-2 1; VI.7.8.4-8. Plotinus is probably making use of *Parmenides* 13 2b7-10 where it is argued that τὸ νοούμενον is prior (logically, though the text is not explicit) to a νόημα of it. Cf. VI.7.40.6: νόησις πᾶσα ἐκ τινός ἐστι καὶ τινός. V.4.2.6-7: ἀόριστος μὲν αὐτὴ [νόησις] ὥσπερ ὄψις, ὁριζομένη δὲ ὑπὸ τοῦ νοητοῦ. In V.2.1.12-3 the logical priority of τὸ ὄν to the "gaze" [θέα] upon the One is clear. It is tempting to gloss τὸ ὄν with τοῦ νοητοῦ above. The explicit identification of the objects of νοῦς with Forms is made at V.9.8.1-4. Cf 1.6.9.41-2; VI.7.15.9-13. H. Oosthout, *Modes, of Knowledge and the Transcendental. An Introduction to Plotinus Ennead 5.3 [49]* (Amsterdam, B. R. Grüner, 1991), 68, puzzlingly, argues against the logical priority of being to knowing, even though earlier (64) he asserts it

25. This is most clearly brought out at VI.7.8.3-8: But supposing [νοῦς] discovered the thought of horse in order that a horse (or some other animal) might come into being here below? Yet how would it be possible for him when he wanted to make a horse to think a horse? For it is already clear that the thought of horse existed if he wanted to make a horse; so that it is not possible for him to think it in order to make it, but the horse which did not come into being must exist before that which was to be afterwards.

26. VI.8.20.9-15. Cf. V.4.2.35; VI.8.7-46-8; VI.8.12.22-3; VI-8.13.6-8; VI.8.16-15, 25, 30, 31, 35 and Krämer (1966: 12-13).

27. On the One as δύναμις of all things cf. V.3.15.33. Also, III.8.10.1; V.1.7.9-10; V.3.16.2; V.4.1.24-5, 36; V.4.2.38; V.5.12.38-9; VI.7.32.31; VI.7.40.13-14; VI.S.9.45; VI.9.5.36-7.

28. V.3.15.31. CE V.2.1.1; V.4.2.16; VI.7.32.14; VI.8.21.24-5.

29. VI.7.17.3-4, 17-18.

30. G. Lerous, *Plotin. Traité sur la liberté et la volonté de l'Un* [Ennéade VI,8 (39)] (Paris: J. Vrin, 1990), 96. 108, seems to unpack the metaphorical representations of the One in terms of eminence, a position that is in conflict with his basic thesis that the simplicity of the One entails its impersonal nature.
31. VI.7.32.13-14. Cf. V.5.12.41.
32. Cf. VI.7.2.40-3: εἰ οὖν μὴ ἔχει (the Forms) αἰτία τοῦ εἶναι, αὐτάρκη δέ ἐστι καὶ μεμονωμένα αἰτίας ἐστὶν, εἴη ἂν ἐν αὐτοῖς ἔχοντα σὺν αὐτοῖς τὴν αἰτίαν. Also, VI.7.17.6-9;VI.7.40.21-4. Cf C. Rutten, "La doctrine des deux actes dans la philosophic de Plotin," *Revue Philosophique* 146 (1956): 104-5 and J. Bussanich, *The One and Its Relation to Intellect in Plotinus* (Leiden: E. J. Brill,1988), 163-5.
33. V.6.5.8-9: καὶ τοῦτό ἐστι νοεῖν, κίνησις πρὸς ἀγαθὸν ἐφιέμενον ἐκείνου. Cf. VI.7.15.11, 16. At V.4.2.4, 12, 13 Plotinus seems to hold that the One is intelligible [νοητόν]. On my interpretation, the One is called νοητόν here because the good is achieved by νοῦς by contemplating, that is, having an intelligible object. At 3.8.9.10-11 Plotinus denies that the One is intelligible. The assertion and denial that the One is νοητόν are parallel to the statements that the One does and does not contain all the Forms and should be interpreted accordingly. I believe this interpretation helps explain why in the notorious text at V.1.7.54 Plotinus should not be taken to be saying that the One looks at itself by turning back upon itself and in this way produces νοῦς. The generation of νοῦς in this passage refers to the achievement of νοῦς in identifying itself with what the One virtually is, all Forms. So G.J.R. O'Daly, *Plotinus' Philosophy of the Self* (Shannon: Irish University Press, 1973), 71-2. On this difficult passage cf. J. Igal, "La Genesis de la Intellegencia en un pasaje de las de Plotino (V.1.7.4-35)," *Emerita* 39 (1971), M. Atkinson, *Ennead V 1: On the Three Principal Hypostases. A Commentary with Translation* (Oxford: Oxford University Press 1983), 156-60), and J. Bussanich, op. cit., 37-43. Should V. 1.6.17-18 be read differently? Cf. A.C. Lloyd, "Plotinus on the Genesis of Thought and Existence," *Oxford Studies in Ancient Philosophy* 5 (1987): 159-60.
34. If this were not so, then a real relation between the One and νοῦς would be erected. It is pertinent to recall *Parmenides* 132de where Parmenides derives a regress from Scorates' agrument that Forms are παραδείγματα wherein their instances are images or ὁμοιώματα of these. Pamenides' argument is that we can consider model and copy καθ' ὅσό the one is like the other. This presumes a real relation is possible. T. Szlezák, *Platon und Aristoteles in der Nuslehre Plotins* (Basel: Schwabe & Co., 1979), 164 n. 539 is too quick to dismiss the containment of Forms in the One as inconsistent with Plotinus' general doctrines. Cf. V. 1.7.10-13: ὧν οὖν ἐστι [the One] δύναμις, ταῦτα ἀπὸ τῆς δυνάμεως οἷον σχιζομένη ἡ νόησις καθορᾷ ἢ οὐκ ἂν νοῦς. Ἐπεὶ καὶ παρ' αὐτοῦ ἔχει ἤδη οἷον συναίσθησιν τῆς δυνάμεως, ὅτι δύναται οὐσίαν and the analysis of this passage by Igal, *art. cit.*, 142ff. As Igal argues, the subject of δύναται is νοῦς. So Lloyd, *op. cit*, 161. Since νοῦς is eternally contemplating Forms, the sense in which the One has all

Forms indistinctly in it ought to mean that goodness for νοῦς is just contemplating Forms and that the One is the cause of the existence of this ἐνέργεια.

35. If I understand Lloyd, op. cit, 175-6, rightly, my interpretation is consonant with his own. Lloyd thinks that it is the One as object of thought which acts on νοῦς and produces οὐσία, whereas I have said that it is the One as object of desire. Perhaps draw amount to the same thing if the desire of νοῦς is just βούλησις, an intellectual desire.

36. On the generation of νοῦς and Forms from the One cf. V.2.1.7-1 I. Also, III.8.9.29-32; V.1.5.18-19; V.1.7.5-35; V.3.10.40-4; V.3.11.4-12; V.4.2-4-7; V.5.5.15; VI.7-17.14-16, 21; VI.7.35.19-23. All of these passages analyze the generation of νοῦς into a twofold process or presume such an analysis. The point of this logical analysis which is couched in temporal terms only for heuristic purposes, is to indicate both the priority of being and desire to knowing and the essential complexity of the ἐνέργεια of cognition. V-9.8.9-22 makes abundantly clear that the derivation of νοῦς is logical.

37. V.4.2.3.

38. Cf. IV.8.3.10; V.1.8.26; V.3.15.11, 22; VI.2.2.2; VI.2.10.11; VI.2.15.14; VI.2.21.7;, 46-7; VI.2.22.10; VI.5.6.1-2; VI.6.8.22; VI.6.13.52-3; VI.7.8.17-8; VI.7.14.11-12; VI.7.39.11-14. There are some very weak arguments for the existence of νοῦς offered at V.9.4.

39. At VI.9.5.16-20 Plotinus says of νοῦς that it is a πλῆθος ἀδιάκριτον καὶ αὖ διακεκριμένον and just as in ἐπιστήμαις πάντων ἐν ἀμερεῖ ὄντων ὅμως ἐστὶν ἕκαστον χωρὶς αὐτῶν. The divisions and separateness of the parts of νοῦς cannot be the same as what is divided in discursive judgment. I think that what it does mean is that νοῦς is virtually divisible in discursive judgments. Cf. VI.4.2.22-3 (with lines 47-9) where Plotinus says that that which participates in true being ὅλῳ οὖν ἐντυγχάνει τῷ ὄντι. A.C. Lloyd, "Non-Propositional Thought in Plotinus," *Phronesis 31* (1986): 362, replying to R. Sorabji, "Myths About Non-Propositional Thought," in M. Schofied and M. Nussbaum (eds.), *Language md Logos Studies in Ancient Greek Philosophy* 1982) and *Time, Creation & the Continuum* (Ithaca, N.Y. Cornell University Press, 1983), 152-6, states the position I am defending with admirable lucidity and precision: "The *totum simul* which is associated with pure intellect neither is nor is known by a collection of propositions, but is what occupies the place of the genus of being. For that can be grasped as a merely undifferentiated whole, while in fact it contains a multiplicity of parts. It is the former aspect, Being as an intentional or phenomenological object, which is the content of the thinking qua thinking and whose non-complexity prevents it from being propositional." Cf. J.M. Rist, "Back to the Mysticism of Plotinus: Some More Specifics," *Journal of the History of Philosophy* 27 (1989): 190-7 and M.R. Alfino, "Plotinus on the Possibility of Non-Propositional Thought," *Ancient Philosophy* 8 (1988): 273-6 also replying to Sorabji.

40. V.9.8.23.
41. V.5.1.42-4: εἰ δ' ἁπλᾶ φήσουσι, δίκαιον χωρὶς καὶ καλόν, πρῶτον μὲν οὐχ ἓν τι οὐδ᾽ ἐν ἑνὶ τὸ νοητὸν ἔσται, ἀλλὰ διεσπασμένον ἕκαστον.
42. V.9.8.18.

Platonism in Late Classical Antiquity
and Some Indian Parallels

Henry J. Blumenthal

The Platonism of late antiquity is, of course, what we now call Neoplatonism. That term is a modern one.[1] All the philosophers whose work comes under this heading thought of themselves simply as Platonists, and the doctrine they were expounding as the Platonic philosophy. For Plotinus, the man normally thought of as the founder of this type of philosophy, all that he might have to say had been said before though it might not have been set out explicitly, and could be found in the text of Plato (cf. V 1.8.10-14). For Proclus in the 5th century, after two hundred years of this kind of thinking, the same view of what he was doing still stood, as it did for Simplicius and Damascius into the 6th. Thus Proclus, in the preface to his *Platonic Theology*, could write of his whole enterprise, and that of his Neoplatonic predecessors, as the understanding and exposition of the truths in Plato.[2]

Given our modern views of Plato and Aristotle, as philosophers whose views developed and whose answers to questions were not always the same, it is important to realize that their ancient interpreters looked at them as creators of fixed systems: though they might recognize that they did not always say the same things about the same questions, they saw such apparent inconsistencies as problems about the relation of disparate statements to an assumed single doctrine rather than about how different doctrines might relate to each other.

Before going on I should perhaps offer three explanations and an apology. The apology is simple: it is to those who know a great deal about Neoplatonism, to whom some of what I shall say is basic common knowledge.The explanations are three.

First, that I am taking late classical antiquity to start in the 3rd century C.E., following an old Cambridge custom of taking ancient Greek philosophy to have ended in the year 180. The second is to say what I am going to do here. It relates to the first. When this view of the limits of classical antiquity still held, the study of Neoplatonism was regarded as rather disreputable, in the English-speaking world at least, and the few apparent exceptions tend to prove the rule. Thus E. R. Dodds' edition of Proclus *Elements*, still one of the great achievements of Neoplatonic scholarship, and the first modern commentary on a Neoplatonic work, was seen not so much as evidence that there was here a rich field for new scholarly endeavour as an indication of that scholar's eccentricity. The common attitude found its expression in the preface to the first volume of W.K.C. Guthrie's *History of Greek Philosophy*, where he relegated Neoplatonism to the realms of the unphilosophical and the un-Greek: "with Plotinus and his followers, as well as with their Christian contemporaries, there does seem to enter a new religious spirit which is not fundamentally Greek...": that was in 1962.[3] "What I want to do is to look at some of the characteristics of Neoplatonism, and to see how the picture of this philosophy, or rather group of philosophies, has changed during the last three decades. I think most would now agree it is basically Greek.[4] As to the importance of the religious and soteriological elements in it, which for many of its adherents was rather small in any case, that is arguable, and its significance depends on the extent to which one regards other forms of ancient philosophy as enquiries into how one should live the best life. What is important is that most of the Neoplatonic writings we have are clearly philosophical rather than religious or otherwise concerned with the supernatural. I shall therefore take it for granted that we are talking about philosophy, and not any of the other things with which Neoplatonism has sometimes, not always wrongly, been associated. We might note, however, that the combination of philosophical and other concerns, which is more marked in Neoplatonism than in earlier Greek philosophy, is also to be found in some Indian systems.

The third explanation concerns the possible Indian parallels in my title. I have already indicated that I regard Neoplatonism as a purely Greek phenomenon. Though some ideas in it may resemble some Indian philosophical ideas, and those that come under the heading of Advaita in particular, there is no evidence that there was any influence in either direction. What is more interesting, and potentially enlightening, is to consider what parallels there may be between the various kinds of Neoplatonism and the systems of Indian thought which might have something in common with it. At this stage I should make it clear that I have no expertise in Indian philosophy, and in that respect I have come here in the hope of learning from those who do. I should, however, like to observe that almost all the discussion that there has been has centred on Plotinus, and that it would be interesting to see whether the differences between his philosophy and that of later Neoplatonists might also be found in those Indian thinkers who have ideas in common with, but not ancestral to or drawn from, later Greek Neoplatonism. A look at the index of *Neoplatonism and Indian Thought* shows over five times as many references to Plotinus as to Porphyry or Proclus, the latter being almost entirely confined to two contributions.[5] Iamblichus, Damascius and the Aristotelian commentators are conspicuous only by their almost complete absence. The commentators are represented only by a single appearance of Simplicius, and that not in his own right but as a source for Proclus. I would also observe that a lot of the comparisons that have been made between Plotinus and Indian philosophy have taken as their basis Advaita-Vedanta as expounded by Sankara who was born about five centuries after Plotinus' death, a chronological fact that is rarely mentioned. It should be, because it, of course, rules out any possibility of influence on Plotinus: as far as I know there is no evidence of influence in the other direction either. In fact this insouciance is characteristic of much work that has been done in the whole area: I hardly need to spell out its implications. Perhaps our work here can improve this unsatisfactory situation.

Let us now return to the new version of Platonism, as it is to be seen in the thought of Plotinus. Of course some of the ingredients of that thought were developed in the interval between him and Plato, but it is to Plotinus that we owe the reworking of these and other ingredients into an original and philosophically coherent whole.

Since we are looking at the development of the picture of Neoplatonism as well as the characteristics of its thought, it is interesting to note that the concept of Plotinus has changed more than once. At one time he was thought of primarily as a mystic, and it was somehow supposed that his experience coloured, not to say, vitiated his philosophy. He then came to be seen as a serious philosopher, inferior in antiquity only to Plato and Aristotle, but unlike them, a philosopher with a system rather than the instigator of a series of enquiries many of which led to no clear solution. Now he is starting to look more like his predecessors, a thinker who was often unable to make up his mind on the right answer to some of the questions which he considered over and over again.

The other striking feature of Plotinus' thought, which is by no means peculiar to him, is that much of it is devoted to a quest for solutions to matters that were problematic in Plato. His successors and I hasten to add that I am using the word primarily in a chronological sense were concerned in their turn not only with these matters but with some loose ends in the new version of Plato that Plotinus had produced. For these reasons I think it may be worth spending some time on Plotinus himself.

Let us begin by looking at some of the rather obvious problems in Plato. The most important in its consequences was the nature and status of the Good (ἐπέκεινα τῆς οὐσίας...ὑπερέχοντος) on the other side of being ... and lying above or beyond it (*Republic* 509B). Most English-speaking students of ancient philosophy would have little trouble with this, and interpret it as meaning that the Good was the Form on the far side of the constituents of the world of Ideas, and so furthest from us, but still a Form. Some in other places would take it to mean that it was beyond the other Forms and so not a form at all.[6] Plotinus and his successors had no doubt that the latter interpretation was a correct one and so turned the Form of the Good into something that was not a Form at all, but an entity, or rather a non-entity, that transcended all the other Forms and was the source of their existence: the second part of this proposition does, of course, have clear support in the *Republic*, most obviously in 509B itself, just before the controversial words. The Good beyond Being was also identified with the first hypothesis of the *Parmenides*, for it was assumed by all Neoplatonists that dialogue contained positive teaching rather than logical exercises or any of the other subjects with which it has at various times been supposed to deal. So clear was this to the Neoplatonists that they eventually came to classify this dialogue, along with the *Timaeus*, as one of the two containing the highest metaphysical truths. It was not, however, a wholly new idea that the *Parmenides* could be interpreted along such lines: attempts to extract positive teaching from the earlier hypotheses had been made in the period before Plotinus, notably by the Neopythagorean Moderatus. But now this approach became standard: the points for discussion were the number of hypotheses that could be interpreted in this way, and what the significance of each, particularly those from the fourth onwards, might be: on the first three there was for a time general agreement that they represented the three primary divisions of the Neoplatonic intelligible world, the One, (νοῦς), Intellect, and (ψυχή), Soul.

As for the One, it is strictly indescribable, and its nature can only be indicated by negating descriptions which apply to Intellect, the sphere of Being in Plato's sense, populated therefore by Forms. Some of the indications of its nature which Plotinus used are taken straight from the *Parmenides*: so, for example, when Plotinus says in various places that the one has no name, and is the object of neither reason, knowledge, sense-perception or opinion, his words echo *Parmenides* 142A: it has no name, no reason, no knowledge, no sense-perception, no opinion the Greek words are the same (cf. e.g. VI 7.41.37f.).

By such and similar means Plotinus was able to offer what he regarded as a satisfactory answer to the request made on several occasions in the *Republic* that Socrates should provide a description of the Good, a request with which he notoriously never complies. Modern readers might well ask what the hypotheses of the *Parmenides* have to do with the *Republic*, and answer "nothing", but that would not have impressed Plotinus, knowing as he did that Plato had a systematic world picture to which different dialogues all contributed in their different ways. To say that one was simply unrelated to another because it was dealing with a different subject was unacceptable at this time, though as we shall see it was later to become a principle of interpretation that each dialogue had its own specific purpose. Even then it should not be incompatible with others. All this was greatly helped by the tendency which ran right through Neoplatonism to follow the letter of Plato and Aristotle while making no serious attempt to be guided by the philosophical context of a given text.

A further striking difference between Platonic and Neoplatonic Platonism is the absence of the political, and so of many of the ethical elements, a difference which once caused Plotinus to be labelled a Plato reduced by half.[7] Political structures were of no interest to most of the Platonists who lived under the Roman Empire, or the earlier centuries of its Byzantine continuation. Themistius, who was a prominent member of the Byzantine governing aristocracy, and was one of the few thinkers to stand apart from Neoplatonism, is for that very reason no real exception.

So far we have been talking about the treatment of problems in Plato and we shall, of course, need to say much more about that. But before we continue we must bring in another ingredient in the compound that constitutes Neoplatonism, namely Aristotle. Its importance was already noted by Porphyry who, in a well known remark in the *Life of Plotinus* (14.4-5) wrote that there are unnoticed Stoic and Peripatetic doctrines present in his works. He goes on to say that the *Metaphysics* are there in condensed form (*Ibid.* 5-7). The Aristotelian views with which we are particularly concerned just now are those about the nature of the unmoved mover, and the soul and its operations, for these are an essential part of the organization of the Neoplatonists' intelligible world.

The self-thinking supreme principle of Aristotle's world from the *Metaphysics*, and the notion that the thinking mind is identical with its objects from the *De anima*, with some refinements made by Alexander, formed the basis of the structure of Plotinus' second hypostasis, or level of being, Intellect. This they did by providing a means by which the components of that structure, namely the individual intellects which were also Platonic Forms, related to each other and formed "parts" of a self-thinking whole.

We can now go back to Plato, to recall some further problems which he left unclear or unsolved. In assessing their relevance we must bear in mind that a Platonic problem was as good a starting point for a Neoplatonic doctrine as was a firm statement of Plato's views. So too was a Platonic answer to a question put for the sake of argument or exploration like those in the second half of the *Parmenides*. And in the case of Intellect Plotinus' intellect all three types of Platonic texts contribute.

To start with the Platonic problem, or rather problems. First, there is the well-known passage in the *Sophist* where Plato is discussing the content of the sphere of being in the fullest sense, (τὸ παντελῶς ὄν) (248E-249A). That should contain (κίνησις, ζωή, ψυχή) and (φρόνησις:) motion, life, soul and intellect, and yet the Forms which must be a part of that sphere. I shall assume that Plato had not abandoned the view that they must be permanent and unchanging. Because of the scope that this passage gave for the introduction of life and thought into the intelligible world, it was to be a favorite text of Plotinus and his successors. Further problems offering scope for interesting if Platonically improbable solutions were available in the first part of the *Parmenides*. The difficulties raised there by Plato himself were serious enough to have led to the rethinking if not to the abandonment of the theory of Ideas. But for Plotinus they offered material for his own philosophy.

We may begin with Plato's first problem, the extent of the world of Forms. Socrates in the *Parmenides* is unwilling to accept the existence of Forms of things which are trivial or undignified; mud dirt or hair are the examples given though *Parmenides* tells him he will learn to accept them when he becomes more of a philosopher. Whether Plato did or did not accept these particular substances as suitable for Forms, there are other doubts about what had Ideal archetypes. Most Platonists accepted Xenocrates' limitation to things that exist in nature (fr.30H). Plotinus simply said that everything that exists here in the physical world exists in the Intelligible too, though in a superior mode, and derives its existence from it: (ἐκεῖθεν ἦν σύμπαντα ταῦτα καὶ καλλιόνως ἐκεῖ) (V 8.7.17). The word (καλλιόνως) simply avoids any problems that might be caused by having undignified and worthless objects prefigured in the intelligible world.

Only in one early treatise, which may contain some other ideas that Plotinus dropped later, or even put up only for discussion, and in a rather disjointed chapter of it at that, are various trivial and offensive things excluded. This is the only place where mud and dirt are mentioned, with the suggestion that things of that kind are imperfections, and so not to be sought in Intellect, but rather to belong to Soul and to arise from its inability to produce anything better from matter (V 9.14.7-17) admittedly a paradox in terms of Plotinus' account of the world. Elsewhere one can find warrant for the inclusion of earth and earthy things, and so of mud (cf. VI 7.11).

Whatever they might be like in this world, the inferior things are present in the higher world in a form appropriate to it. Whether or not each individual object or person was also represented there, is a different matter, but I should say it was one of those questions on which Plotinus never finally made up his mind. In any case the apparently simple answer that whatever is here must be there too is not simply a move to avoid facing a Platonic problem. It is a necessary part of a fully monistic system in which everything derives from the One and nothing has an independent existence like the receptacle in Plato's *Timaeus*: one might describe it as non-dualism. When Intellect emerges from the one the kind of Being that is the result of its procession is Form, and not just the form of something, but of everything, with nothing excluded (V 5.6.1-4).

The next problem raised in the *Parmenides* is participation, but before looking at that it may be helpful to explain why a world whose constituents are Forms is described as Intellect, a description which is unremarkable in a Neoplatonic context, but would clearly have puzzled a classical Platonist. In terms of Platonic loose ends we may begin yet again with a *Parmenides* problem, namely the one about the difficulties in thinking of the Forms as thoughts (νοήματα) which would be located in souls. It is presented as a possible solution to previous difficulties, but naturally turned down because it would deny to the Forms the self-subsistent status which was essential to them. But if a Form is a νόημα, it cannot be a thought of nothing, so goes the argument, and if it is to be a thought of something, it must be a thought of something that is: it would then be a thought of the one single Idea discernible in its several objects, and that would be the Form. Since for Plato thoughts and their objects are not identical, the original thought could not be a Form after all. A further objection is that if particulars participate in Forms in the way participation is envisaged by Socrates, a reference to *Phaedo*-type participation then they too would be thoughts. If they did not there would be thoughts that do not think (νοήματα ἀνόητα). That, Socrates is made to say, would make no sense, and so the proposal is abandoned (132B-C).

If we now return to Plotinus, we find that not only the proposal itself, but some of the consequences which Plato regarded as unacceptable, are taken on board as appropriate to Forms as he conceived them. It is here that the Aristotelian input is most marked. The extent to which the *Parmenides* problem influenced Plotinus appears most clearly in the Treatise "That the intelligibles are not outside the Intellect, and on the Good" (V 5) which discusses both the nature of the contents of Intellect and their internal relationships. Whether or not the intelligibles were contained in Intellect, or were outside, had been a matter of controversy, and both positive and negative answers seem to have been given as interpretations of Plato: we have Porphyry's account of how he was converted to Plotinus' view by a fellow student, Amelius (*Life* 18.10-22). We are not now dealing simply with the Middle Platonist notion that the Ideas were the thoughts of God, *inter alia* because for Plotinus Intellect was not the supreme principle.[8]

The starting points for this discussion are usually taken as the Demiurge's model in the *Timaeus* and Aristotle's self-thinking Intellect. While the latter is, as we have already indicated, important both here and elsewhere, the section of the *Parmenides* we have just considered has clearly been one of Plotinus' points of departure. That emerges at the very start of the treatise, where Plotinus asks whether Intellect could think things which do not exist and whether it could be not-intelligizing, an expression which recalls the thought which do not think in *Parmenides* 321C. Plotinus takes the answer to both questions to be negative and says that therefore Intellect must know itself (V 5.1.3-6). It cognizes intelligibles, which must be like itself because if they were not it would be impossible to do so: to cognize what is other and external is characteristic of sense-perception rather than intellection. The kinds of beings that are to be found at this level must be intelligible (νοητά) else they could not be parts of, Intellect (Νοῦς)" of they are not intelligible and without life, how can they be beings, asks Plotinus (*Ibid.* 37f). In a later chapter Plotinus spells out that intelligence and being are the same: so we have one kind of thing, nature, all being, and truth (V 6.3.1f.). In an earlier treatise he had already argued that intellect and being entailed each other: if there is being, then there is intellect: if intellect, then being (V 6.6.21). Forms are identified with Intellect in other places, most notably in the long discussion of the contents of Intellect in the treatise on "How the multitude of Forms came into being, and the Good" (VI 7, cf. esp. ch. 2 passim).

Thus for Plotinus Ideas are indeed thoughts, and since all Ideas are both thought and objects of thought all are νοήματα, and none of them (ἀνόητα). In other words Plotinus has accepted an identification which was unacceptable in the *Parmenides* and turned it into a description of essential features of his second hypostasis. In all the placers we have just referred to the identity of the contents of Intellect both with the whole and with each other rests on the Aristotelian identity of thought and thinker, as set out in the (*De anima*). It is this which makes sense of the notion that any part of Being, as soon as it is conceived as an object of thought, becomes itself an intellect. One could discuss at some length whether Being or Intellect is prior: the short answer would be that it depends on the context, but the question is only a real one if one considers the procession of the hypostases quasi-chronologically otherwise it does not matter. That intellect, as a whole, is based on the self-thinking (νοῦς) of *Metaphysics Lambda*, should by now be clear enough. It differs in two ways: in not being the supreme principle, and in having acquired some content for its thinking.

Participation problems raised in the *Parmenides* are also soluble if one operates with Plotinus' suppositions. Two difficulties about participation are raised. The first is that if each particular participates in the whole of a Form, then that Form will be split up: none of the attempted explanations is accepted. Alternatively, each particular might be thought of as participating in part of a Form rather than the whole of it. In that case paradoxical consequences appear to result: a small particular, for example, would be in possession of a part of smallness smaller than the Idea of smallness itself. Part of Plato's trouble was that he was still inclined to think of immaterial entities as though they had material attributes. Plotinus, who no longer did, was able to think of immaterial entities being omnipresent in the material world. The treatise, split by Porphyry into VI 4 and 5, which he wrote to explore the implications of such omnipresence is now known by a title which may well be taken from the problems, of this part of the *Parmenides*. Admittedly the title is Porphyry's, though Porphyry's claim that the titles of his edition were those by which the treatises were generally known does not exclude that it was originally Plotinus' own. The title is περὶ τοῦ τὸ ὂν ἓν καὶ ταὐτὸν ὂν ἅμα πανταχοῦ εἶναι ὅλον, on Being being one and the same at the same time everywhere. The sentence in which Plato expresses the difficulty he sees in participation in whole Forms runs: ἓν ἄρα ὂν καὶ ταὐτὸν ἐν πολλοῖς καὶ χωρὶς οὖσιν ὅλον ἅμα ἐνέσται, so Being is one and is at the same time present in many things which are separate (131B): the resemblance is too close to be entirely coincidental. The complete and simultaneous presence of the intelligible applies not only to the contents of Being in the strictest sense, namely the collection of individual beings which constitutes the second hypostasis, but also the larger collection of the same entities existing in a more diffuse form in the third. In fact in this treatise Plotinus is not particularly concerned with differences between these two hypostases, but more interested in the nature of the intelligible as a whole, and as opposed to the sensible. A tendency to blur the distinction between these two hypostases was to be one of the loose ends in Plotinus that was picked up by later Neoplatonists. What is of interest in our present context is that the presence of beings (ὄντα) in a more diffuse form in Soul makes it easier to think of them as omnipresent at the even further diffused level of existence which is the physical world. When a Form is in the individuals it somehow becomes multiple, like the impressions made by a single seal. It might also be regarded as analogous to the presence of a single soul in each part of its body as opposed to a quality like white which is divisible (cf. VI 5.6.1-15).

Strictly speaking Plotinus would say that the body, or whatever, was in its soul: here he follows the lead of the *Timaeus* (34B and 36D) where the world is said to be in its soul, an idea which Plotinus developed into the general principle that a lower kind of being is always in a higher one rather than vice-versa. While closer examination might reveal difficulties in the notion that any one particular is in the Form that makes it what it is, it does make it possible for Plotinus to escape from the problems presented by the splitting of Forms in the *Parmenides*.[9] A further section of the *Timaeus* was also helpful here, namely the well-known passage on the ingredients of soul at 35A. The correct interpretation of this passage is, of course, unclear, but what Plotinus found in it included a distinction between what is divisible only in so far as it is distributed around bodies, which is soul, and what is actually divided in bodies, that is sensible qualities. This interpretation of *Timaeus* 35A is applied to omnipresence as a whole at IV 2.2.39-42, though there it is clearly at the level of souls. It does, however, help to show how Plotinus sees the presence of the intelligible in the sensible world.

In any case the ability to explain how an intelligible entity can be present as a whole in more than one place means that the arguably unreal difficulty about pieces of Forms being better representations of some things than the Forms themselves disappears. Let us return for a moment to VI 4-5, where chapter 8 of VI 5 provides some further comment on the whole or part problem. The Idea, writes Plotinus, gives none of itself to matter because it cannot be broken up. Being itself one it has the capacity to inform what is not one with its own unity, and to be present with all of itself in such a way as to inform each individual part of anything with the whole of itself (cf. VI 5.8.35-39). In any case, as he had argued earlier in the treatise, an entity which is immaterial must be exempt from all the *pathë*, affections, of the body of which the most important is divisibility: what has no magnitude cannot be divided (VI 4.8.15-22). A further argument depends on the nonspatial nature of the intelligible: what is not in space cannot be divided if division means, as it does, that one part of a thing is in one place and another in another (*Ibid.* 33-36).

At this point one might ask how a Form can be present as a whole everywhere without replicating itself, and giving rise to one of the variants of the "third man" problem, the alleged need for an extra Form to account for the relation between the original Form and its descendants. Plotinus' answer would be in terms of the way in which lower entities could partake in, or receive higher ones. The participating one participates to the extent that it can, and takes on as much of that in which it participates as it is able, although the whole is present (VI 4.3.10-11). As much as, is not it should hardly need saying a reference to the size of a piece of Form or soul, but of the extent to which it is available to the participating subject.

So far we have been looking primarily at Plotinus' responses to some of the problems raised in the first part of the *Parmenides*, and these are the most interesting in so far as they show how what had been problems were either explained away or even adopted as positive contributions to parts of Plotinus' own philosophy. But before we go on we should look again at the way in which material from the hypotheses was used to delineate the features of the several hypostases. We have already seen how this worked in the case of the negations used to speak about the ineffable One. In the same way the second hypothesis will give Plotinus some of the distinctive characteristics of Intellect, and its appendix, sometimes taken as the third, of Soul. Soul, however, relates to the dialogue much less clearly than Intellect and the one.

The unity of Soul is such that diversity will appear in it, while that of Intellect is greater, to the extent of the unity there predominating over the diversity and multiplicity of the individual intellects or Forms which are to be found there. Plotinus most often distinguishes Intellect as εἷς καὶ πολλοί, one and many (both masculine), from Soul which is (πολλὰ καὶ μία), many (neuter) and one (feminine), but at V. 1. 8.23-27 he refers to the Platonic *Parmenides* distinguishing the first one, which is more properly one, the second which he calls ἓν πολλά, one many, and the third which is ἓν καὶ πολλά, one and many (neuter in both cases). The *Parmenides* says of the one that is that it is ἓν πολλά one many, at 144E, in the second hypothesis, while at 155E the "third" talks of a one that is and is many, ἓν καὶ πολλά. The rest and movement in Intellect, perhaps primarily drawn from the *Sophist*, may also be found in the second hypothesis: this one must be in motion and at rest (145E).

Plotinus did not, of course, write commentaries as such, but an extended discussion of how his intelligible hierarchy related to various texts from Heraclitus to Plato, many of them perversely interpreted, may be found in the treatise "On the three primary hypostases", V 1. That he did not write commentaries was no bar to his works being treated as commentary by his successors, who expressed themselves in that medium more and more as time went on. Not only were they convinced that they were merely expounding the philosophy of Plato: while doing so they were often explaining and, where necessary, reconciling with Plato's doctrines the writings of the Platonist philosopher Aristotle.

It is time to move on from Plotinus to the rest of the story: I have spent so long on Plotinus because he produced outlines and guidelines for later Greek philosophy. That is by no means to say that he was followed in every detail. Of course he was not: guidelines were sometimes abandoned, and outlines obscured. The first point to stress again, one well-enough known to those who occupy themselves with the thought of later antiquity, is that the new Platonism was not an undifferentiated mass. It is not so long since that was how it was regarded, and even a pioneering historian like E. Vacherot, who was well enough aware of some of the differences, could lump all the Neoplatonists together under the heading of Ecole d'Alexandrie,[10] though, to be fair, he did make some attempt to sort them into less comprehensive categories, as did E. Zeller, in different versions of his *Geschichte der Philosophie der Griechen*, influenced perhaps by Hegelian preconceptions rather than the facts of philosophical history.[11]

Even among those not unfamiliar with the field there was a tendency to think of two kinds of Neoplatonism, a Plotinian-Porphyrian variety and a late and nasty kind beginning with Iamblichus and losing itself in the highly complex structures of Damascius. A further, but as it now turns out, partly misguided attempt to sort later Neoplatonists into groups defined by their approach to philosophical problems as well as the geographical locations in which they studied and taught was made by Karl Praechter in a well-known article published in 1910, entitled 'Richtungen und Schulen im Neuplatonismus'.[12] Among others Praechter distinguished a more scholarly from a speculative strain of Neoplatonism, and associated the former with Alexandria, the latter with Athens. The thinkers who most clearly represented these tendencies were Proclus and Damascius at Athens, and the Aristotelian commentators at Alexandria. The first was responsible for an ever increasing complexity and multiplication of entities as well as, one might add, an interest in dubiously philosophical matters, the second for a more sober approach which restrained these inclinations. This picture was generally accepted, even after H. D. Saffrey, in an article published in 1954, had demonstrated the extent of the connections between the two centres: not only was there considerable movement between them by persons who studied at one and subsequently taught at the other: there were even family connections between them.[13] One obvious problem for anyone working within this theoretical framework is as Praechter realized what to do about Simplicius, superficially an Alexandrian by virtue of his output, but an Athenian by location and association. Praechter himself, in an article on Simplicius written nearly twenty years later, in Pauly-Wissowa's classical encyclopedia, sought to distinguish an Alexandrian strain manifested in Simplicius' commentary on Epictetus' *Encheiridion* from an Athenian one in the other works. This is a matter to which we must return: let us now go back to the beginning of post-Plotinian Neoplatonism.

The old view of its development, and this includes Praechter's, saw Porphyry not only as the editor of Plotinus' works, but as a faithful disciple of his master, following him rather closely but admitting, or allowing greater scope to, tendencies which Plotinus had avoided, like the major excursion into allegorical interpretation in the exposition of the Odyssean Cave of the Nymphs in the work of that name.

More recent work on Porphyry has seen him prepared to depart from Plotinus in a reorganization of the intelligible world which led to the reduction of Plotinus' three hypostases to two, by treating Soul and Intellect as one: even the One and Intellect were not, on this view, as clearly distinguished as they needed to be if they were to be kept clearly apart, as they are not in the Turin fragment of a *Parmenides* commentary attributed to him by Professor P. Hadot.[14] This so-called telescoping of the hypostases, expounded by Professor A. C. Lloyd in the *Cambridge History of later Greek and Early Medieval Philosophy*,[15] was widely accepted, but has been questioned in some subsequent work, which would see Porphyry preserving the Plotinian structure. Another area where Porphyry did move on from Plotinus was in the explanation of the body-soul relation: this was one of the Platonic loose ends which Plotinus had difficulty in tying up, for reasons which are perhaps too obvious to state, namely the difficulty of establishing a satisfactory relation between the incorporeal and the material, an old problem which merely became less obtrusive in Neoplatonism because of its monism. Porphyry's solution was produced by the use of his doctrine of ἀσύγχατος ἕνωσις, unconfused unification of things that were in fact uncombinable.

That was a doctrine that did not find favour with later Neoplatonists, who preferred the more Platonic notion of some sort of juxtaposition, obscured by some of them by the interposition of extra levels of soul, of which the last was almost an Aristotelian entelechy.[16] They did, however, adopt and sometimes extend a doctrine that was first taken seriously by Porphyry, that between soul and body there was a quasi-material vehicle made of some sort of πνεῦμα. What is interesting from the point of view of the development of Neoplatonism is that both these questions, the body-soul relationship and the distinction, or lack of it, between the hypostases Intellect and Soul, were ones on which the answers given by Plotinus were either unclear or conspicuously inadequate inadequate of course to late Platonists, not to us, who would generally find their solutions even worse. They were therefore questions which presented a challenge to later Neoplatonists in just the same way as problems in Plato had presented a challenge to Plotinus himself.

In two ways Porphyry may be seen as departing from Plotinus, if not necessarily from the Platonic tradition, in directions where later Neoplatonists were to follow. One was in the adoption of Aristotle's categories into the Platonist system. Plotinus himself had rejected them as inappropriate. The other, not unconnected, was the practice of writing commentaries on Aristotle, two of them in addition to the Introduction on the *Categories* itself. In his treatment of Aristotle he also seems to have moved further in the direction of later Neoplatonism, by taking the line that Aristotle and Plato were really expounding the same philosophy in different words: the lost commentary, or part commentary, on *Metaphysics* Λ would have made it easier to assess both the scope and the practical effects of that hypothesis.

Before continuing it might be useful to say some more about why the relation between Intellect and Soul in Plotinus may be called a "loose-end". The answer is that though Plotinus insisted that there were three hypostases, neither more nor fewer, his treatments of the second and third vary according to context in such a way that one may be equipped with the attributes of the other.[17] Thus when Plotinus is concerned with the structure of his world, they are kept clearly apart. On the other hand, where he is trying to show how all things are present in the Intellect, he will put into it the dynamic aspects of the intelligible which more properly belong in Soul. Conversely, when he is dealing with the transcendence of Soul above the material world he will emphasize the static elements of intelligible being which more properly belong to Intellect. Lest this seem merely careless or irresponsible, we should note that it arises in part from the difficulty of distinguishing different kinds of immaterial existence, a difficulty which sometimes led Plotinus to say that they differed by otherness alone. Such untidiness was not acceptable to later Neoplatonists, who felt no inhibitions about multiplying the number of immaterial entities, and levels of immaterial existence, which they admitted to their philosophy.

The most important steps in this direction were taken by Iamblichus. Here again our picture of the development of Neoplatonism has changed. Partly because of the accidents of survival, the credit or discredit for these changes once tended to be attributed to Proclus. Iamblichus, whose strictly philosophical work was represented by fragments in Stobaeus and the reports of his successors while productions like the *De mysteriies* and works on Pythagoras survived, was held responsible for the corruption of Neoplatonism by superstition and occultism. During the last twenty years there has been a process of rehabilitation[18] in my view it has gone a little too far and concentration on what we can learn about Iamblichus' interpretation of Plato and Aristotle, and the philosophical views expressed therein, has shown that he was responsible for at least two of the characteristic features of later Neoplatonism, namely the elaboration of the structures of the intelligible world, and the exposition of Neoplatonism in a course where Aristotle was studied as a preliminary to the study of Plato's dialogues, arranged in a fixed curriculum leading to the highest insights of the *Parmenides* and *Timaeus*, with each dialogue being assigned a peculiar purpose, as were some of the works of Aristotle. Just how far all the details were worked out by Iamblichus himself is uncertain, but that he provided the initial framework is clear enough. So is the fact that Proclus, however much he may have esteemed him, did not always agree with Iamblichus. Less clear is the extent of the contributions of Proclus' master Syrianus: these are now receiving more attention and looking correspondingly more important.[19]

Even those who have some expertise in Neoplatonism have all too readily thought of Iamblichus as the immediate precursor of Proclus. In fact Iamblichus may have been a student of Porphyry's at the end of the 3rd century: Proclus was not born till the 5th. What happened between them is by no means clear, and such attempts as have been made to trace the philosophical history for pagans of the intervening period have been hindered by the lack of surviving works and the paucity of other evidence, particularly for the 4th century.

It may in any case be true that not a great deal happened before the study of Platonism was revived at Athens, probably by the Athenian Plutarch the son of Nestorius late in the 4th century or early in the 5th: the case for attributing the revival to him is strong, if not impregnable.[20]

At Alexandria, though there was a continuous tradition of, at least, Platonist mathematics, from which emerged Hypatia at the end of the fourth century with her pupils Synesius and probably Hierocles, most of the interesting developments took place later. Many of those involved, and the case of Hierocles is particularly worth noting, had been students of Plutarch and his Athenian disciples, Syrianus and Proclus, most importantly Ammonius not, of course, the mysterious Ammonius Saccas, whom I have deliberately left out of this account.

Let us return for the moment to the restructured type of intelligible hierarchy associated with Iamblichus and Proclus, but present in one form or another in most of those who came after Plutarch. We have already referred to its greater degree of elaboration. In it souls and intellects were clearly distinguished, and furthermore divided into different kinds of each, in a framework of triadic structures in which entities were grouped by virtue of participation or lack of it: various orders of gods, all of which could be linked to the *Parmenides*,[21] were also worked into this system. The highest member of a vertical triad would be distinguished by being unparticipated: the second by participating in the first and being participated in by the third, the third by being merely a participant. The separation of an unparticipated level meant that the aspect of soul or intellect that was to be found there was separate from what came below, notwithstanding the apparently conflicting principle that higher entities acted at a greater distance than lower ones. Thus everything could be kept in its own place, and the demarcation problems that arose in the case of Plotinus' second and third hypostases no longer applied. At the same time horizontal triads formalized the relation between different aspects of a given level of being, a system already prefigured in the more informal discussions in Plotinus, of Being, Life and Thought in the hypostasis Intellect. Here again Porphyry began the more formal and rigid treatment of questions which had been explored without firm conclusions by Plotinus, and one might see this too as a part of the process of tying up loose ends even if the outcome was a degree of complication that we might think required radical simplification.

That the structures of Proclus were a conscious move towards greater order appears in his comment that Syrianus had cleared up some of the vagueness and confusion of his predecessors: "he set determinate limits to what was undetermined in the speculation of our predecessors, and put the confused state of the various orders into a condition where they could be distinguished intellectually" (*Platonic Theology*, 1.10-42.4-20S-W). Similar comments may be found elsewhere. That one might accuse Proclus of causing confusion by having too many entities is another matter. In one respect he had fewer than Iamblichus, for Iamblichus took the creation of new entities to the highest level, and invented a one above the one, a lead rejected by Proclus but followed later by Damascius.

Another piece of tidying up that should be mentioned here, though it is well-enough known, is the rejection of Plotinus' view that a part of the individual human soul could remain transcendent, either at the level of Soul or Intellect, another point on which Plotinus may not have come to a final decision. This view, which Plotinus admitted to be unorthodox (cf. IV 8.1.13), allowed each person a permanent place in the intelligible. Apart from the fact that this broke through the boundaries of the Neoplatonic world, it had other consequences which were regarded as unacceptable by Iamblichus, Plutarch, Syrianus, Proclus, and Simplicius: among their complaints were that it entailed permanent intellection on the one hand, and impeccability on the other.[22] For Iamblichus there is just one text that points in the opposite direction, though it may be a mistake by Simplicius.[23] Otherwise there was a wide consensus, which had implications not only for the means by which some Neoplatonists thought one might ascend to the highest levels but also for the interpretation of Aristotle.

The interpretation of Aristotle brings us back to the question of the two schools of Athens and Alexandria: were they the repository of different kinds of Neoplatonism, and if so how did the Alexandrian kind diverge from the sort of philosophy which we have sketched in relation to Proclus?

Until about fifteen years ago it was generally accepted, following Praechter, that the two groups were philosophically different, and that the Alexandrians were distinguished by having a simpler metaphysical system in general, and not believing in a transcendent one in particular. In some cases these characteristics could be attributed to the fact that their works were commentaries, so that they might have been keeping their own views in the background. I think their methods of work are now sufficiently well-known for it to be apparent that that is not likely to be the correct explanation. Here too views have changed, and the picture of an Alexandrian commentator, of whom Simplicius was taken to be a particularly good example, carefully if somewhat verbosely expounding the text of Aristotle in a basically scholarly way is no longer on display: not long ago many would have thought that a perfectly reasonable assumption, and one equally valid for most of the commentators. Now that it is coming to be recognized as false even by those without a special interest in late Neoplatonism, there is a corresponding realization that the personal philosophies which find expression in the commentaries may differ. We shall look briefly at a few examples of such differences, which must serve to cast doubt on the notion of a specifically Alexandrian line. That there was such a line, to be opposed to an Athenian one, is *prima facie* questionable if one considers the extent of the cross-fertilization between Athens and Alexandria. In any case closer examination of two works which Praechter had put forward as examples of Alexandrian metaphysics, the *Encheiridion* commentary by Simplicius to which we have already referred, and Hierocles' on the Pythagorean *Carmen Aureum*, has shown that they are not. Not only is it true that the more complex metaphysics present elsewhere are not always relevant. The existence of a One can be shown to be either implicit or clearly required in some passages of each. That was demonstrated ten years ago by Mme. I. Hadot,[24] and in itself invalidates an important part of the till then traditional distinction. It does not, I hasten to add, prove that there were no differences between the two centres, or that Athenian metaphysics was not sometimes more elaborate than Alexandrian: this is still an open question.

With these points in mind let us come back to the man who is generally credited with the responsibility for the Aristotle industry at Alexandria, Ammonius. Ammonius had learnt from the Athenians by two routes: his father Hermias had studied with Syrianus, and he himself with Proclus. He was moreover related to them through his father's marriage to Aidesia, a kinswoman of Syrianus. Further connections of this type may be seen in the careers of Hierocles who, as we have already noticed, was taught by Plutarch, and, in the reverse direction, those of Simplicius and Damascius who were taught by Ammonius at Alexandria.

Ammonius presents two problems, firstly why he inaugurated the concentration on Aristotle which was to be continued by his pupils, and secondly how much of the vast bulk of commentary he and they produced between them is attributable to him. Since some of the commentaries were published by Philoponus, purportedly based on Ammonius' lectures but in most cases "with some additions of his own", while only two have come down to us under Ammonius' own name, it is not easy to disentangle his views: this also applies to the *Metaphysics* commentary of Asclepius, and even to those commentaries of Philoponus which have come down under his own name exclusively.[25] A start on this difficult task has been made, but much remains to be done.[26] It is complicated by the fact that Philoponus will treat Ammonius as a different person from the commentator even in work which is labelled as his. That could, of course, be the fault of the transmission rather than Philoponus, though one wonders if he was not in some cases trying to present a front of Neoplatonic respectability by presenting his own work as that of his master. His disputes with both the dead Proclus and the living Simplicius provide a reason why he might have wished to do so. Though recent work on Philoponus has tended to highlight his individuality, and the influence of Christianity on some of his ideas, it is important to remember that the framework of his thought was a Neoplatonism to most of which both Proclus and Simplicius would have subscribed, even if in his commentaries he did not go as far as Simplicius in seeking to demonstrate the agreement of Plato and Aristotle.

The other question about Ammonius is less complicated, but likewise admits of no clear answer. It had long been believed, since an article by P. Tannery at the end of the last century,[27] that Ammonius and his school devoted themselves to the study of Aristotle as the result of a deal with the ecclesiastical authorities by which they undertook not to teach Plato. The only evidence we have for any sort of deal is a well-known, if not well understood, remark by Damascius that Ammonius "being disgracefully avaricious and always acting with a view to making money, made an agreement with the person in charge of the dominant view", that is Christianity. In so far as it comes in one of the snippets from the *Life of Isidore* in Photius (cod. 242.292),[28] there is no context. In any case the view that it meant no Plato teaching is merely an inference from the amount of work on Aristotle done at Alexandria. We know that Ammonius himself lectured on the Gorgias at a date almost certainly later than the supposed deal: the time of that is uncertain, and the one most often used the patriarchate of Athanasius (490-97) depends on a piece of textual juxtaposition which may or may not be correct. The deal might equally well have had something to do with the conditions under which Christian pupils could attend, or be sent to attend, Ammonius' lectures: no attacks on their religion is a possible ingredient. Or even just a special elementary course? Whatever the answer the traditional explanation must be regarded as unproven.[29] There are, in any case, other possible explanations for the concentration on Aristotle, apart from the obvious one that Ammonius might have been particularly interested in the subject. One is that the Alexandrians felt that there was little to add to the Plato commentaries already available, most notably those of Proclus: that did not, however, deter Damascius at Athens, or Olympiodorus in the next generation at Alexandria.

Since we are concerned with differences between individuals, we should not omit the quarrel between Simplicius and Philoponus, both pupils of Ammonius but violently at odds over the eternity of the world and the related question of the existence of a fifth element, which came to be known by the Latin calque translation 'quintessence'.[30] I do not intend to discuss again the importance or otherwise of Christianity in determining Philoponus' opinions. Suffice it to say that his by now unorthodox view that the world had a beginning in time is a perfectly possible interpretation of the *Timaeus*, and one that can be taken seriously now: another unsolved problem in Plato.

Philoponus' attack on Proclus in the *De Aeternitate Mundi* is part of the same dispute. Since it is securely dateable to 529 it has sometimes been seen as either a precipitating cause of the imperial edict of that year forbidding the teaching of philosophy by pagans, or a protective gesture to defend the Alexandrians against it. In view of that possibility the work has often been connected with the question of Ammonius' deal without good cause.

What about the edict itself? Everybody once knew that it put an end to Greek Philosophy, at least at Athens. That view survived as a historical fact till the late 1960s, when Alan Cameron produced arguments to show not only that pagan Platonism continued afterwards, but that it continued at Athens.[31] This latter part of his thesis is highly questionable, and it is better to admit that we do not know where the philosophers who left Athens shortly after the edict resumed their activities. The latest candidate, much favoured in France since 1984, is the border city of Harrān, but the case rests primarily on the testimony of an otherwise admittedly unreliable Arabic source, al-Mas'udi and some rather over-confident inferences from references to calendars in Simplicius.[32]

Alexandria continued to be the home of Aristotelian commentators, some of whom wrote on Plato too, and may even have received some of the Athenians. On this note of uncertainty, we must end the story. I do not, of course, claim to have presented an exciting new discovery or new light on a specific problem. What I hope I have done is to show in outline what late antique Platonism looks like now, and some of the ways in which its appearance has changed. I think one can assert with some confidence that if anyone tries to do the same thing in ten year's time, the picture will have changed again. That is a measure both of the number of unanswered questions and of the rate at which they are now being approached. Comparisons with Indian thought seem to be in a similar condition.[33]

Endnotes

1. 'Neoplatonist' and 'Neoplatonic' first appeared in English and French in the 1830s. The *Shorter Oxford English Dictionary* gives 1837 for the first occurrence of 'Neoplatonist' but 1845 for 'Neoplatonism'.
2. Cf. too In *Alc.* 227.18-21, where Proclus writes that we must not attribute certain things to the soul, in order that we should be interpreters of Plato and not explain him in accordance with our own views.
3. (Cambridge 1962) 24.
4. This proved not to be the case at the conference itself since most of the Indian participants, as well as the usual minority of 'western' scholars, thought that there were crucial non-Greek elements in the thought or not-thought of Plotinus. But, in the absence of clear textual evidence for more than the occasional possible parallel, let alone demonstrable influence in one direction or the other, I remain unconvinced.
5. R. Baine Harris, ed. *Neoplatonism and Indian Thought*. Studies in Neoplatonism: Ancient and Modern (Albany 1982).
6. One thinks particularly of the work of the so-called Tübingen School, and especially of the writings of H.J. Krämer, cf. e.g. *Der Ursprung der Geistmetaphysik* (Amsterdam 1964) 351-69; *Platone e i fondamenti della Metafisica* (Milan 1982) 184-98.
7. By W. Theiler, 'Plotin zwischen Plato und Stoa' in Les *Sources de Plotin*. Entretiens Hardt sur l'Antiquitvé Classique 5 (Vandoeuvres-Geneva 1960) 67.
8. On the history of this problem before and in Plotinus cf. A.H. Armstrong, 'The background of the doctrine "That the intelligibles are not outside the Intellect"', in *Les Sources de Plotin* (see n. 7) 391-424.
9. For a discussion of this difficulty as handled in the *Parmenides* cf. F.M. Schroeder, 'The Platonic *Parmenides* and imitation in Plotinus', *Dionysius* 2 (1978) 51-73, esp. 52-54.
10. *Histoire critique de l'école d'Alexandrie* 3 vols. (Paris 1846-1851).
11. Zeller saw Plotinus as the thesis, Iamblichus the antithesis and Proclus as the synthesis. Vacherot's groups were chronological.
12. In *Genethliakon C. Robert* (Berlin 1910).
13. 'Le chrétien Jean Philopon et la survivance de l'école d'Alexandrie au VI siècle'', REG 67 (1954) 396-410.
14. 'Fragments d'un commentaire de Porphyre sur le Parménide', *Revue des Etudes Grecques* 74 (1961) 410-38.
15. (Cambridge 1967) 287-93.
16. Cf. e.g. Simplic. in *De an.* 90.29-91.4.
17. Cf. A.H. Armstrong, 'Eternity, life and movement in Plotinus' accounts of Nous', in P. Hadot and P.M. Schuhl, edd., *Le Néoplatonisme. Colloques internationaux du CNRS* (Paris 1971) 67-74; H.J. Blumenthal, 'Nous and Soul:

some problems of demarcation' in *Il Neoplatonismo in Oriente e in occidente. Accademia nazionale dei Lincei: Problemi attuali di scienza e di cultura 198* (Rome 1974) 203-219, reprinted in *Soul and Intellect* (see n 33), Study 11.

18. Cf. H.J. Blumenthal and E.G. Clark edd., *The Divine Iamblichus. Philosopher and Man of Gods* (Bristol 1993) introduction and passim.

19. Cf. esp. R. L. Cardullo, 'Siriano nella storiografia filosofica moderna e contemporanea', *Siculorum Gymnasium* 40 (1987) 71-182.

20. Cf. my '529 and its sequel: what happened to the Academy', *Byzantion* 48 (1978) 373-75, reprinted in *Soul and Intellect* (see n 33), Study XVIII.

21. Cf. the introduction to vol.1 of H.D. Saffrey and L.G. Westerink's edition of the *Platonic Theology*, xv ff., especially the tables on xviii f.

22. Cf. e.g. Proclus' *Elements of Theology* 211 and *Timaeus* commentary, III.334.3ff., Simplicius, In *De an.* 6.12ff.

23. In *Cat.* 191.9-10, where Iamblichus is bracketed with Plotinus.

24. In *Le Probleme du Néoplatonisme Alexandrin. Hiéroclès et Simplicius* (Paris 1978).

25. On the attribution and authorship of 'Ammonius' commentaries cf. my 'John Philoponus: Alexandrian Platonist?', Hermes 114 (1986) 325-28.

26. Cf. K. Verrycken, 'The metaphysics of Ammonius son of Hermeias', in R. Sorabji, ed., *Aristotle Transformed. The ancient commentators and their influence* (London 1990) 199-231 and 'The development of Philoponus' thought and its chronology', *Ibid.* 233-74.

27. 'Sur la periode finale de la philosophic grecque', *Revue Philosophique* 42 (1896) 226-87.

28. 352a 11-14=VI 53H.

29. On this matter see further my 'John Philoponus: Alexandrian Platonist?', (see n. 25 above) 321-24.

30. On this see particularly P. Hoffmann, 'Simplicius' Polemics', in R. Sorabji, ed. *Philoponus and the rejection of Aristotelian science* (London 1987) 57-83.

31. Cf. 'The last days of the Academy at Athens', *Proceedings of the Cambridge Philological Society* n.s.15 (1969) 7-29.

32. Cf. M. Tardieu, 'Sabiens coraniques et "Sābiens" de Harrān', *Journal Asiatique* 274 (1986) 1-44 and 'Les calendriers en usage à Harrān d'après les sources arabes et le commentaire de Simplicius à la Physique d'Aristote' in I. Hadot, ed., *Simplicius. Sa vie, son oeuvre, sa survie* (Berlin/New York 1987) 40-57, where he argues from Simplicius' references (*In Phys.* 874.32ff.) to four different beginnings of the year, that of the Athenians, 'which we use', at the summer equinox, the Asians' at the autumn one, the Romans' the winter and the Arabs' the spring: these were all used at Harrān, therefore Simplicius must be there. Cf. now the judicious remarks of P. Foulkes, 'Where was Simplicius?', *Journal of Hellenic Studies* 112 (1992) 143.

33. An earlier version of some parts of this paper was given as a lecture to the Society for the Promotion of Hellenic Studies in London, England. A compressed version was read to the conference. Another article based on the original lecture will appear in my *Soul and Intellect. Studies in Plotinus and later Neoplatonism*. Variorum Collected Studies (Aldershot/Brookfield VT 1993).

The *Sadhana* of Plotinus and Sri Aurobindo

Arabinda Basu

Plotinus and Sri Aurobindo are both mystics. They are also philosophers, though not quite in the same sense. For Plotinus philosophy is a way of life, what in India is called *sadhana*, a way leading the philosopher to a vision of, and union with, what he calls The One. Sri Aurobindo takes philosophy as what it means in the modern world. It is primarily rational, an attempt to think about the nature of reality whatever that may be knowledge, ethics, religion, beauty, etc.

Some philosophers may, and do, construct a system of ideas about these subjects, others deny the possibility of building such a system. Sri Aurobindo, while regarding philosophy as a useful intellectual construction, considers it to be too much indulging in abstractions and hair-splitting analysis of concepts which for the most part do not have much to do with actualities of either existence or of life. Plotinus was very well acquainted with the doctrines of Greek philosophers and was influenced by many of them. Nevertheless for him philosophy was not mainly *theory*, not even *theoria* but *praxis*. The philosopher led a certain kind of life in preparation for a knowledge of the Reality by direct experience.

Though Sri Aurobindo thinks that philosophy is basically rational, when he speaks of the Upanishads, he regards them as intuitive philosophy. What Plotinus regards as philosophy Sri Aurobindo calls *yoga* and spiritual *sadhana*. But this is mainly a matter of terminology. The difference in the meaning which Plotinus and Sri Aurobindo give to the term 'philosophy' should not cause confusion to an intelligent student of their respective systems. Both of them hold that discursive reasoning cannot give direct knowledge of Reality and that whatever faculty can attain that kind of unitive apprehension has to be developed by a moral and contemplative discipline.

Sri Aurobindo's yoga is much more complex than the philosophical practices of Plotinus both in its disciplines and in its aims and objectives. This is mainly due to the fact that his concept of The Supreme Reality of Sri Aurobindo appears more comprehensive than that of Plotinus. I may mention in passing that Sri Aurobindo had not read the writings of Plotinus; yet there are many points of agreement between their respective systems which to my mind furnish eloquent evidence of the universal character of some mystical experiences.

Several comprehensive studies of Plotinus and Sri Aurobindo have been published by Indian and foreign scholars. I do not propose to follow their footsteps. My purpose is to point out briefly the agreements and differences between the yogas of Plotinus and Sri Aurobindo. However, since I have said that Sri Aurobindo's concept of the Supreme Reality is more comprehensive than that of Plotinus, and that that is the main reason for the greater complexity of his *sadhana*, I should say something, however briefly, about the two doctrines of God.

First, as regards the points of agreement. For both our mystic-philosophers Reality is self-existent, ineffable, self-aware. Plotinus says that *monos*, One, does not know itself though it has what he has termed self-intellection which Sri Aurobindo describes as self-awareness, beyond the duality of subject and object. It is both repose and dynamic and unity-in-diversity on a certain level of its whole existence.

Sri Aurobindo makes a distinction between self-awareness and self-knowledge in God. Self-aware is what is known in Vedanta as *cit*, Pure Consciousness in Sri Aurobindo's English rendering, in which there is no manifest self-knowledge of God. But in Sat-Chid-Ananda *cit* is also *Cit-Sakti*, Consciousness-Force. It is by this inherent Consciousness Force that Consciousness becomes Self-Conscious. God is both his own subject and his own object containing both aspects in him and yet transcending them. Similarly, he posits a status of God beyond the One which of course Brahman is, though no name can be given to this aspect of God. The term Parabrahman is used to indicate this status of Sat-Chid-Ananda which is according to Sri Aurobindo the first manifestation of the Supreme Reality to awakened human consciousness. He says that the One and the Many are the last two antinomies through which the spiritualised mind of man looks at the Absolute *Parabrahma*. As the Rigveda X.82.6 has it: In the navel of the Unborn the One was placed and there in that One all the worlds abide: *ajasya nabhavadyekamarpitam yasmin visvani bhuvanani tasthuh.*

Plotinus places the One beyond being (Being in the interpretation of some writers on Plotinus) which however, he is careful to point out, does not mean that the One is nonexistent. I understand Plotinus' statement to mean that the status of the One is transcendent of that level in which the Many emerge ideally in the Intelligible World, for he employs the term 'being' in regard to this second hypostasis, the nous. If the term 'being' is specifically applied only to the Intelligible-World, then the One is certainly above being. But if the word is employed to indicate that which is the ultimate Principle depending on nothing for its existence, then it can be certainly used for the Vedantic Sat-Chid-Ananda. Sri Aurobindo applies the term to Sat-Chid-Ananda, Being or Existence-Consciousness-Bliss.

Another difference between Plotinus' and Sri Aurobindo's conceptions of God is the following: the former places the Universal principle and therefore the Universe at a level lower than the One, viz. the nous, or Intelligence. For Sri Aurobindo Brahman is Transcendent, Universal and Individual. I have indicated what the Transcendent is in Sri Aurobindo's philosophy. It is beyond not only the universe but also beyond its source; it is however also the All, the Universal. The Universe is an equal extension of the Brahman in which there is yet no individual concentration. But Brahman is also the Individual centration of the Universal God.

Sri Aurobindo describes the Individual Self as the Divine as Individual or the Individual Divine. Plotinus does not speak of any individual self which is an aspect of the One. The individual self first emerges in the Intelligible World, is a content of that world and is itself also (an) Intelligence. Plotinus places the World-Soul below Intelligence and the Intelligible World. Sat-Chid-Ananda is the Soul of the world, the Cosmic Consciousness in Sri Aurobindo's system.

Plotinus distinguishes between the higher soul and the lower soul. Sri Aurobindo would agree with this distinction in principle. But the word soul has a different connotation in his philosophy, which I shall explain presently. Let me just mention here that the soul or the psychic being is an evolutionary entity. Though a portion of God in essence, it is in this world as a being which evolves to the human level from subhuman planes and to its spiritual destiny through many births and through several levels of Consciousness.

Consciousness descends to the many levels of its nature in which it becomes progressively less and less manifest till it reaches that of Matter in which Consciousness is present but completely unmanifest. Of course a yogi with the right kind of development of his psycho-spiritual means of knowledge can see Matter as a concrete and sensibly seizable form of Conscious Energy, of the Force of Consciousness. While Plotinus in metaphysics considers Matter to be pure negation of being and in ethics as the source of evil, to Sri Aurobindo's spiritual vision, Matter is revealed as the physical vesture of God and the earth as the venue of his unveiled manifestation. This difference in the respective points of view of Plotinus and Sri Aurobindo should be kept in mind, especially when the aim of spiritual life according to the two mystic philosophers is considered. I have said above that in Sri Aurobindo's spiritual vision God is both Plenitude and Plentiful. This description implies that God is both Impersonal and Personal. In Plotinus' doctrine the One is Impersonal and hardly evinces any character of being a Person. In my view this affects his *sadhana* and the fruits of his idea of the state of union with Intelligence and the One, as I shall try to show later. But even on the doctrinal plane the two philosophies are very different in an important respect.

According to Plotinus there is no intention in the One to create the universe understanding the phrase "to create" to mean bringing into being something out of nothing but only the "emanating" of what is already contained in the source of emanation. The world is the product of necessary and spontaneous emanation from the Intelligence as are light and heat from the sun. Sri Aurobindo rejects the view that the world is an emanation from God. On the contrary, it is the product of a deliberate choice on his part to manifest himself as the whole furniture of heaven and earth. Plotinus disagreed with this concept for an apparently good reason, namely, that to wish to create or in Sri Aurobindo's terms, to self-manifest, implies a want and therefore an imperfection. This may be, indeed, is true in the case of finite beings.

But the infinite Plenitude and Plentiful wills to manifest himself not because he lacks anything but because he exercises his super-abundant creative energy to make himself known to beings manifested from his own essential being and nature. He does it for the sake of Delight. For there is a Delight of Being which is the very nature of God and also a Delight of Becoming. If there be a joy in Repose, there is also bliss in Love. Sri Aurobindo says that the selfbecoming of Ishvara does not denude him one iota but leaves him as he always was, is and will be, just as Plotinus says that the emanation does not affect the One at all.

Plotinus has given scant attention to social and political issues. True he has said that political virtues must be developed before one can begin the contemplative life. This corresponds generally to the idea of the practice of *dharma*, in this case by people of a certain order of the society in the Indian scheme of life. Sri Aurobindo on the contrary is intensely interested in the future society as is evident from his book *The Human Cycle*. He has also written a book called *The Ideal of Human Unity*. Both these books furnish ample proof that Sri Aurobindo is convinced that God has a purpose to achieve in the world. The spiritual destiny of the individual human being is sketched out in his *The Synthesis of Yoga* which also describes some of the disciplines and practices of his integral yoga. His idea of the plan of the Divine in the collective, i.e. in society and in humanity is expounded in the two works mentioned above.

Though Plotinus quietly and in a most exemplary manner lived a contemplative and active life, he felt that intellectual and artistic works are a distraction. This certainly is true while a seeker is journeying towards the Intelligence and through that luminous realm, to the One. However, all kinds of work can be done from the state of union with God moved by the inspiration of the Master of Works, be it intellectual, artistic, apparently social and political work. I say 'apparently' because to the *karmayogi* in union with the active Divine, the work he does is fulfilling God's command, though it may appear to others as capable of being brought under human category of mundane works.

Devotion also has hardly any place in the scheme of *sadhana* found in the *Enneads*. The yoga of Plotinus resembles very much the *jñānavoga* as practised in India (actually, it is found in non-Indian mystical disciplines also). But there being no concept of God as a Person who has relations with his emanations or with the individual spiritual *jivas* in Indian terms, any kind of bhakti-yoga cannot be found in Plotinus' *sadhana*. God is both Impersonal and Personal according to Sri Aurobindo. The yoga of abstractive knowledge leads to the Impersonal aspect, to identity with Brahman as in Shankara or a most close union with the One in Plotinus. Bhakti enables the seekers to have close relation with the Personal.

It is not easy to understand how in Plotinus' idea of spiritual life the souls do not have any kind of personal relation with the One, since their existence is not denied, for if it were then souls cannot be said to emanate from the One at all. True, in one sense emanation from the One is denied. But this means that the lower self is transcended or in Indian terms the separative ego-sense, *ahamkāra* is left behind. But in the yoga of bhakti the higher soul, when liberated from its association with the lower soul, finds its true relationship with God. Sri Aurobindo accepts the possibility of identity, unity-in-distinction and distinction-in-unity with Brahman as viable spiritual states. In his own integral yoga all the three experiences are to be attained and harmonized. This can be done not by means recognized in all mystical disciplines but by what Sri Aurobindo, for want of a better term, has called the supermind.

I have said above that Brahman is Pure Consciousness, self-awareness but also self-consciousness, and self-knowing. God's knowledge of himself is the Supermind. Infinite self-awareness must first translate itself into an infinite faculty of knowledge but also the integral knowledge that God has of himself and of the world his self-manifestation, the method and means of the self-manifestation and its goal. For the cosmic manifestation is moving towards a consummation as foreseen and planned by the Divine. But before I say something about God's purpose in the world, I would like to emphasize that the supramental realisation of God is integral in that one who has that realisation knows God directly as Transcendent, Universal, Individual, Static, Dynamic, Impersonal and Personal, Qualityless, and Qualitied, Nameless and all Names, Formless and all Forms.

A capital difference between the respective concepts of the ultimate spiritual destiny of man of Plotinus and Sri Aurobindo is that the founder of Neoplatonism has no doctrine of cosmic evolution while one of the most important doctrines of the founder of the Integral Advaita Vedanta is that he is firmly of the view that God has a purpose in the world in a cosmic way. Brahman, as and through the Supermind, his integral Knowledge-Will and the source of the Universe, manifests himself by a process of downward evolution as a hierarchy of principles of consciousness and being till it reaches the state of the Inconsistent Ocean, of the *apraketa salilam* of the *Nasadcyasakta*, Rv. X.129.1-5.

That One, *tadekam* progressively descends through the Supermind. Mind, Life, Psyche, into the state of Matter which is formed out of the unconscious Waters over which the spirit of God broods and moves to bring the world into manifestation. The formation of Matter is brought about so as to provide the stable basis for the progressive manifestation, the upward evolution, of the involved Consciousness. This thrust of Consciousness or rather consciousness involved in the world, whose essence is less manifest on the different levels of its own involution and evolution, manifests Life and Mind in the world.

The appearance of Mind is really the emergence of Man, the progeny of Manu, Mind. Below the level of Mind, evolution is subconscious; in man it has become conscious. He can choose to collaborate in what Sri Aurobindo describes as the Yoga of Nature, the collective yoga. Yoga is a method of quickening evolution. Subconscious evolution is a tardy movement of universal Nature which in man can make a more conscious and deliberate march towards a further evolution of Consciousness of which the mental is one stage. That higher level of consciousness is the Supermind. In this integral Knowledge-Will there is no diminution of being, consciousness and bliss. It is in effect God as both the material and efficient cause of his self-manifestation as the world.

One of the innumerable powers of God is self-limitation. It is by deliberate self-limitation that the Supermind becomes Ignorance, Avidya, mental Maya. The world is in the grip of Ignorance. It is not a principle and power *essentially* different from Knowledge. It is from the involutionary viewpoint limited Knowledge and from the evolutionary standpoint developing Knowledge.

Sri Aurobindo holds the view that Consciousness involved in Mind is pressing for a more open manifestation of itself. In other words it is evolving towards the Supermind. When that evolution is accomplished, those who will be supramental souls will live for God and from a state of union with him in Knowledge, Will, Peace and Delight. Their life will be a movement from knowledge to more knowledge and not as man's life is now a seeking of Knowledge from within Ignorance.

It is painfully obvious that Mind cannot control the affairs of the world and the many-faceted life of man and mankind. It therefore cannot be its creator and controller. The supermind is the veiled creator and the hidden principle and power of the life in the world. Whatever is involved must evolve. The Supermind concealed in Mind, Life and Matter must also manifest itself here.

The Will of the Supermind which is full of Knowledge of God and the world is the instrument of bringing about a radical transformation of our ignorant nature comprising Mind, Life and Matter. The ultimate aim of the *sadhana* of Sri Aurobindo is the complete transformation of the physical consciousness in the human body. That is to say, the physical body of the superman will be fully conscious, vibrant and full of divine peace established in its cells in such a way that their decay will be arrested, their disintegration stopped and consequently death will no longer be inevitable. Instead of being the source of embarrassment and shame the physical body too is potentially capable of knowing the Divine and manifest him in it. There is nothing of this idea and ideal in Plotinus. His sadhana culminates in the passing of the alone to the Alone. In the yoga of Sri Aurobindo the seeker has first to get his own liberation from ignorance and achieve union with God in many modes. He is the lone pilgrim. But he says that to seek one's own liberation is the last act of egoism. The integral yogi's ultimate aim is to realize God on all the planes of being and become a channel of the integral supramental Knowledge-Will for the transformation of consciousness inwardly and of the collective being[1] and life outwardly. The Divine is both Solitary and All. The integral yoga aims at realising God as spirit ensouling a glorified physical body and as the collective Soul, directly guiding a spiritual society in all aspects of its life.

To fulfil God in life is man's manhood, says Sri Aurobindo and fulfilling God means fulfilling his purpose which is manifesting himself in all levels of consciousness and being in the universe including the physical. The life of the supramental community will be a life expressing the Divine in its existence, activities and plays of joy.

Endnotes

1. The phrase collective being occurs in the *Enneads*. But as I understand it means the intelligible world and not a human society in this world, where we live, more and have our being.

Plotinus' Neoplatonism and the Thought of Sri Aurobindo

John R. A. Mayer

> *"To rest in the apparent and to mistake it for the real is the one general error, root of all others and cause of all our stumbling and suffering, to which man is exposed by the nature of his mentality."*
> (Sri Aurobindo, *The Human Cycle*, Chapter 5, p.37, Sri Aurobindo Birth Centenary Library, Pondicherry, 1971)

The present conference is dedicated to a task in comparative philosophy, namely to compare and contrast two traditions, Neoplatonism and Indian Philosophy. Each of these traditions is rich, with many diverse individual contributors; so that under this heading an almost unlimited amount of scholarship is possible. The present paper represents a reflection about the significance of the fact that there are a variety of philosophies from a variety of traditions which can be explored both for finding similarities and for contrasts which have in common the fact that they can be seen as a metaphysical monism. Plotinus' and Sri Aurobindo's thoughts are exemplars, to which references will be made. It is not our purpose herein to present a detailed exposition of the thought of either. Rather, we shall outline our own reflections, which are also informed by phenomenology, post-modernism, and without doubt, by a strong empathy with monism. The significance of the influence of post-modernity on this author is that he recognizes and admits that whatever is meant by the term "truth" may well be beyond coherent rationalization. Therefore the presence of formal inconsistency in the serious articulation of a philosophical position should not be considered an immediate ground for rejection of that claim; rather, it is incumbent on the open listener to attend not merely to the text and its formal characteristics, but when finding an inconsistency, attempt to reflect on the preideational adumbration from which the author writes, and which is addressed by the text, so as to empathize and find meaning in the expression. Rejection of a position does not signify its falsity; it signifies essentially the failure of the imagination of the rejecter, and the relative lack of success of the communication intended by the speaker. While truth is subjective, and depends on "having the ears to hear", it is not merely private, but is interpersonal, accessible to everyone, provided that the medium of communication succeeds in focusing the attention of the listener-reader to the same "area" from which the speaker-author constructs his address.

Aurobindo Ghose (1872-1950) was given a deliberately European education. In a convent school by age five, he was sent to England at age seven, where he stayed until 1893, eventually studying at Cambridge. He returned to India when he was 20 years old, and only then began to study his cultural heritage. It is therefore clear that he had direct knowledge of Western Neoplatonism as well as of Indian philosophy. It is, however, certain that the Indian intellectual-spiritual tradition was the more directly influential element in his later thought. Once in Baroda, he began to study Sanskrit seriously, and immersed himself in the texts of the Upanishads, the Gita, and the writings of Ramakrishna and Vivekananda. At first he was also involved as a very active nationalist in the political movements of his time, eventually even giving up his post as Vice-Principal of Baroda College in order to be more fully able to participate in the political life of India. It was in the first decade of our century that he gradually withdrew from his political activities in order to pursue his spiritual development. He devoted himself exclusively to spiritual exercises and to philosophical writing for the last forty years of his life, from 1910 to 1950.

Both Plotinus and Sri Aurobindo are authors of speculative metaphysics, in the sense that they have developed and presented in a systematic and thoughtful way their view of the nature of reality. Both of these views may be characterized by the label "monism", in that they identify the ultimate as a singular being, the One or Brahman as the case may be. Both recognize that this singular being is dynamic, involved in a process, that Aurobindo calls the Life Divine. This concern with activity, process, change, evolution and becoming is the reason why their thought in particular is worthy of comparison. Plotinus' monism is in contrast with that of both of his great intellectual predecessors, Plato and Parmenides of Elea, in that Plotinus asserts activity and dynamism on the part of the Ultimate, while the two earlier thinkers denied change or process as appropriately characterizing Being or the Forms. Aurobindo's philosophy also stands in some contrast with the earlier Advaita Vedanta of Shankara, exactly in the sense that for Advaita change or process is an aspect of *maya* or illusion, while for Aurobindo Brahman is both Being and Becoming. "This absolute manifests itself in two terms, Being and Becoming. The Being is the fundamental reality, the Becoming is an effectual reality. It is a dynamic power and result, a creative energy and working out of Being, a constantly persistent yet mutable form, process, outcome of its immutable formless essence." (*Life Divine*, p. 785 f.)

Our aim in this paper is to demonstrate that in spite of the differences in the way of understanding Plotinus' One and Aurobindo's Brahman, namely that the former conception seems less specifically theistic in its language and envisionment than the latter, we claim that the two systems are compatible, and are but different articulations of fundamentally similar experience. Of course, experience is subjective, and we can have no access directly either to the experience of Plotinus or to that of Sri Aurobindo. However, it is our conviction that articulation and reflection, especially about that which is not strictly and narrowly empirical, is based on an apprehension which is direct, not mediated by thoughts or concepts, but which then serves as a stimulus and guide for articulation and intellectualization. Our claim is fundamentally phenomenological. If we but explore how it is that we give utterance to our thoughts and how our thoughts present themselves to us as plausible, coherent, persuasive and functional we discover that there is a preconceptual adumbration, which guides and forms our reflections which eventually gels into speech or script. Not unexpectedly, our speech and thought patterns are the joint product of this pre-conceptual and root experience and our exposure to our culture, our traditions. From the tradition we extract what seems useful for describing the adumbration; and our audience, our listeners understand our speech or script only to the extent that their experience to some extent confirms what they hear. Otherwise the speech heard will seem to be nonsense, or at least, totally implausible and unconvincing. The fact that monistic speculation has happened in many cultures and many societies is evidence that there is some fundamental experience other than the merely empirical informing us of multiplicity, diversity, differences and particularities. There must be a complementary intuition that however convincing and interpersonal the world of multiplicity is, there is something that is not given in the empirical appearances, but which we can know just the same. Such an intuition is not merely a private whim, but is widely shared, and it is our belief that with the appropriate discipline and attitude, every person can develop to the selfsame intuition. It, like all intuitions, presents itself as important and meaningful; it might not be directly accessible, yet it will influence the way we open ourselves, and in the way we shape our actions and thoughts, including our speech. This transempirical adumbration is what discloses the meaning in the claim that appearance and reality are not synonyms but rather, antonyms. Reality then is not merely appearance, but is accessible through an intuition that the apparent discloses something that is transcendent to it. How we constitute in thought and language this intuition of transcendence is challenging. However, the very origin of the word "transcendence" and its meaning is evidence of the fact of such an intuition. Given it, one's speculative thought especially concerning metaphysics is deeply influenced. It is this intuition which has lead some thinkers, though not our two, to the belief that multiplicity, process and the empirical domain is merely illusion. In the case of our two authors their contention, grounded in the same intuition, is that the natural world and its empirical multiplicity is not exhaustive of reality, and is not separate from it. What I have called "intuition" presents itself as an intellectual disposition. It is a complex of feeling-thought, which when we discover it in ourselves draws us to an empathetic disposition toward speculative monisms. When we attempt to rearticulate the basis of this tendency, our own speaking or writing is guided exactly by that reality which permits even those paradoxical claims which seem on the surface to be logically inconsistent to be asserted on the one hand, and to be understood on the other. That there are such inconsistencies in the various monisms that we encounter is demonstrable. But these inconsistencies ultimately are not barriers to the acceptance and appreciation of the speculative tradition, they serve rather to intimate the limits of rationality and the less than ultimate adequacy of ideation and language for the fullest expression of the experiences which persuade us of their veracity, their viviality. Thus every speculative monism has to be somewhat less than crystal clear about the relationship between the One and the Many; the bases of the contrasts within the manifold, if there is ultimately only one substance or being or ultimate. Whether we read Plato or Plotinus, Shankara or Aurobindo, we can spot logical problems in the texts if our openness toward them is characterized by a critical skepticism. On the other hand, if we ourselves turn to that inner mirror from which we are capable of understanding what we hear or read, and which we use to guide the formulations of our own serious speaking, we are in touch with exactly that anamnetic ground-source of our intuitions and knowledge which Plato desired to redirect us to, which, when we listen to the wisdom tradition, turns out to be not merely private and subjective, but universal, even if it is not always easily accessible, and which in Maharishi Mahesh yogi's terminology is called "the source of creative intelligence". That this is not rational knowledge, but that which lends rationality and plausibility to conceptually formulated claims is clear from all accounts. Therefore, let us now turn to how Plotinus reacts speculatively to the adumbration of the nature of reality from which his philosophy finds its formulation.

While for Plotinus the first emanation of the One is *nous*, or mind; the second, *psyche* or soul, and the third, *physis*, or nature, it would be useful for us to stop and reflect on the meaning of these terms rather than merely translate them from the Greek into their conventional English. If mind and soul are the first two ".products" or outpourings of the One, is it plausible for us to think of it as other than Spirit, or Consciousness ? Clearly Plotinus avoided both of these terms as descriptives of the One, because he wanted to avoid suggesting any positive descriptions, since each of these would ultimately be intelligible as a limitation, and the One is not limited. However, the tendency to think that the ground or source in the Plotinian conceptualization is impersonal would be a mistake. Now it is true that text asserts the One as being beyond all distinctions, including the one of personal and impersonal. Our tendency, therefore, is to think that the answer to the question "Is the One personal?" should be negative. But the answer to the question "Is the One impersonal?" should be exactly the same. Thus if our imagination is limited to thinking either in terms of personal or impersonal, then the negative answer to the question about the personal nature of the One should not draw with itself the implication of the impersonality of the One. The fact that the first two emanations have characteristics that are more to be associated with subjectivity, consciousness or mind suggest that the One is more proximal to Mind than it is to mere objective existence. Thus Plotinus' philosophy is not to be understood as radically differing from that of Aurobindo.

Aurobindo, on the other hand, calls the ultimate Brahman, and sometimes refers to it as "Supermind". This ultimate is characterizable by three diverse human perspectives. The Transcendental, the Universal and the Individual. It should be clear that each of these three characterizations is dependent on the human perspective from which whatever is transcendental is transcendental, and so forth. Aurobindo suggests that human liberation, *moksha*, is the destiny of the Individual, producing the inevitable emergence of a developed society, functioning through the operation of the principle of love, and the purpose of the evolutionary process. From matter to life, to mind, to Higher Mind, Illumined Mind, Intuitive Mind, Overmind and Supermind. All this is understood as a seamless process, the reversal of the original involution of Brahman into unconscious matter. Here Aurobindo's teaching seems to coincide with that of Hegel. Hegel suggests that the dialectical process initiates itself by the Absolute as pure abstract Spirit, othering itself from itself into its opposite, concrete, unconscious matter, and thereafter each of the separated elements strives to unite itself with its opposite. Matter becomes conscious, first in life, then in selfconscious life, while spirit expresses itself into matter as art, culture, civilization. The restoration, or synthesis is an elevated reintegration of that which originally cleft itself from itself into otherness.

In Plotinus also, we have the presentation of the reunion of the original overflow or emanation. While reason and intellect serve to guide the way back as far as *nous*, beyond *nous* to the One reason and intellect no longer suffice, as the satisfactory means for the restoration. Only love is the sufficient means of effecting the full return. This Plotinian description is indeed similar to Aurobindo's claim that surrender is the only means to achieving the higher stages of the evolutionary process. The ordinary mind and ordinary intellect, however useful they may be in some spheres, are not adequate to this task. But the end of evolution is not the elimination or destruction of the lower stages; rather it is the harmonious integration of all into a mutually interpenetrated whole, characterized by Satchitananda. Multiplicity, even though it is a less than complete appropriation of the way reality is, is, however, not unreality, but the very way of the Brahman self-manifesting in all its varieties and richness. Thus motion, change and history are not illusions, they are of the way of the Being of the One, which is in fact dynamic, processual, and in a continuous and emergent partial self-disclosure, whose characteristic feature is intensification; the emergence of fuller, more complete and more integrated self-disclosure, which transcends but does not deny process. Multiplicity and particularity does not exclude its simultaneous unity and co-participation in the totality and oneness of Brahman.

Parmenides, as is well known, has maintained that motion and change are but illusions. The real is eternal and unchanging. Zeno, an Eleatic Parmenidean, has developed this thought further, demonstrating the rational unintelligibility of motion and change, and using his paradoxical conclusions as evidence and persuasion for the rejection of the apparent as the basis for truth. It was the analogous paradox concerning the reality of identity and an unchanging substance as expressed by Heraclitus in his famous dictum that one can never step into the same river twice, which contributed to Plato's formulation of his own metaphysics, which can be considered as a reflective synthesis of the Parmenidean denial of change and the Heraclitean assertion of the universality of flux. Traditional Platonism though dynamic even within Plato's own corpus of writings, can be characterized as a kind of two-storey universe, with the priority being given to the permanent and unchanging, perfect realm of Forms, under the primacy of the Form of the Good, the True and the Beautiful, all aspects of the same single supreme. Time, the moving shadow of eternity, characterizes a lesser domain, the chaotic unformed, which in its striving to emulate the eternal, gives form to matter, which however, forever fails in its attempt to mirror the Forms because of its debilitating limitations as matter. Materiality prevents the temporal realm from being a perfect reflection of the Ideal, thus resulting in the flux of temporality in its ceaseless effort to more adequately mirror the perfect formal original. Thus change, process, characterizes only this lesser domain, which serves as but an imitation, and an unsuccessful one at that, of the higher true being. Knowledge of the Form of the Good is possible in the Platonic envisionment, but the full formulation and articulation of such a knowledge is elusive, even if formulations are inspired by the unformulated and only partially accessible possession of exactly that which stimulates us in the further search and attempt to know and speak it, as well as to act and live in its service. Plato never makes clear how he understands the original nature of the chaotic, the character of unformed matter, and the reason that human souls find themselves embodied and mired in the temporal domain. His hint is that the soul becomes embodied in consequence of some sort of wrongdoing, though this is problematic.

For if the soul is originally a preexistent in the domain of the eternal, then in fact it cannot be active, it cannot be engaged in "doing" of any sort, much less in wrong-doing. If the soul is originally, even prior to physical embodiment somehow different from the Form of the Good, and in being a lesser Form, subservient to it, then these lesser forms are not wholly forms at all, because they are active. Thus Plato's philosophy, though inspired to some extent by a monism, cannot be thought of as consistently monistic. Plotinus, in transforming Platonism into what is now known as Neoplatonism rejects the inertia associated with the Platonic ultimate, and suggests the notion of "emanation" as a basis of the emergence of multiplicity and differentiation. However, this emanation or overflow of the One is balanced by the need and desire to return and reunite with the One that characterizes particular beings, *physis*, *psyche*, and *nous* alike.

However, Plotinus' speculative thought is much more explicitly monistic than Plato's. What interests us here is how it is possible that in spite of the evidence of multiplicity and the apparent manifoldness of the world of conventional experience, both some sages, but even more surprisingly, many ordinary and common folk have a strong inclination to doubt or reject the ultimacy of the apparent manifold, and generate arguments as well as accept claims of the transempirical reality of the singularity of the ultimate, in which we each live move and have our being.

Monistic philosophies have arisen from different cultural and intellectual backgrounds, and it is my belief that these have often developed in relative independence from one another. Also, it is the case that a variety of speculative monisms have not only been formulated by thinkers, but have found sympathetic and admiring followers. How are these facts to be understood? Why is it that the "natural standpoint" from which it is persuasive that there is an "out there" world of many diverse things has been questioned and rejected in favour of philosophies which assert that the apparent multiplicity of the seemingly independent entities is not the final perspective; rather, that the truth of the matter is, that this vast diversity of appearances all belong together, and are aspects of a "One" which is the ground, the source, the ultimate reality; to which all belong, and from which they are never really sufficiently separated to make the "return" a merely temporal future event. In truth the separation and "descent" is coextensive with a transcendent unity, in which the separations are but perspectival differences. Time is the requirement primarily for the acquisition of the wisdom to realize the truth of the unity of Being. While that wisdom is occluded from the apparently individual consciousness of the not-yet enlightened being who glories in his/her separateness and individuality, such a glorying is but a moment to be overcome in the growing development of the individual who is eventually to see through the vanity of his individuality.

But where do we get such ideas from? And why are they appealing at all? Surely prior to any and every theoretical and articulated monism there must be some personal, existential adumbration of the notion that things are not what they seem, or that there is more to the ultimate nature of things than meets the ordinary consciousness of the ordinary human beings. A sense of the interdependence of all, of the belonging together not only of the many synchronous entities, but the belonging together of all throughout all time, time past and time future is part of a sensibility which may not be equally and universally accessible to all human beings, but which is sufficiently common and regular in a culture-independent manner as to generate the diversities of monistic philosophies such as those of Spinoza, Shankara, Plotinus, and even such early figures in the Western tradition as Thales and Anaximander.

For to understand the famous fragment of Thales that all is made of water, we must not interpret this to be a shallow and naive materialism; rather, it is the sophisticated insight that what we know as water can take on many distinct and diverse forms, be these solid as in ice or frost, liquid, as is the case of the primary sense of "water", (and here we should remind ourselves how different a river is or a lake from that little vesselful which we drink for our sustenance, or that liquid in which we render most of our raw foodstuff edible and digestible), or gaseous, as in steam or cloud or fog or mist. Indeed, if all is made of water, the clear liquid we associate with the term is not distinctively any more "water" than is any and every other thing. This is why Anaximander's renaming of the single ultimate as the *"apeiron"*, or boundless, is indeed an intellectual advance in description even if not in the basic insight of the ultimate unity of being. Furthermore, even the modern realistic materialist will admit a universal "substance", namely matter, as the invariant "foundation" of items as diverse as the Rock of Gibraltar, the gentle breezes which melt the winter snows, and the body of a living human being, such as myself, or that voluptuous "Other" for whose smile and gratitude even the labours of Hercules would gladly be undertaken. Thus the so-called "Absolute

Idealism" of a Bradley is not the only kind of intellectual system which has been developed in consequence of the surmise of the illusory character of the sheer multiplicity and apparent independence of what the Taoist has called "The Ten Thousand Things". Indeed the fact that the problem of the One and the Many has been recognized as one of the core issues of philosophical reflection is evidence that there is a lure of the One not only for the mystic or the scholar of Neoplatonism, but even for all who would use language, and name two distinct moments by the same name. It is this insight which inspired the famous Heraclitean dictum "You can never step into the same river twice". Thus the very fact that humans have a proclivity to language, to speaking, to naming, to claim identity with those former moments which we conventionally call "my" childhood, "my" biographical data, is evidence that there is unity in the very heart of multiplicity and diversity. The very notion of difference hinges on non-differentiation. Thus when I claim that this thing differs from that thing, and insist on the truth of that claim, the very claim is made against the horizon of the thingness of both this and that, in other words, that behind their differences there is also a commonality!

Prior to all speculation, prior to all theorizing, there is an irreducible and prearticulate awareness of transcendence, of unity and of the mutual interdependence of the multiplicity of particulars. It is this which grounds the theorizing, the rational articulation, the specification of the doctrines which are the features of a variety of schools of thought. Our task as philosophers is to read carefully, openly and sympathetically those texts of the traditions which seem to address us, and to learn from them, and at the same time to reformulate and integrate them into the very stuff that constitutes our own life, actions and thoughts, and which will nurture the heritage for its evolutionary goals.

The Theoria of Nature in Plotinus and the Yoga of the Earth Consciousness in Aurobindo

Daniel Kealey

The word "contemplation" usually brings to mind techniques to facilitate the return to Source, God, Brahman, the One, and this association is usually correct. But it can also connote the apparently opposite movement. That is, contemplation is not only the way by which the lower returns to the higher, but the way the higher forms, and interacts with, the lower. It is the added consideration of this second meaning of contemplation that constitutes an integral view of the spiritual life. The integral view is not missing from Plotinus, even though he and his interpreters have emphasized the one-way ascent to the heights. My intention here is to resuscitate this integral reading of Plotinus and, as an aid to my reading, I will invoke the vision of the great philosopher and yogi of Integralism, Sri Aurobindo. I will not be simply comparing these philosophers. Better scholars than I have already done so. Dr. S. K. Maitra has written a very informative comparative essay in his book, *The Meeting of the East and the West in Sri Aurobindo's Philosophy*, and Professor Pritibhushan Chatterji contributed an illuminating essay on these two luminaries in *Neoplatonism and Indian Thought*.

Plotinus inherited Plato's ambivalence about the value, significance, and purpose of material existence, on the one hand expressing the negative regard towards the body as found in the *Phaedo*, and at other times expressing the positive regard towards material existence as the manifestation of the Divine, as found in the *Timaeus*. It is in these positive views (*Ennead* IV. 8, for example) that we find the integral Plotinus. It is my impression that Plotinus had an integral vision, and he did give it some intellectual expression in his system, but that his will did not fully go along with the vision. I would venture to say, furthermore, that this ambivalence which Plotinus inherited, has been inherited by us. This is a problem we all struggle with to one degree or another.

Our will is wounded, or it behaves as if it were. The spiritual traditions of both East and West have, for the past 2500 years at least, fallen prey to the mood of resentment. Resentment, as revealed by Nietzsche and Scheler, is an attitude that rationalizes our unwillingness to accept the highest and noblest vision of the good life available to us. That vision of nonduality discloses the essential divinity of material existence and our mission to manifest this in our lives here. Because of the difficulties and the frustrations we have faced in this mission, we recoil from the task of manifestation and seek instead to fulfill some more manageable agenda. That these "manageable agendas" have tended to be different in East and West should not obscure the fact that they are fundamentally the same reaction of unwillingness to embrace the life of integral nonduality. Whether we are talking about Plotinus's flight of the alone to the Alone, Christian redemption, the dualism of Samkhya-Yoga, the negation of Maya in Advaita Vedanta, or the modern obsession to conquer nature through science and technology, we are talking about the same rejection of the divinity of material existence.

Seen in the context of this pathology of consciousness universal to the human race, the advent of Sri Aurobindo's Integral Nonduality is, at the very least, a hopeful sign of healing. I would even go so far as to suggest that Sri Aurobindo's personal attainments are an attempt on the part of undivided Divine consciousness to introduce a new force of healing into the fractured state of human consciousness. It is in this spirit of healing and integral nonduality, then, that I will turn to find those elements in Plotinus that resonate closely with this vision of wholeness. I will do this by focusing on Plotinus's concept of *theoria*, or contemplation.

Since it is nonduality that we seek, we must find what it is that bridges the fundamental dichotomy of subject and object. In Plotinus it is contemplation which links each level of reality with its corresponding level of consciousness (except in the case of the One which transcends all differentiation). Plotinus not only links the subjective and objective poles of reality in this way but states further that these subjective sides of reality are ontologically prior to their objective manifestations, these latter being likened to poor images of their archetype. Plotinus called the states of consciousness *theoria*, contemplation, and their objective manifestations *theorema*, which can be translated as either work of contemplation, object of contemplation, or result of contemplation. The world as theorema is the product of contemplation. But the world stands to contemplation not only as product, for it too contemplates. To one degree or another all things contemplate and aspire to contemplation. This is the thesis by which Plotinus begins his treatise "On Nature and Contemplation and the One."

> Suppose we said, playing at first before we set out to be serious, that all things aspire to contemplation, and direct their gaze to this end not only rational but irrational living things, and the power in plants and the earth which brings them forth and all that attain to it as far as possible for them in their natural state, but different things contemplate and attain their end in different ways, some truly, and some only having an imitation and image of their true end could anyone endure the oddity of this line of thought?[1]

Interestingly, Plotinus proposes this thesis as a play. Play is here proposed to be a more effective means than is seriousness for leading the inquirer into the experience of contemplation, and this probably for at least two reasons: 1) it encourages the use of imagination, and 2) it frees the mind from more or less exclusive concentration on the given conditioned sensuous aspect of objects so that the playful nature, of the world in its wholeness can be fully participated in. In any case, an argument over whether seriousness or playfulness is the best approach to realize the truth should not distract one from the point that "one plays and the other is serious for the sake of contemplation."

This accent on play is also found in Aurobindo's philosophy. This Lila, or Divine Play, is not to be understood as an arbitrary imposition of a wanton God sadistically enjoying the sufferings of creatures made to dance according to His bidding, but is rather the perception of creation as a mutual agreement between the Divine Purusha and all individual Purushas.[2]

> If we look at World-Existence...in its relation to the self-delight of eternally existent being, we may regard, describe and realise it as Lila the play, the child's joy, the poet's joy, the actor's joy, the mechanician's joy of the Soul of things eternally young, perpetually inexhaustible, creating and recreating Himself in Himself for the sheer bliss of that self-creation, of that self-representation Himself the play, Himself the player, Himself the playground.[3]

Seeing creation as play automatically shifts the perspective on life away from the serious business of escaping the tragedy of the cosmic fall or mistake to one which sees oneself as a co-creative participant in the Divine Unfoldment.

Actions, writes Plotinus, are a "shadow of contemplation and reasoning" (III.8.4). People engage in action and have their minds distracted by the purely superficial aspects of manifest action because "their souls are weak and they are not able to grasp the vision sufficiently, and therefore are not filled with it, but still longing to see it, they are carried into action, so as to see what they cannot see with their intellect" (III.8.4).

By exhorting us to see action as a shadow or image of contemplation, Plotinus is encouraging us to awaken a symbolic mode of knowing. A symbolic mode of knowing would try to understand actions as images of a higher life concealed in their working as their essence and origin. Of the different forms of symbolic knowledge, Plotinus spoke highly of the power of art to lift the Soul with the wings of beauty. Beauty is the domination of matter by Form, or Form made visible to the sensitive soul. Even the weak soul sunk in the dissipated consciousness of sensual action can be stirred by the power of beauty of bodies, images, music and excellent actions. Beauty is something which the soul becomes aware of even at the first glance and recognizes and speaks of it as if it understood it already (I.6.2). It welcomes beauty and adapts itself to beauty as if it recognized beauty to be of the same nature as itself. Sri Aurobindo views on Beauty are nearly identical:

> Beauty is the special Divine manifestation in the physical as Truth is in the mind, Love in the heart, Power in the vital.[4]
>
> The search for beauty is only in its beginning a satisfaction in the beauty of form, the beauty which appeals to the physical senses and the vital impressions, impulsions, desires. It is only in the middle a satisfaction in the beauty of the ideas seized, the emotions aroused, the perception of perfect process and harmonious combination. Behind them the soul beauty in us desires the contact, the revelation, the uplifting Delight of an absolute Beauty in all things which it feels to be present but which, neither the senses and instincts by themselves can give, though they may be its channels for it is suprasensuous nor the reason and intelligence, though they too are a channel for it is suprarational, supra-intellectual but to which through all these veils the soul itself seeks to

arrive. When it can get the touch of this universal absolute Beauty, this soul of Beauty, this sense of its revelation in any slightest or greatest thing, the beauty of a flower, a form, the beauty and power of a character, an action, an event, a human life, an idea, a stroke of the brush or the chisel or a scintillation of the mind, the colors of a sunset or the grandeur of the tempest, it is then that the sense of Beauty in us is really, powerfully, entirely satisfied. It is in truth, seeking, as in religion, for the Divine, the All-Beautiful in man, in nature, in life, in thought, in art; for God is Beauty and Delight hidden in the variation of his masks and forms.[5]

Turning again to Plotinus we find that beauty and soul are related in so far as they are both productions of Form. It is the participation of the things of this world in Form, which have their station in *Nous* (Intellect, sometimes, under influence of the German *Geist*, translated as Spirit), that endow the things with beauty. The more completely a thing participates in Form the more the beauty inherent in Form is manifested in its recipient nature. Conversely, the less a thing is dominated by Form, the more ugly its appearance. In the Platonic tradition Form is reality or Being. Truth, Beauty, and Goodness are the chief characteristics or Forms of Being and, consequently, the more a thing participates in, or partakes of, the experience of Being, the more it will exhibit these characteristics. "Beautifulness is reality" (I.6-6). Both Soul and the things it contemplates as beautiful or ugly have their common origin in the One, the source of Being. Intellect (*Nous*) is the One's first emanation or hypostasis in Being. Plotinus sometimes refers to *Nous* as God, that which is most like the One under the condition of the Many. The one is beyond Being, or beyond God. Hence, the true beauty of the Soul is to be found in its own highest being which is the Intellect; and to the extent that it is perfectly conformed to Intellect, says Plotinus, so is it truly soul. "For this reason it is right to say that the soul's becoming something good and beautiful is its being made like to God, because from Him come beauty and all else which falls to the lot of real beings" (I.6.6).

To posit that manifestations of beauty (the objective) and souls (the subjective) are alike by virtue of a common third element, Form, only gives us a static, logical explanation which is insufficient for portraying the more dynamic aspect of their relationship. In the treatise "On Beauty" Plotinus portrays the dynamic (*dunamis* in Plotinus is the contemplative power of Forms) relation as one of a procession of Beauty from the One (which is also characterized as the Good) to Intellect, where it is recognizable as Beauty, and which, in turn, gives beauty to soul, the second hypostasis. Everything else below the purely psychic (Soul) dimension is beautiful by the shaping of Soul. In fact, Soul tries to make everything it grasps and masters beautiful (I.6.6). The psychic dimension refers not only to individual human souls but to the World Soul or Cosmic Soul and to pure disembodied (abstract) soulness alike, although the latter is sometimes identified with *Nous* by Plotinus. In any case, beautifulness is soulness, and the beauty of this world is a reflection of Soul or the imprint, of Soul, which by the power of Forms that inhere in it, gathers the dissipated and relatively unformed matter (theoremata deformed by lapse of time) into organized wholes which, relative to their less formed parts, are beautiful. Thus, whether the beautiful thing is a work fashioned by a human soul or a natural beauty fashioned by the World Soul, the beauty is in each case the work of Soul and an image of soulness. When a human soul experiences beauty it is, consciously or unconsciously, actually being stimulated by universal soulness; it is suddenly edified by its own nature which is beautiful. We might ask here, why is it that if Soul is beautiful it needs to be reminded of its inherent beauty by an extraneous sort of beauty?

The chief characteristic that differentiates Soul or Psyche from *Nous* is duration or time. *Nous* is non-durational or eternal (notwithstanding Plotinus' various contrary assertions, which he tries to justify as necessarily paradoxical, the logic of the Divine transcending the logic of science), and as such is omniscient and omnipresent, having all contents of knowledge altogether at once, which constitutes perfect contemplation. Soul, however, is unable to maintain that intellectual quietude necessary to reflect the whole at once, for it has a "restless power" which does not want, or cannot have, the whole to be present to it altogether, but prefers to experience the whole successively in one form after another in an infinite number of different ways. By thus dividing up, measuring the illimitable it loses its integrity and dissipates the unity of the whole into ever weaker extensions and part-formations. Soul thus betimes first itself and then reality; time is the life of the Soul (III.7.11).

The Soul's activity of "betiming" is also a work of art, for the reality which has been worked or betimed is an image of what is before time, the eternal Forms of Intellect. Time for Plotinus, as it was for Plato in the *Timaeus*, is the moving image of eternity. Time is the One contemplating under the limitations of Soul. Soul's contemplation is temporal. The essential character of the Soul's activity is contemplation of the whole under particular temporalized Forms. However while its essence (in any particular instance) is the whole under a particular temporalized Form, the Soul's contemplation is inherently distracted and cluttered by its own past acts of contemplation.

The cluttered state of mind is a problem for Soul because the intuitions of different times are not completely conformable to each other, each being the contemplation of the whole from a different perspective. An act of contemplation in the present cannot be isolated from past acts of contemplation which help constitute the present one and which thus render it as ambiguous or over-determined. This problem obtains only under the condition of time, because for the Soul which is conformed to Intellect there would be no past acts of contemplation, Intellect being beyond severed time. At the level of Intellect, therefore, the Platonic concept of recollection would not make any sense. On that account Plotinus replaces recollection with direct intuition. Noetic intellection is beyond time, and so memory is not in order there, for all is present. "Intellect, therefore really thinks the real beings, not as if they were somewhere else; for they are neither before it nor after it" (V.9.5). There is no ambiguity in noetic intellection.

The embodied soul, however, must rely on memory in the attempt to compensate for its weakened intuition. Memory is a Soul power (*dunamis*) which weakens in direct proportion to the soul's degree of absorption in the sense level of experience. The soul's power is fully actual in Intellect, but when embodied its actuality loses ground to potentiality, which is a more passive state of being. The more the soul is merely passively perceiving and remembering the superficial appearances of things, the further it strays from seeing things in their real being. Soul only knows things completely and fully in Intellect, which is to say, when it perceives their eternal being as identical with its own being. Such knowing also constitutes the soul's actualization of its power and this, notes Plotinus, confirms Parmenides' alleged statement that "thinking and being are the same thing."

Thus the soul self-limited to perceiving instrumentally through the senses is blind to real beauty, and can see only its faint reflection, matter. In order to perceive real beauty the soul must develop a "passionate love for the invisible" (I.6.4). This passion of love, *eros*, seems to be a necessary predisposition that renders the soul receptive to the ubiquitous but otherwise hidden splendor. Plotinus adopts Plato's philosophy of eros, with some minor differences. Eros in Platonism is not just a passion of deficiency seeking for satisfaction but is also a logos, which is to say that it is not merely a passive potentiality but is partly an active *dunamis* by virtue of its constitution as an expression of a rational principle; a delegate, as it were, from the Intellect in the world of embodied souls (to adapt a phrase from Aurobindo). Love is not merely a delegate, however, even though it often forgets itself and becomes enamored of superficial beauty. Ultimately it is of the very essence of reality. The Good, for Plotinus, is not only lovable, *erasmion*, but is eros. "He is at once lovable and love and love of himself" (VI.9.15). Hence for the Soul eros is not merely the conveyance towards the Good, upon the attainment of which eros is dropped, but is, the end and perfection which the soul will conform to eternally (VI.7.22).

While Soul is naturally attracted to beauty, it is beauty in conjunction with goodness, which inflames love. Beauty without goodness may either mislead the soul towards, and entrap it in, the non-being of externality (I.6,8; V.5.12), or it may leave the soul cold and unenthusiastic with a mere passionless attraction (VI.7.22). This applies equally to intelligible as to physical beauty. The attraction exercised by the Good is primal and ubiquitously constant (because it has all power), whereas the attraction exercised by beauty is of a derivative power, not as deep and is intermittent and relative. The power of the Good to attract need not be perceived to be effective, and it is always at work, whereas the power of beauty can only be effective when perceived (V.5.1.2). Beauty, then, functions most appropriately when it is a means of experiencing an even deeper level of being, namely, the Good:

> Just as with bodies here below our desire is not for the underlying material things but for the beauty imaged upon them. For each is what it is by itself; but it becomes desirable when the Good colors it, giving a kind of grace to them and passionate love to the desirers. Then the soul, receiving into itself an outflow from thence, is moved and dances wildly and is all stung with longing and becomes love and is truly winged (VI.7.22).

True eros is the love of the Good, a love which carries within it its own principle of purification and perfection. It is a logos, and as such is deeply connected with the reality underlying all things. The more life a beautiful object possesses, the more beautiful it is because life has "soul, and because it has more the form of the Good; and this means that it is somehow colored by the light of the Good, and being so colored wakes and rises up and lifts up that which belongs to it" (VI.7.22).

The beauty of physical objects, then, is a reflection of the beauty of the Forms. But in the Intellectual or Spiritual world of the Forms themselves, Plotinus argues in VI.7.32, beauty is not just one Form as a part amongst others, but must be that which generates Form; and that which generates Form is the principle of Form and as such must be formless. Consequently,

> when you cannot grasp the form or shape of what is longed for, it would be most longed for and most lovable, and love for it would be immeasurable. For love is not limited here, because neither is the beloved, but the love of this would be unbounded; so his beauty is of another kind and beauty above beauty. For if it is nothing, what beauty can it be? But if it is lovable, it would be the generator of beauty. Therefore the productive power of all is the flower of beauty, a beauty which makes beauty (VI.7.32).

"How, then, shall we find the way?" asks Plotinus in introducing the method of contemplation. "Let him who can, follow and come within and leave outside the sight of his eyes and not turn back to the bodily splendors which he saw before. When he sees the beauty in bodies he must not run after them; we must know that they are images, traces, shadows, and hurry away to that which they image" (I.6.8). This gives us a brief sketch of Plotinus's practical instructions on the method of contemplation. Already we begin to see his failure to carry through with his vision and a tendency to resort to a one-way ascent by way of the *via negativa*. The essential point, however, is that external looking at beauty must be complemented by internally-directed looking.[6]

This seeing inwardly, the seeing of beauty within one's own soul, is not a mere passive looking, but an active intervention, an education or drawing out of potential beauty, a process Plotinus likens to "working on your statue" till one sees the "divine glory of virtue" shining within oneself. Working on oneself could be understood as developing one's power, or actualizing one's potential. In the matter of the affections this would involve transforming them from their merely passive states (i.e., purely reactive to external situations) into active states, of which love is the primary exemplar (III.5.7). An active affection is one which most exhibits the higher Soul qualities, and these qualities are Soul expressions and reflections of the perfect contemplation of *nous*. Affections are more real and active the more they arise from the unitive level of Soul, which is to say, the more they approximate the contemplative power of *nous*.

Plotinus's views on beauty and love illustrate the sort of symbolic knowledge that he is encouraging philosophers to bring into play when, for example, he exhorts one to see physical objects as shadows of a greater reality. Because it involves faculties usually excluded from "serious" knowledge, (i.e., the passions, imagination, moral and aesthetic sensibility), Plotinus's theory of knowledge goes beyond the prevalently cognitive views philosophers tend to have of knowledge. That is so in that he does not ground knowledge in sense perception, as do empiricists, nor in the laws of reason, as do rationalists, but finds the source of knowledge in the transcendent One whose act of knowledge is identical with himself. True knowledge is undifferentiated absolute identity. This superknowledge, if it can still be called knowledge, is the perfection of knowledge. The nisus of knowledge on all levels of being is towards identity which is complete knowledge. The standard by which the degree of truth of any knowledge is measured is the identity of the knower and the known: knowledge is truer as knower and known become more identical.[7]

The primary model of knowledge so-called, however, is *nous*, because in *nous*, there is plurality and differentiation, conditions usually presupposed for the possibility of knowledge. The differentiation in *nous* is not opposed to unity, but expresses unity in the most perfect degree possible for any multiplicity. The simplest difference that can be generated from the absolute unity of the One is that between contemplation of the contemplator and the contemplated, *theoria* and *theorema*. In its origin this difference is a mere difference-in-unity, for in *nous* the contemplator or contemplation, "must be the same as the contemplated, and Intellect the same as the intelligible; for, if not the same, there will not be truth; for the one who is trying to possess realities will possess an impression different from the realities, and this is not truth. For truth ought not to be the truth of something else, but to be what it says" (V.3.5).

By identity of theoria and theorema Plotinus means not the overpowering of the latter by the former, as in epistemological idealism, but that the theoremata contemplated are themselves also theoriai or contemplations of the whole. If theoremata do not become identical with theoriai then they remain merely objects in another subject and, even if living objects, they would not be self-living. In *nous* all is self-living, for *nous* is the fullest life (III.8.8). Plotinus employs images to depict this highest level of contemplation in order to provide the soul with some contemplative aids, though these images can only give an external representation which must be "dematerialized" to allow the identification of the soul and what it is contemplating to be realized. For example, Plotinus likens *nous* to "something all faces, shining with living faces" (VI.7.15). Each "face" or Form is a particular power, which makes *nous* a multiplicity, yet each is all and in perfect harmony with the whole because identical with it (which makes *nous* also a perfect unity) even while remaining a part. *Nous* is perfect unity-in-diversity. Each maintains the appearance of a part, "but a penetrating look sees the whole in it" (V.8. 4). This heaven world of *nous* is not another place, but as the last quote makes clear, this very world of appearances seen with complete penetration. So heaven is this world of men, animals, plants, sea and earth, but now seen in and as *nous*, heavenly.

> All things There are transparent and there is nothing dark or opaque, everything is clear, altogether and to its inmost part, to everything, for light is transparent to light. Each There has everything in itself and sees all things in every other, or all are everywhere and each and everyone is all, and the glory is unbounded. The sun There is all the stars, and each star is the sun and all the others. One particular kind of being stands out in each, but in each all are manifest (V.8.3).

Since heaven or *nous* is this world as experienced in perfect contemplation, there is no type of appearance "here", however lowly or loathsome, that cannot be, "saved". This is to say, every existent can be experienced as having inherent divine value, but the degree to which the inherent value of things can be known depends on the degree of one's contemplative intuition. To see all things as heavenly, as the living substance of God, is not to collapse the value distinctions of all things into a single value. Distinctions in value remain on the surface of each being, in their appearance, even though in their common depth they are seen in and as oneness. Differences in value are "according to their nearness to the first principles". Hence a god is greater in value than is a man or animal because more totally *nous*. Even an irrational and animate thing is a living thought in Intellect, and since at a deep level *theoremata* are identical with *theoria*, "is a particular kind of *nous*," and as such does not cease to be *nous*, and as *nous* the *nous* of all, although in a particular way.

> For it is actually one thing, but has the power to be all: but we apprehend in each what it actually is: and what it actually is, is the last and lowest, so that the last and lowest of this particular *nous* is horse (for example), and being horse is where it stopped in its continual outgoing to a lesser life, but another stops lower down (VI.7.9).

An important consequence of perfect contemplation, where the contemplated is the same as the contemplation or where thought and being are the same, is that whatever is thought "There" necessarily comes into being. Simply by being what it is, contemplation, *nous* produces. *Nous* does not intend or choose to create; yet if the intelligibles subsist, the sensibles will ensue from a necessity inherent in contemplating intelligibles (VI.7.8). Contemplation, *theoria* is at the same time production, *poiesis*. In this respect *nous* imitates the infinite, supremely active *dunamis* of the One whose formlessness is productive of all Forms and hence of the existence of all things. Plotinus emphasizes that this outflow of Reality from the One is not the work of a Creator, nor a matter of chance, but is rather a spontaneous but perfectly natural expression of the nature of the Origin, and is without temporal beginning or end. As a natural expression of the One the procession of Reality, cannot terminate until everything that could possibly come into existence on all the levels of being has actually done so. Each of these levels, furthermore, must be complete in its turn: *nous* containing the totality of being in a timeless eternity, Psyche or Soul under the conditions of temporal succession, and sensible Nature under the conditions of spatial extension.

Poiesis, the productive aspect of contemplation, is in another view *tolma* the impulse of self-assertion. The self that is asserting its desire for existence is always a part of its originary context. Plotinus tends to see this tolmaic aspect of contemplation as regrettable, but not to the extreme extent of the Gnostics for whom the concept was equivalent to the principle of evil. In any case, he leaves out this "moment" of contemplative production (i.e., the self-assertion) from his model of poiesis, according to which the best action is accomplished by the non-action of resting in oneself. "But that true All is blessed in such a way that, in not making, it accomplishes great works and in remaining in itself makes no small things" (III.2.1). In moral works this principle is followed by and exemplified in the highest type of man who always does the right thing immediately and spontaneously without having to think about it. That is because his soul is intimate or united with *nous*, and in *nous* action and contemplation are identical, and thus in perfect equilibrium.

Sri Aurobindo places much more emphasis on this constructive work of the Way, and we see it in the importance of Karma Yoga in his system where it serves far more than the traditional purpose of mere return, becoming an expression of Divine will and action on earth. The reason why Plotinus emphasizes the "return" moment of contemplation (which is self-negating, the *via negativa*) over the tolmaic moment of self-assertion, is that with the descent of soul the former wanes while the latter waxes in strength, and philosophy must endeavor to bring these powers back into balance. Moreover, since the outward movement of self-expression happens more or less spontaneously, the key to right action is the controlling, forming element of contemplative vision, the depth of inwardness determining the rightness of outward action.[8] From an Aurobindonian point of view, however, it is erroneous to think that manifestation will happen automatically, for if the human will is not aligned with Divine purpose, then the creative self-expression of the Divine will be blocked and distorted in those areas where humans are called to be co-creators with God.

As contemplation weakens, the gap between theoria and theorema, contemplation and action, becomes more marked, to the point where contemplation becomes absorbed by outer action, where action, the contemplated, becomes for all practical purposes the only form of contemplation. That is why Plotinus calls action at this level a mere shadow of contemplation. Even though it is a straying from contemplation, however, action never leaves contemplation entirely behind and tries to return to contemplative intimacy by producing works which will be enjoyed by contemplation. Works are performed ostensibly for the preservation and enhancement of self-existence through a process of possession, and possession is a tendency towards identity or union, which is perfect contemplation. Contemplation is the end of action. The more action is attuned to contemplation the less the need of the soul to go out of itself in action (i.e., the greater the quality of action the less the quantity of action[9]) (III.8.6). Contemplation is, both the origin and end of action, for *poiesis* is the application of rational Forms to potential matter, and this is an activity of contemplation, "for creating is bringing a Form into being, and this is filling all things with contemplation" (III.8.7). Hence, the originative principle (Form, Logos, contemplation) is for all things the goal, which is to say that the whole life of the universe is philosophy, or, as Sri Aurobindo puts it, "All life is yoga."[10]

What I hope has been clearly brought out in this meditation on Plotinus is that the role of the hypostases for the practical life is not merely that of serving as guide posts for the return journey to the Absolute. They also function as indispensable powers to be used by the contemplative actor in his creative involvement with the world. While Plotinus did not develop this aspect of the spiritual life, Sri Aurobindo made it a central feature of his Integral Yoga. It is this emphasis that prompted him to remark that his yoga begins where all the others end.

According to Sri Aurobindo the Integral Yogi does not merely use the involutionary dimensions as stepping stones to the infinite, but brings the insight and puissance (*cit-sakti*) found there by the elevation of his consciousness to bear on manifest nature in order to further the evolutionary progress not only of himself or even humanity, but of all life and even physical nature itself. The involutionary dimensions, populated by gods, constitute part of the mechanism of grace, which plays a necessary part in facilitating spiritual development. The help that the beings of the involutionary planes can render to the evolving earth consciousness is severely limited, however, by the lack of conscious cooperation with them on the part of humanity. This lack of cooperation and the consequent difficulties we have in manifesting the Divine in the material world constitutes a negative feedback loop that reinforces the *resentment* world views of dualism and materialism.

In Conclusion, if Neoplatonism is to be revived as a viable contemporary philosophy, I believe it needs to develop the neglected aspect of that philosophy outlined in this essay, and Sri Aurobindo's Integral philosophy would serve as an indispensable guide in this endeavor.[11]

Endnotes

1. *Ennead* III.8.1. A. H. Armstrong, translator. (Harvard University Press, Loeb Classical Library, 1980). Subsequent references to this translation will be placed in parentheses after the citation.
2. *The Life Divine*, Book Two, Part 1, chapter IV. "The Divine and the Undivine" (p.369 of the 1951 New York edition).
3. Centenary Edition, 18:102-3.
4. *Collected Works*, 9:491.
5. *Ibid* 15:135.
6. Cf. Plato's *Symposium* 210.
7. See John Deck, *Nature, Contemplation, and the One*, (Toronto, 1967) p.20.
8. This contemplative understanding of action is virtually identical to the concept of *nishkama karma*, desireless action, of the *Bhagadvad Gita*, and mutatis mutandis, to the *wu-wei*, non-action, of Taoism.
9. "Yoga is skill in action." (*Bhagavad Gita* II.50)
10. In a note to his translation of *Ennead* III.8.7, Armstrong observes that "by making *theoria* the end of all perception and action Plotinus abolishes, no doubt consciously and deliberately, Aristotle's distinction between *praktike* and *theoretike episteme*, or *dianoia*...and makes the whole life, not only of man but the universe philosophy in Aristotle's sense." "All Life is Yoga" is the epigram to Sri Aurobindo's book, *The Synthesis of Yoga*.
11. Another lacunae in Plotinus that Aurobindo's thought would help to fill is in the area of spiritual sociology and a philosophy of history. These are consequences of Plotinus's concentration on the static, nontemporal (Shiva) aspect of the Divine and his failure to appreciate the dynamic temporal (Shakti) aspect.

The Four Dimensional Philosophy of Indian Thought and Plotinus

I. C. Sharma

At the very outset I would like to define Indian thought as that ethico-metaphysical philosophy, which has its roots in the four Vedas, Rig, Sama, Yajur and Adharva Samhitas which express the four-dimensional essence of the experiences of the sages, engaged in the spiritual search of God, Nature and Man. Further, this very thought has its roots in the Brahmana Granthas which are the explanatory and definitional part of the Vedas: in the Aranyakas, the philosophical experiential conclusions, drawn by the forest dweller practitioners of the fourfold knowledge stated above, and in the Mahavakayas (the universal statements), experienced, expressed and stated in the Upanisadic part of the Vedic tradition. Let it be pointed out that the Vedic tradition the Vedic Truth is called Sruti, the revealed Truth. This truth was attained by the practice and experience of the Ultimate Reality, the groundless Ground of everything that exists, lives and has being; it is again four-dimensional. This ancient most ethico-metaphysical philosophy has the following four divisions:

1) The Mantras or hymns;
2) The Brahmanas or the explanatory notes;
3) The Aranyakas or the books written by the forest wellers;
4) The Upanisads or the philosophical conclusions.

The Mantras or hymns are the oldest aspect of the Vedic literature and have been classified into the four major collections stated above, (i) Rig (ii) Sama (iii) Yajur and (iv) Adharva Samhitas. These Samhitas cover a very wide field, ranging from the social problems of marriage, love and gambling to metaphysical theories of creation. But most of the hymns are addressed to gods, who on a close examination turn out to be the names of the various entities or powers of one Supreme God. This Supreme Ruler of the universe, again, is not a person but a central Reality, the Master of the creation that resides in the very core of everything that exists. According to Plotinus as well, gods are the entities arising from light; and light is equivalent to Brahman.

The Brahmanic literature explains the various rituals and analyses, the various terms used in the hymns. But unfortunately, this literature has been neglected, not only by the Western, but by Indian scholars as well. In fact, Brahmanas are a link between the Vedic hymns and the Upanisadic Philosophy. In the absence of a systematic study of the Brahmanas, the apparent conflict between the ritualistic philosophy of the Vedas and the *Atma Vidya* (the science of self) of the Upanisads, which places knowledge above action can never be resolved.

The four dimensional philosophy of the Vedas and Upanisads, though chronologically prior to the four-dimensional mystic philosophy of Plotinus with the three hypostases of the One, the Nous and World Soul plus the concept of Nature or Matter as an emanation from the World Soul, is not only similar to, but almost identical with the latter. Before explaining the mystic experience and its purpose the union of the individual soul with the One the Supreme Being, the Supreme Abode of Man and Nature it seems necessary to allude briefly to the four dimensional basis and background of metaphysics, ethics, psychology, epistemology and sociology of the Vedic and the Upanisadic philosophy.

The four dimensions of the Vedic tradition stated above, point to the identity of the Vedic and the Upanisadic four-dimensionality with that of Plotinus. The Vedas, the Upanisads and the Bhagavadgita, the three foundational philosophical texts comprising the Indian tradition, agree in accepting the following four fold-nature of the Brahman, the Supreme Being as:

(1) *Avyava* Brahman (the Eternal Infinite Ground of all), corresponding to Plotinus' One, and even transcending the One;
(2) *Aksara* Brahman (the Indestructible Cause), corresponding to Plotinus' Nous;
(3) *Atmaksara* Brahman (the Supreme Self), endowed with the potentiality of creation, preservation and destruction, and hence a Creator, not yet differentiated as subject and object, corresponding to the World Soul of Plotinus; and
(4) *Visvasrit* Brahman (the Cosmic Manifestation), the extended material world of universes, super galaxies, and individualities, as an emanation and irradiation of just one spark of the Supreme Self, corresponding to the ensouled matter or Nature of Plotinus.

A word of caution in this context seems to be necessary to distinguish between the Plotinian Hypostases and the four-dimensional nature of Brahman, even though both Plotinian philosophy and Indian thought are firmly rooted in the mystic experience, the sole purpose of which is the return of the four-dimensional Self of man to the four dimensional Supreme Self the One. The *Avyaya* Brahman is not to be confused even with the One or with Unity, since It is also beyond One. Even Plotinus agrees with this transcendence of the One in his writings. Thus the One of Plotinus can be regarded as closer to the *Avyaya* Brahman, even though it is not wholly identical with it. The *Avyaya* Brahman is also designated as the *Paratpara Brahman* (the Brahman beyond the beyond). *Aksara Brahman* is the Absolute and Indestructible the unmanifested potential Cause. This very *Aksara* manifests or transforms Itself as the Parama *Purusa* (the Supreme Self or the Supreme Person).

Lest the comparison given above be misunderstood, a clarification seems necessary. The *Atmaksara* is wholly identical neither with the World Soul, nor with the *nous* though it is closer to the *nous* than to the World Soul, because it is the emanation from the *Aksara* Brahman, which is both the One and also the *nous*.

It would help to clarify why the entire gamut of Indian Thought (including Jainism, Buddhism and the materialist Carvaka philosophy) has been comprehended in the Upanisadic philosophy, which expounds the Pancakosa Theory of the Self i.e., the Theory of the *Annamaya Kosa* (the bodily Self), the *Pranamaya Kosa* (the biological Self), the *Manomaya Kosa* (the Mental or Psychological Self), the *Viinanamaya Kosa* (the intellectual or rational Self), and the *Anandamaya Kosa* (the Spiritual or Blissful Self).

The final *Kosa* or Sheath, the highest stage of the individual self, consists of bliss. It is within the intellectual, mental, biological and physical self and is the subtlest of all. It corresponds to the *Praiapati*, the center of centers and the truth of truths. The realization of the spiritual or blissful Self leads to God-realization, having attained which the aspirant rises above all contradictions and antinomies. The two stages of self-realization, *Moksa* or *Jivanmukti* (liberation while living in the body) and *Videha Mukti* (final liberation or release after physical death), have been recognized by all the schools of Indian Philosophy. Thus the Upanisadic thought is the very rock and foundation of the metaphysical as well as the ethical concepts of all the systems of Indian philosophy.

The Upanisads also regard man as four-dimensional by combining the causal intellectual ego and the spiritual Self as Atman. Society as an organic whole is constituted by *Atman* (Soul as the spiritual organ), *Buddhi*, (the administrative organ, the causal intellect), *Manah* (Mind, the skilled labour organ) and Sarira (the physical labour organ), retrospectively designated as the four castes, Brahmanas (the spiritual class), Kshatriyas (the administrative class), Vaishyas (the skilled labour class) and Shudras, (the labour class), based entirely on their bent of mind and voluntary adoption of a particular occupation.

The Vedic and Upanisadic Brahman are identical because of this four dimensionality viz., (1) The Ground (2) The Cause (3) The Supreme Self and (4) The Cosmic Form, corresponding to the Plotinian One, Nous, the World Soul and ensouled Matter or Nature.

This parallelism holds good as far as the constitution of man is concerned. According to the Vedas, Upanishads and Bhagavadgita, Man is microcosmic Brahman, whose four-dimensionality is constituted by the sum of *Atman* (Pure Being), *Buddhi* (the Casual Self), *Manah* (creative psyche the mind), and *Sarira* (the physical body with five sense organs and five organs of action). It is noteworthy that in the Vedic tradition, the gradation from *Avyaya* Brahman (the Pure inexhaustible Ground of everything) to *Visvavrit* (the Cosmic form inclusive of the World Soul and Matter), that is from the One to Nature, in Plotinian language, is from the subtle and most fundamental to less subtle and dependent. The Plotinian concept of matter confirms this very gradation:

> "That which is taken to be material, is in reality the Soul. It is an extension of Soul down below the normal level of Soul, or better, it is Soul in its lowest possible level of being. Just as all of the level of Soul is an extension of Mind down below in its normal level, so Mind is the One in an extension down below its normal level, or the One in its lowest possible level. Thus Plotinus' Ultimate is transcendent in its level as the One from all determinate being, but it is immanent in it as *Nous*".[1]

The Upanisads, as stated above, regard *Atman* (the Self or Purusha) as identical with man as miniature Brahman. The gradation in the case of Brahman from Avyaya to Visvasrit is from subtle and most fundamental to less subtle and dependent as already stated. In the case of man, called Adhyatma, the gradation is from the most subtle to the most gross. Based on this fourfold cosmic metaphysics and human nature, are the fourfold social, ethical, philosophical and mystical systems in the Vedas, Upanisads and Bhagavadgita. Unlike Plato, the social system in the Vedic tradition is not threefold, but fourfold, because of the spiritual, the intellectual, the mental and the physical aspects. The fourfold values parallel to Platonic virtues are *Artha* (economic value) controlled by temperance; *Kama* (love), depending on courage and temperance; *Dharma* (ethical duty), depending on justice and courage; and Moksha (spiritual perfection), depending on wisdom. The Upanisads also state the fourfold nature of knowledge, based on the four levels of *Jaqtad* (waking consciousness); *Svapna* (dream consciousness); *Susupti* (deep sleep consciousness or unconsciousness); *Turiva* (supra-consciousness, associated with the spiritual self, the causal self, the mental self and the physical self, respectively). The word *Cit* (consciousness) applies both to waking and dream consciousness and the word *Acit* (unconsciousness) as the ground of *Cit* (consciousness), is not to be understood as devoid of consciousness. *Turiya* is beyond the concept of *Cit* and *Acit*. Incidentally, Plotinus's gradation of the stages from the physical to the level of the One, so far as soul's journey back to the One is concerned, seems to be parallel to this hierarchy.

It seems important to mention that the philosophy of the Bhagavadgita propounds four, not three parts, as it is commonly believed. These four paths or methods or Yogas, of attaining enlightenment are: the Buddhi Yoga, corresponding to the spiritual aspect of man (the Buddhi here may mean Nous, which is closer to the One); Jnana Yoga corresponding to the intellectual or rational aspect, Bhakti Yoga, corresponding to the mental aspect; and Karma Yoga, corresponding to the physical nature of Man. It is pertinent to point out that the first six discourses of the Bhagavadgita are devoted to the Buddhi Yoga, the seventh and eighth discourses explicate the Jnana Yoga, the ninth to the twelfth discourses explain the Bhakti Yoga, and the last six discourses expound the Karma Yoga. This four dimensional trend of metaphysics, ethics, sociology, and practical spirituality in Indian Thought is undoubtedly based on the mystic experience of the One Ultimate Reality, as experiential and is not a figment of imagination. The same explanation applies to the Plotinian metaphysics.

The One propounded by Plotinus as the basics of the Intelligence Nous, the World Soul and of Matter, is not a product of mere imagination, but that experiencible indestructibility and everlastingness which pervades every being everywhere. It would be appropriate here to compare the notions of Matter and Brahman in both the Hindu tradition and Neoplatonism. The Isopanishad says "All this living and nonliving (existence) is permeated with Isa (God as Supreme Being), hence the way to the Supreme is to enjoy everything with an attitude of non attachment."[2]

According to Plotinus this everlastingness is present in Matter or Nature as well as in the Soul and Nous. While defining Matter Plotinus says "Matter then, makes the greatest contribution to the formation of bodies...so here in the material world, the many forms must be in something which is One...we can see that this is so because in our present experience things that are mixed together come to identity by having matter, and there is no need for any other medium, because each constituent of the mixture comes bringing its own Matter".[3]

The Bhagavadgita very clearly points out that the One's indestructibility is immanent everywhere: "Know that (Being) to be indestructible in which everything is rooted; no one is capable of annihilating It."[4]

Further, the substrate according to the Bhagavadgita is both potential and actual Being and becoming as coexistent ontologically:

"Nasato Vidyate Bhavo
Nabhavo Vidyate Satah
Ubhyorapi Drishto Antah
Tunyo Tatva Darshibhill"

That is:

Non-being cannot exist,
Nonexistent cannot be;
The seers have accepted this...ontology.[5]

Amazingly, Plotinus also arrived at this ontological notion of the substrate. He says: "One speaks of potential and actual existence; and one speaks of actuality in the class of existing things. We must consider therefore what potential and what actual existence is. Is actuality the same as actual existence, and if anything is actuality, is it also actually existent? or are the two different and is it not necessary for that which is actually existing to be actuality? Further, it is clear that there is potential existence in the World of Things perceived by the senses, we must not speak of potential existence simply; for it is not possible to exist potentially without being potentially anything...It is better and clearer to use "potential existence" in relation to "actual existence" and "potentiality" in relation to "actuality".[6]

It looks as if Plotinus is providing an intellectual explanation of the intuitively discovered nature of the substrate as both being and becoming or being and existence potentiality and actuality. As a matter of fact, his notion of the substrate was an intuitive discovery rather than an intellectual construct.

This very substrate is the receptacle of all. In the words of Plotinus, "What is called 'matter' is said to be some sort...of 'substrate' and 'receptacle' of forms...As for the question whether intelligible matter is eternal...intelligible realities are originated in so for as they have beginning, but unoriginated because they have not a beginning in time; they always proceed from something else, not as always coming into being like the universe, but always existing, like the universe There."[7]

Thus Plotinus points out that all the individual ties arise from the unmanifested substrate and that this substrate is the matrix of all the experiences of the senses and of the mind. The Bhagavadgita calls this nature the 'lower' nature or *apara prakrti*...So far as the substrate of the individuality is concerned, this nature is called Avyakta or unmanifested material ground known as Pradhan in Sankhya system and Avyaktha in the Bhagavadgita: "*Avyaktat vyaktayah sarvah prabhavanti.*" That is, all the individualities arise out of the unmanifested substrate.[8]

As lower nature or *apara prakrti*, this substrate has been beautifully expressed in the Bhagavadgita:

" *Bhumiraponalo vayuh kham mano*
Buddhirevaca ahamkara itivam me
Bhinna prakrtirastadha"[9]

That is, earth, water, fire, air, space (ether) mind, intelligence and ego are the eight different types of Nature. It is further stated that these are the lower nature which are dependent upon and rooted in One Supreme

Brahman. The point to be noted here is that the immanence of the One Ultimate Being in all the levels of existence from Matter to Nous and vice versa in the case of Plotinian philosophy and from the Avyaya to Vishvasrit and vice versa in the case of Indian Thought, has been propounded solely on the basis of immediate intuitive and mystical experience. This fact must be highlighted in the context of comparative study of Plotinus and Indian Thought especially because Plotinianism is an unique expression of Plotinus' Four-dimensional Philosophy. Any imposition of other influences on Plotinus would be out of place.

It is claimed that Plotinus's teachings were the culmination of ancient Greek and Roman philosophy, since Plotinus followed chronologically Plato and his successors. But this culmination was not a mere summary of what the previous writers had stated. It may be granted that Plotinus' ideas derived their inspiration from Plato, whose philosophy he thoroughly studied. The greatness of his teaching, however, does not depend on his study of Plato nor on the observations of contemporary Christian traditions. Plotinus's philosophy was primarily the outcome of his personal inner experience and his spiritual development. His own intuitive experience, his meditation and the glimpses of the divine light, led him to his fundamental convictions, concluding that God is the source of all existence.

Plotinus's cosmology reveals the presence of individual differences and plurality of souls in the spatio-temporal world, emanating from one God, who is Himself infinite and undifferentiated. This One is also the Supreme God, identified with the light above light. Beyond this however, he tried to avoid the use of any positive concept to define God, lest it conceptually limit Him. Human soul individuates from the World Soul, which itself is an emanation from the infinite God. Before being incarnated, the soul was in a state of constant contemplation of the eternal Nous (Mind), and had complete knowledge of the good. Having separated from God and descended into the material world, it is now on its journey back to God and passes through various births in its ascent towards its Supreme Source. In the state of ecstasy, the soul is raised above all limitations and merges with the soul of God. Only thus reunited with its source can the soul retain true knowledge. These ideas cannot be labelled as the mere summary of a theoretical study of Plato or Aristotle on the part of Plotinus. Rather, they are the expression of intuitive inner experiences arising from the link of the individual consciousness with the cosmic current.

When the intuition is honoured, and when the inner experience corroborates the external observation, the diversity is understood in its right perspective. Differences and duality are not abolished, but an insight into the underlying unity weaves a coherent and consistent pattern into the differences. Truth is then established as an organic whole of various interrelated parts, which are neither mutually exclusive nor absolutely independent. Reality is fundamentally One and essentially eternal.

Endnotes

1. R Baine Harris, Ed. *The Significance of Neoplatonism*, Vol. I in *Studies in Neoplatonism—Ancient and Modern*. SUNY Press, Albany, NY., 1976, p.5.
2. Isopanisad hymn 1.
3. Armstrong, ed. *Plotinus* London, 1966 II:4:12.
4. Gita 2:17.
5. *Ibid* 2:1.6.
6. *Plotinus* op. cit, vol. II: pp 155-157.
7. *Ibid*, Vol. II, 1 to 5, pp 107-117.
8. *Gita*, 8:18.
9. *Ibid* 7:4.

Plotinus' Criticism of Materialism

Christos Evangeliou

I

In *Vita Plotini*, Porphyry provides us with valuable information about Plotinus' habits as a teacher and a writer.[1] From Porphyry's sympathetic presentation, Plotinus emerges as an inspired and inspiring teacher who, like Pythagoras, Socrates, Ammonius Sakkas, and other philosophers before him, was reluctant to commit his thoughts to writing.[2] Late in life, he was persuaded by his students to write down and circulate his advanced doctrines among the selective members of a small inner circle.[3] When they do not express his mystical experiences in metaphorical language, Plotinus' writings reflect the conversational style of the school discussions which would review the opinions of various Hellenic philosophers of the pact on a given subject, and invariably end up in presenting the Platonic position as understood by Plotinus. Only two of the fifty-four treatises are engaged in polemics, *Enneads* II.9 and VI.1, and in both cases Plotinus assumed the role of the defender of Plato and genuine Platonism of the Old Academy. The former of the polemical treatises attacks the Gnostics for their misunderstanding of Platonic texts, while the latter criticizes both Aristotle and the Stoics for their audacity to propose radically new sets of categories as a substitute for the Platonic "genera of being".[4] Elsewhere I have analyzed the arguments and explained the reasons for which Plotinus found it necessary to criticize the Gnostics and to reject the Aristotelian doctrine of categories.[5] At the present I would like to consider the specific objections which Plotinus raised against what he considered as a Stoic set of categories in *Ennead* VI.1 which has not received much attention compared with his criticism of the Aristotelian set.[6]

These two sets of categories are functionally comparable in that each of them attempts to provide an ontologically adequate account of the sensible world, but they are equally unacceptable to Plotinus who, being convinced of its truth, wanted to revive the ontology of ancient Platonism with its emphasis on immaterial, incorporeal, and intelligible beings. It will become clear from our discussion that the debate had to do less with logic and more with ontology which at the middle of the third century A.D. was about to take another turn away from the prevailing materialism. The time was ripe for the rebirth of Platonism of the Old Academy and Plotinus was ready to fight all opposition to such a revival. But before we come to consider Plotinus' specific objections to Stoic monistic and materialistic conception of the Cosmos, it would be helpful to place our discussion in its appropriate context.

II

Ennead VI.1.I opens with a paragraph in which Plotinus looks back at the history of Greek philosophy and sums up the opinions held by various philosophers regarding the number and nature of beings: "Some said there was one being, some a definite number, and some an infinite number; and in each of these groups, some said the one being was one thing and some another, and the same applies to those who said the number of beings was limited and those who said that it was infinite."[7] Plotinus asserts that the relative merits of each of these positions had already been considered by others who rejected, with good reasons, the two extreme views which claimed that being is one or infinite in number. The consensus was that the number of categorically generic beings is limited and definite, but there was disagreement as to their correct number between the most important schools, the Peripatetic, the Stoic, and the Platonic, which had respectively declared for a tenfold, a fourfold, and a fivefold division of reality. Hence the problem. In his effort to solve this ontological problem and to prove that the Platonic division is philosophically sounder than either of the alternative divisions, Plotinus had to display great dialectical dexterity and a pugnacious spirit which are not typical of him.[8]

Plotinus' strategy develops in three phases. In *Ennead* VI.1. he criticizes both the Aristotelian tenfold and the Stoic fourfold divisions of beings or rather sets of categories[9] for many reasons but basically because neither of them seems to pay sufficient attention to the intelligible and immaterial realm which has, for the Platonists, the most important beings; in *Ennead* VI.2 he expounds and defends the Platonic fivefold division of beings as found in the *Sophist* 254c-255d, *to on, tauton, heteron, kinesis*, and *stasis*, because it articulates clearly the ontological relations of the intelligible beings; and in *Ennead* VI.3 he returns to consider the sensible realm of becoming for which he attempts to provide a new set of five categories which differ from the Aristotelian categories.[10] This fact in conjunction with the fact that only six of the thirty chapters of *Enneads* VI.I are devoted to criticizing the Stoic division of categories indicates that, for Plotinus, the real threat to the revival of Platonism was not the crude monistic materialism of the decaying Stoa, but the more subtle and sophisticated Peripatetic ontology which gave priority to sensible substances over the pure Platonic Forms.[11]

It is true that such Stoic doctrines as the unity and sympathy of the sensible cosmos, the function of *logos* and of providence in ordering and guiding all nature and the ideal of the wise man who practices *arete* and finds happiness in this life, did influence the thought of Plotinus. Some of these doctrines as well as many Aristotelian doctrines did find their way into the *Enneads* so that Porphyry is justified in stating "His (Plotinus') writings are full of concealed Stoic and Peripatetic doctrines. Aristotle's *Metaphysics*, in particular, is concentrated in them."[12] However, since the categorical doctrine is not among those Stoic doctrines which influenced Plotinus' philosophy, it would seem that he had serious ontological objections against it.

III

According to *Ennead* VI.25, 1-6, the Stoics distinguish four genera or categories of beings which he identifies as follows: substrates, substances or "subjects" (ὑποκείμενα) qualia or qualified things (ποιά); disposed things or "things in a certain state" (πὼς ἔχοντα); and relatively disposed things or "things in a certain state in relation to others" (πρὸς τι πὼς ἔχοντα).[13] Plotinus also claims that these genera are subsumed under a super genus, "the something" (τὶ) which is supposed to encompass both the corporeal, existent, and real things of the sensible world, as well as the incorporeals; void, time, place, and the famous λεκτά.[14] This supposed super genus became the target of his first attack:

> For, really, how incomprehensible and irrational this something of theirs is, and how unadapted to bodiless things and bodies. And they have not left any room for differences with which they will be able to differentiate the something. And this something is either existent or non-existent; if then, it is existent, it is one of its species; but if it is non-existent, the existent is non-existent. And there are innumerable other objections.

Well, we should leave those for the present and consider the division itself (VI-1-25, 6-12).[15]

In order to appreciate Plotinus' arguments against the stoic division of reality, we must keep in mind the basic tenets of their philosophy of nature.[16] For the Stoics the real world is one, living, finite, and corporeal being located in the infinitely expanded void, "like the seed in the womb."[17] It is permeated by the divine and vital πνεῦμα which is also material but active and responsible for the differentiations and qualifications of matter which gives rise to elements, living beings, and rational beings, all sympathetically related as parts of an integrated Cosmos.[18] In other words everything real is either matter or qualified matter, but the qualifications of matter are due to influence of *pneuma* which is to be understood as a material like firy-air.[19]

With this picture of the Stoic conception of the world in mind, it will be easy to understand the reason for which Plotinus concentrates the fire of his criticism on the first two genera: the ὑποκείμενα identified with material bodies and ultimately with matter; and the ποιά identified with the qualified material bodies; while he is rather brief in his treatment of the other two categories, "the things in a certain state" and "the relatives". For instance, he is aware that the Stoics try to distinguish between "the certain state", as it applies to matter which produces the qualia, and as it applies to qualia which produces specifically what they call "things in a certain state." But, Plotinus objects, since the qualia themselves are nothing but "matter in a certain state", it would follow that "the things in a certain state" are ultimately related to matter. Besides, even if the positing of the third category is accepted as legitimate, Plotinus finds totally unacceptable its claim to substitute for such diverse Aristotelian categories as quantity, quality, place, time action, passion, position and possession, although in *Ennead* VI.3 he did not admit most of these categories into the fivefold list which he accepted as final.[20] He concludes with a remark about the fourth category:

> But as regards the relative, if they did not class it under one genus with the other (things in a certain state) it would take another discussion to enquire if they give any reality to such (relative) states, since they often do not do so. And again it is absurd to put a thing which is subsequent to things already existing into the same genus as the things which were there

before: for one and two must be there first for there to be half and double." (VI.1 30, 24-28)

Plotinus' brief comment on the fourth category of relation and the relative contrasts with its importance for Ancient and Modern Skepticism and the enthusiastic treatment which it has received."[21]

However, about the other two categories especially the first one, Plotinus has something more interesting to say. Utilizing dialectically the Aristotelian distinctions between genera and species, prior and posterior, potentiality and actuality, substance and accidents, and matter and form, Plotinus is able to look critically at the Stoic category of ὑποκείμενα.[22] To summarize and paraphrase his argument (VI.1 25-27), it seems to Plotinus that the Stoics are mistaken in giving priority to matter by considering it as a first principle and at the same time as a genus of being to be classified with material bodies to which it gives rise, thus mixing carelessly what, in their account, is prior to that which is posterior. Furthermore, they speak of *hypokeimena* in plural, while the singular would be more appropriate, since their conception of matter is one continuous and indivisible mass.[23] It is also absurd to give priority to matter which is potentiality, instead of giving it to actuality, that is, the forms, the *rationes seminales* or the divine λόγος.

The absurdities seem to multiply for the Stoics who identified matter with body which itself is a composite of matter and some form or other unless, Plotinus remarks, they use the word "body" with a new meaning different from the common one which associates natural bodies with three-dimensionality and resistance.[24] Above all, by giving ontological priority and the place of honor to that which in indefinite, obscure, shapeless, lifeless, and mindless, that is, sheer matter, the Stoics reduce everything else including God to "matter in a certain state."

To Plotinus it does not make sense to hold, as the Stoics do, that substantiality is decreasing as one moves from matter to body, from bodies to living beings, and from living beings to rational beings because it is contrary to intelligible reality and its priority as he understands it. He describes as follows the root of the Stoic absurdities and the gulf which separates theirs and the Plotinian approach to reality and to the really real beings:

> The cause of this is that sense-perception became their guide and they trusted it for the placing of principles and the rest. For they considered

that bodies were the real beings, and, since they were afraid of their transformation into each other, they thought that what persisted under them was reality, as if someone thought that place does not perish. Yet place also does persist for them, but they ought not to have considered that what persists in any kind of way was real being, but to see first what characteristics must belong to what is truly real, on the existence of which persistence for ever depends... But the most extraordinary of all is that, though they are assure of the existence of each and every thing by sense-perception, they posit as real being what cannot be apprehended by sense, for they do not rightly attribute resistance to it; resistance is a quality. But if they say they grasp it by intellect, it is an odd sort of intellect which ranks matter before itself and attributes real being to matter but not to itself. So, since their intellect is not real for them, how could it be trustworthy when it speaks about things more authentic than itself and is in no way related to them? (VI-1, 28, 5-26)

Regarding the second category, the qualia or qualified things, Plotinus proceeds in a similar manner. He raises a series of questions about the nature of the qualia and how they differ from the substrates in order to make the point that Stoic materialism has turned the world really upside down. To paraphrase his argument again, it runs as follows: Since the Stoics posit qualia as a second category, it must be different from their first category, the substratun which was shown to be material, passive and composite. Therefore, the second category must be simple, active and incorporeal. But that is not what the Stoics assert, when they talk about ἔνυλοι λόγοι and characterize their second category as qualified matter and qualified substrata. If their λόγοι are nothing but "matter in a certain state," this would make the second category indistinguishable from the third. Plotinus' opponents must face the dilemma that either the λόγοι are real beings before they unite with matter in order to produce the qualified things, in which case they will have to give up their materialism; or the λόγοι are not real, in which case they must abandon their division of the categories because all of them are reducible to "matter in a certain state." But, Plotinus asks poignantly:

> Who then, asserts this? Not, presumably, matter. But perhaps matter does assert it: for matter in a certain state is intellect; though the "in a certain state" is a meaningless addition. Matter, then, says this and understands it. And if talked sense, it would be surprising how it thinks and does the works of the soul, when it has neither intellect nor soul....But, as things

are, matter does not speak, but the speaker speaks with a large contribution from matter, to which he entirely belongs; even if he has a bit of soul, he speaks in ignorance of himself and of the power which is able to speak the truth about such things. (VI.I. 29f 27-36)

The irony with which Plotinus speaks in this passage highlights the gap which separates the philosophy of Platonic idealism which he wanted to revive from the decaying philosophy of stoic materialism.

IV

From the above observations and comments it follows that Plotinus did not treat the Stoic set of categories with much care nor did he approach it in the same serious manner as he did the Aristotelian set. The reason for this differential treatment perhaps has to do with two related factors which are: first, his adherence to the ontological interpretation of the categories, as opposed to the logical and the grammatical interpretations which were adopted by other Platonists;[25] and, second, his commitment to revive the philosophy of Plato which, in his interpretation, gave priority to the incorporeal and the intelligible being, while it gave to the sensible and corporeal cosmos a status of dependence. This commitment placed Plotinus in polar opposition to Stoic corporealism and materialism which he considered as unworthy of serious attention by any philosopher with some sense of self respect as an intelligent human being, a being capable of seeing reality as it really is by using not only discursive reason and also intuitive *nous*.

Accordingly, believing that the Stoics were trying to conceal the sheer materialism of their philosophical system by drawing divisions upon divisions of beings within the same materialistic framework, Plotinus was unprepared to study the Stoic doctrine of the categories in the scholarly and dispassionate manner which his student Porphyry, for example, and Simplicius later, displayed in their numerous commentaries on Aristotle's works. Unlike these commentators, Plotinus shows no interest and makes no effort to understand the Stoic position correctly, let alone sympathetically. For him nothing ontologically sound could come from a philosophy which put the feet in the place of the head, unless and until the system were to be turned around or rather literally up-side down.

Evidently Plotinus was able to do to Stoicism what Marx did to Hegelianism in modern times but in the reverse order. This clearly indicates that the long battle between materialism and idealism is by no means over. However, the signs of our troubled times seem to favor the revival of the Plotinian version of Platonism whose categories and ontological priorities are destined to remain, as they have always been, opposed to materialism in all its shapes, Stoic or Epicurean, Marxist or Maoist, Ancient or Modern. More than any possible historical connections between the two, what makes Plotinus a permanent ally of the Indian genius is his determined opposition to materialism and his successful effort to revive the Platonism of the Old Academy with its emphasis on things immaterial, such as the Soul, the Intellect, and the one Absolute.

In conclusion, it would seem that Plotinian philosophy and Indian wisdom are destined to work together in assisting the human mind to comprehend the cosmos, to find its appropriate place in it, and to give meaning to its existence by seeing that the true, the good, and the beautiful all stem from the same ineffable Source. By the strength of their common wisdom, tolerance and enlightenment, Plotinian Platonism and Indian Spirituality can help post-modern humanity overcome anxious existentialism, atheistic materialism, and monotheistic fanaticism in any form of intolerant dogmatism.

Endnotes

1. See *Vita Plotini* in *Plotinus*, 7 vols., ed. and translated by A H. Armstrong, Cambridge Mass.: Harvard University Press. 1978-1986. Unless stated otherwise all quotations will be from this edition.
2. The art of writing should be considered as distinct from the art of dialectic and the art of speaking. For one can be a great teacher, like Socrates and Ammonius, or a great thinker, like Heraclitus and Heidegger, without being a great stylist. In this sense, Plato was exceptional.
3. Porphyry was the most trusted of his students and accepted the responsibility of ordering and editing the treatises after the teachers death, which became known as the *Enneads*.
4. In fact, the title of the three related treatise *Ennead* VI. 1, 2 and 3, is "On the Genera of Being."
5. See my *Aristotle's Categories and Porphyry*, Leiden: J. E. Brill, 1988, 2nd ed., 1994, especially part Two; and "Plotinus' Anti-Gnostic Polemic and Porphyry's *Against the Christians"* in *Neoplatonism and Gnosticism*, Richard Wallis and Jay Bregman, SUNY Press, 1988.
6. The general perception that the Stoic categories, unlike the Aristotelian categories, played no significant role in the development of Stoic logic might explain the lack of interest. On this see B. Mates, *Stoic Logic* (Berkeley, 1953), p. 18; and I. M. Bochenski, *Ancient Formal Logic* (N. Holland, 1951), p.87.
7. Although Plotinus does not identify which view was held by whom of the Pre-Socratics, it is not difficult to guess, since he seems to follow the pattern used in the first-book of Aristotle's *Metaphysics*. See also Armstrong's footnote information on this in his *Plotinus*, Vol. 1, p. 12.
8. Other scholars have noticed that this part of the *Enneads* is difficult and taxing reading. E.g. W.R. Inge, *The Philosophy of Plotinus* (New York, 1923) p. 194. Part of the difficulty relates to the fact that in his criticism of the Stoics and the Peripatetics Plotinus presupposes many commentaries which, although are not extant for us, were available and read in his school as a basis for the discussions to follow, as Porphyry informs us *Vita Plotini* 14.
9. Since he intends to apply the term *genos* to the intelligible realm of being which is more unified than the sensible realm of becoming, Plotinus prefers to refer to the Aristotelian and the Stoic divisions as *kategoriai*. For more on this important distinction I refer to my book, *op. cit.*, pp, 93-99.
10. "The Plotinian Reduction of Aristotle's Categories," in *Ancient Philosophy*, 7 (1988) 146-162

11. Beginning with Porphyry, Plotinus' followers tried hard to reconcile Platonism and Aristotelianism by rehabilitating the doctrine of categories, as I have shown in my book *Aristotle's Categories and Porphyry.*
12. *Vita Plotini* 14.
13. The same names of the fourfold division is mentioned by Simplicius *In Aristotglis Catagorias commentarium*, ed. C. Kalbfleisch (Berlin, 1907), pp. 66-67. Modern discussions on the subject include: M. Pohlenz, *Die Stoa* (Goettingen, 1948-49), vol. 1, pp. 69-70 and vol 2, pp. 39-42; P. De Lacy, "The Stoic Categories as Methodological Principles," TAPA, 76 (1945): 246-263; J. M. Rist, *Stoic Philosophy* (Cambridge, 1969), pp. 152-172; S. Samburzky, *Physics of the Stoics* (New York, 1959), pp. 17-20; A. A. Long, *Hellenistic Philosophy* (London, 1974), pp. 160-163; A. Graeser, *Plotinus and the Stoics* (Leiden, 1972), Chapter Four; M.E Reesor, "The Stoic Categories," *American Journal of Philosophy* 78 (1957): 63-82; and G. Reale, *The Systems of the Hellenistic Age*, tr. J. R. Catan, (Now York, 1985) pp. 226-229. For the fragments see H. von Arnim, *Stoicorum veterum fragmenta* (Berlin, 1905).
14. In SVF II, 501; also II, 333, the scholion from an anonymous commentary reads as follows: τρία δὲ τὰ καθολικώτατα ὁμώνυμα, ἕν, ὄν, τί. Κατὰ πάντων γὰρ τῶν ὄντων φέρεται ταῦτα, κατὰ μὲν Πλάτωνα τὸ ἕν, κατ' Ἀριστοτέλη τὸ ὄν, κατὰ δὲ τοὺς Στωϊκοὺς τὸ τί.
15. It would seem that Plotinus utilizes here Aristotle's argument against those who posit being (τὸ ὄν) as a genus capable of synonymous predication: οὐχ οἷον τε δὲ τῶν ὄντων ἓν εἶναι γένος οὔτε τὸ ἕν οὔτε τὸ ὄν, *Metaphysics* 998b 22, also 1003& 23-24, 1017a 22-27, 1028a 10-b 7.
16. Plotinus' ontological approach to Stoic categories is closer to Subursky's than to De Lacy's interpretations in the works cited in note No. 13. The former has tried to analyze the Stoic physics and the latter the Stoic ethics in terms of their doctrine of categories with some success.
17. SVF I, 87a, Stobaeus uses this beautiful metaphor to indicate the place of the divine Λόγος in matter, but it could be applied to the whole world nested in the infinite abyss of void.
18. For more details on the stoic cosmology, see Sambursky, Long, Pohlenz, and Reale as cited in note No. 13.
19. SVF II, 359; II, 399-401; and II, 449.
20. On this see my "The Plotinian Reduction of Aristotle's Categories." *Ancient Philosophy* 7 (1988) 146-162.
21. E. G. Long, *op. cit.*, p. 163, writes "For this reason the fourth of the Stoic categories has the widest and most interesting implications. Where all things are interdependent, an idea which has today taken on a particular ecological significance, the concept of relationships is a fundamental one." See also Sumbursky, *op.cit.*, p. 18-20.

22. It seems to me that Professor Reesor, *op.cit.*, is inordinately critical of Plotinus because of his use of non-Stoic criteria in his criticism of the Stoic doctrine of categories.

23. Ὄγκος is the word used here by Plotinus which gives the impression that, in his mind, the Stoic emphasis on matter and bodies seemed to reduce Platonic ontology to tumorous oncology.

24. Plotinus was perhaps irritated that the old Platonic definition of real being, "that which has the power of acting and being acted upon," *Sophist* 248c, was appropriated by the Stoics and applied to material bodies. On the Stoic conception of body, see also Sambursky, *op. cit.*, pp. 29-44; Long, *op.cit.*, pp. 152-158; and Reale, *op. cit.*, pp. 237-259.

25. I have dealt with this problem in "Alternative Ancient Interpretations of Aristotle's Categories." In *Language and Reality*, ed. K. Boudouris (Athens, 1985), pp. 163-173.

Plotinus and Vedanta

S. R. Bhatt

Every system of thought is basically a product of the felt needs and aspirations of its age and of the sociocultural milieu. In its rise it may envelop its past and may also gather influences from its surroundings. There is nothing wrong or unnatural about it. It is in this background one should view the striking similarity in fundamental ideas between Plotinus and Vedanta. The doctrinal affinity in respect of the Vedic and the Vedantic 'Tadekam' and the 'One' of Plotinus is remarkable and attracts comparative studies. The half century old controversy as to whether Plotinus was influenced or not by Indian thought and whether Plotinus is himself Vedantic seems not very worthwhile.

In their metaphysical reflections both Plotinus and Vedantic thinkers regard the One negatively as unknown and undefined and positively as unity of Being, Thought and Bliss (*Sat, Cit.* and *Ananda*). Both ascribe *freedom* (*svarat*) and *volition* (*Kama*) to the One. Both insist that the One is immanent and transcendent in many.

This reference to doctrinal affinities, however, should not lead one to overlook the fact that the setting and the conceptual framework within which these two philosophies operate are different from each other and therefore any far fetched interpretation has to be avoided in the zeal to point out their similarity.

Plotinus and Vedantic thinkers highlight the need for metaphysics. Every thinking person sooner or later asks himself the questions, "Who am I?" "Why am I here?" "How did I get here?" "What is my future?" etc. These questions inevitably give rise to other questions about the nature of existence of both self and the world. Both Plotinus and Vedantic thinkers held the deep conviction that, as Plotinus put it, "We have undoubtedly to believe that the truth has been discovered by some of the ancient and blessed philosophers." But he cautions us by adding that, "It is advisable to see who were those who found it and how we can ourselves reach it." (*Enneads* III.6.1.13-16). In the Nasadiya Sukta of the Rgveda the seer poses a query about the supreme truth as follows: "Who knows it directly?

Who would answer the questions: Out of what sort of cause has it originated? From where did this creation take place? The gods themselves came into this existence after this creation has taken place. Who can therefore say as to wherefrom all this originated? That out of which this origination took place, did it undertake this creation or did it not also not do so? Only its Lord who resides in the Supreme heavens knows that; or maybe He too does not."

But soon the Vedic seer recovers faith in the ultimate existence of one Supreme Being (*Sat*) which is all-pervasive (*Brahman*) and which is the essence of *all* (*Atman*).

In India, philosophy was always a faith by which people lived. Even when it was a critique of faith and questioned the old faith, it always created and substituted a new faith. Buddhism is an instance of this tendency. Faith alone leads to certainty and experience. Faith anticipates that we will reach the truth embodied and presupposed in the act of faith. This is what the Gita teaches, "The faith of each is in accordance with his nature, 0 Bharata, man is made of his faith, as a man's faith is, so is he." (XVII 7.3). The Chhandogya Upanishad declares, "When one has faith then one reflects, without faith one does not reflect. One reflects only when one has faith". (CL7.19). Plotinus also holds, "Thus we arrived at a proof. But are we convinced? A proof entails necessity but not conviction. Necessity resides in the intellect and conviction in the soul." (*Enneads* V.3.6.8.10; VI.1.4.32)

Faith, thus, must precede all ultimate knowledge (*paravidya*) which is a spiritual experience. Faith has to guide it, serve it as its criterion. But it is not a blind or irrational faith. It is a faith which is compatible with reason and which is grounded in spiritual experience and which seeks its culmination in that experience. Plotinus writes, "With my reason I find God. After I have found him I have not the same need for my reason as previously. God can be found by means of the laws of logic but these laws cannot analyze him. The power and indispensability of logic are freely granted; but in the case of simplex it is powerless; because its function is to analyze and a simplex is incapable of analysis. After I have reached the simplex by the power of my reason I contemplate that simplex because there is nothing else left for me to do." This is exactly what the Katha Upanishad says, "*Drsyate tvagryaya buddhya suksmaya*" (I.3) or, "*nayamatma pravacanena labhyo na mcdhaya na bahuna srutena*" (I.2)

There is such a striking similarity as if Plotinus were actually translating the Katha Upanishad.

In the primacy of experience reason, faith and scriptures all become mutually corroborative and supportive. But this experience is not applicable to sense experience which is incurably subjective, finite and ineffective, since it is based on exclusive attention to a few isolated brute facts with a total neglect of multifacetedness and unitive nature of things. *Paravidya* is not accumulation of more information but entering into new dimensions of reality; a unitive or integral experience which transforms the entire being, changes one's whole life and attitude. Professor K. S. Murty refers to it as commotion producing power (*The Indian Spirit*, p-134). Plotinus says that 'true knowledge' is the immediate intuition of the unity of beings. "In participating in true knowledge we are real beings; we are all together real beings and constitute but one being." Thus according to Plotinus the universal being is that in whose bosom every difference is absorbed, in which every distinction between subject and object comes to a complete end. Such an identity of self with universal being is not a rational conclusion reached by the discursive intellect but a special intuition arising from contemplation. It is not knowledge in the usual sense of the term since it is knowledge concerning the very subject of knowledge and the act of knowledge. It is the very presupposition in all knowledge (*Tasya bhasa sarvamidam vibhati*). As the Upanishads say, How can it (discursive intellect) know him through whom it knows everything? How can it know that which knows? You can not see that which sees in seeing, nor learn that which learns in learning, nor understand that which understands in understanding. There is no other outside of it to see, to understand and to know; "whoever does not know it knows it. Unknown by him who knows it is known by him who does not know".

In conclusion, it must be pointed out that this is not a metaphysics which is created in a library or in an armchair; but developed in the laboratory of real life situation with all concreteness. It is not an empty or barren speculation which could be in the west under the onslaught of logical positivism. It is not an abstract intellectual play with isolated and brute facts but an illumination of them in their inter-relatedness and interdependence. It is a way of life based on an integral view of life. It is a theory of action based on practical wisdom acquired through reflection on concrete experience, whether that experience pertains to a battlefield as in the Gita or to the court of a king as in Brihadaranyakopanishad; or to the hermitage of a seer as in Chhandogya Upanishad or to the laboratory of a practicing scientist as in the Vaisesika thinkers experimenting on matter and motion; or to Caraka experimenting on vegetation. It is a darshana, a Weltanschauung, a way of life wherein one finds unity, peace, perfection and plentitude.

Plotinus and Sankara
Some Significant Affinities and Divergences

G. C. Nayak

Plotinus and Sankara, two thinkers from the ancient past, have in recent times often been dismissed too lightly by modern philosophers.

Neoplatonism has fallen into disrepute even in the West. It has been accused of not being faithful to Plato, of not being philosophy at all, and so on. Vedanta, especially Sankara's Advaita Vedanta, has been charged by some contemporary scholars, of propagating and promoting illusionism and destroying our normal outlook on life as a whole.

Some Western scholars, like P. R. Coleman-Norton for example, dismiss Neoplatonism as poetry rather than rational philosophy. "This is poetry, not philosophy, when rapture is exalted over reason, and in this essential process of Neoplatonism ancient philosophy abdicates".[1]

As for Indian philosophy, a band of self-appointed custodians of philosophy customarily dismiss the whole of Indian philosophy as mere mysticism, poetry, primitive thinking and so on.

It is in this context that we seek to revive the thoughts of these two great ancient thinkers. The question of their very relevance in the present-day world dominated by science and technology has first to be settled. Unless some relevance to current concerns can be established, there is little point in discussing or examining the substance of their thinking.

One must, however, ask the question: What is the ground of the claim of science and technology to pose as the final arbiter of relevance? Why should everything be tested on the anvil of science and technology? Even if we concede some dominant role to science and technology in determining relevance, that role cannot be all pervasive. For example, science and technology cannot dictate to us in such a way that no one is allowed to cherish classical music, or classical art and poetry.

Contemporary relevance or the absence of it cannot be predetermined, before one has some grasp of the content of the thought of these ancient masters. Contemporary relevance, to my mind, cannot be affirmed simply on the grounds, for example, that present day scientific findings are found to be in conformity with the Vedantic Wisdom of the past. This in itself, even if it were the case, cannot prove anything. Neither Vedanta nor Science, to my mind would gain a sort of invincibility or sacrosanctity simply because they may perhaps seem to corroborate each other in and through some surface resemblance of theirs when differences are lost sight of. Science, after all, is ephemeral, and prone to change. It is, to say the least, falsifiable, in the words of Popper.

There is nothing like final or ultimate knowledge, Wisdom or explanation in science, nor is it a fact that there is a single unitary principle available in science as a key principle for the solutions of all possible problems. The scientist can dream of a time in future where such an explanation can be found, and this is nothing but a fond hope, I should say, on the part of a scientist with an inbuilt inveterate optimism. Hawking, one of the greatest cosmologists of the present day, thus gives us the hope that, "if we do discover a complete theory (of Physics), it should, in time, be understandable in broad principles by everyone, not just a few scientists. Then we shall all, philosophers, scientists and just ordinary people, be able to take part in the discussion of why it is that we and the universe exist. If we find an answer to that, it would be the ultimate triumph of human reason—for then we would truly know the mind of God".[2]

Even this hypothetical situation is controverted by scientists like Davis who think that "rational explanation for the world in the sense of a close and complex system of logical truths is almost certainly impossible. We are barred from ultimate knowledge, from ultimate explanation, by the very rules of reasoning that prompt us to seek such an explanation in the first place".[3] If this is what science is, what corroboration for ultimate principles in metaphysics, whether it is Neoplatonism or Advaita Vedanta, can be expected from the results of scientific pursuits? Perhaps we take to the wrong direction when we turn to science for either corroboration or criticism of a metaphysical theory. Neither Neoplatonism nor Vedanta can take pride simply because it is somewhat in a vague sense corroborated by the direction taken by present-day science. I am therefore, of the opinion that we have to seek criteria for their relevance, if any, elsewhere.

Moreover, there is one peculiarity about philosophy which needs to be noted *vis a vis* science. Scientific techniques, methodologies and findings may get outdated or outmoded, but this does not happen in philosophy, at least not in the way it happens in science. Philosophers and their philosophies, especially those who really count, seem to have a tendency to persist, even if they at times are undermined or shown to be of greater relevance at a particular time. Both Neoplatonism and Vedanta have persisted in spite of their summary rejection, so to say, at the hands of some self-appointed custodians of philosophy, whether in the West or even in India itself.

As I understand the situation in philosophy, what survives in any philosophy worthy of its name, in spite of attacks from different angles and from various sources, is its adventure, so to say, in the world of thought, the conceptual shock or jerk and the intellectual commotion or upheaval effected by such an adventure. What survives is the novel way of looking at things, a direction given which may not be of any immediate utility but which may simply be the guiding spirit for in-depth researches to be carried on in future.

A pioneer shows the way in an experience hitherto unnoticed, engineers a value-shift that would bring about a fundamental change in our ordinary day-to-day outlook, life and experience; provides an insight or a coordinating thought that incessantly beckons us to take a dive into its immeasurable depth. All these and similar other factors in a genuine philosophical enterprise are those that survive against all odds, and even seem to have a tenacity that lasts for centuries. These factors are either neglected as simply useless or are welcomed as extremely relevant only because it serves a specific need of the time. Philosophy acquires importance, no doubt, in accordance with its contemporary relevance, but what I want to say is that philosophical enterprise can and should be assessed independently and irrespective of their contemporary relevance alone, for their merit is not merely confined to such utility in the contemporary world. The adventure in the domain of thought is in itself laudable, to say the least.

Shall we say that it is the mystical that has survived in both these thoughts, viz. Neoplatonism and Vedanta, and has been a constant source of attraction and enticement for many as much as it has also been a butt of ridicule by the so-called votaries of reason? Well, it may be so. There are elements in both these thoughts which can be construed as mystical from a certain point of view. And that mystical element continues to entice and excite us throughout the centuries.

But it would be wrong to put everything in Vedanta and Neoplatonism in one basket, under one blanket term viz. mystical. It is not exactly the mystical aspect of these great thinkers which I would like to highlight here, although I do not deny that the mystical in itself has its own attraction. I would here like to draw the attention of all concerned to that aspect of Plotinus' philosophy where he has highlighted the life and conduct of "a Sage, a Master in Dialectic" as Plotinus calls him. "Once a man is Sage," says Plotinus, "the means of happiness, the way to good, are within, for nothing is good that lies outside him. Anything he desires further than this he seeks as a necessity, and not for himself but for a subordinate, for the body bound to him, to which since it has life he must provide the needs of life; not, however, the needs of the Sage himself, but only of his body. He knows himself to stand above all such things, and what he gives to the lower he so gives as to leave his life undiminished."

This is very significant indeed because it draws our attention to a type of life that is not ordinary in any sense. "A thousand mischances and disappointments may befall him and leave him still in the tranquil possession of the Term", says Plotinus. "The Sage", according to him, "sees things very differently from the average man: neither ordinary experience nor pain and sorrows whether touching himself or others, pierce to the inner hold. To allow them any such passage would be a weakness in our soul". It is important to note that, according to Plotinus, "pleasure and health and ease of life will not mean any increase of happiness to him nor will their contraries destroy or lessen it. When in one subject, a positive can add nothing, how can the negative take away?" The Sage is "ever cheerful, in order of his life ever untroubled, his state is fixedly happy and nothing whatever of all that is known as evil can set it awry—given only that he is and remains a Sage." What is noteworthy about him is that he "can never be deprived of his vision of the All-good."

"For man and especially the Sage", says Plotinus, "is not the complement of soul and body: the proof is that man can be disengaged from the body and disdain its nominal goods". The Sage thus "can be fearless through and through. Where there is dread there is not perfect virtue, the man is some sort of a half-thing." Although it is true that the Sage "will give to the body all that he sees to be useful and possible", at the same time it is to be noted that "he himself remains a member of another order." Referring to Plato in this connection, Plotinus points out in unmistaken terms what Plato rightly taught, that he who is to be wise and to possess happiness draws his good from the Supreme, fixing his gaze on that, becoming like to that, living by that".[4] This conception of Plotinus, though not identical with, is somewhat similar to and reminds us of the conception of *Jivanmukti* in Indian thought, especially in the advaita

Vedanta of Sankara. Let us see at some length what Sankara has to say about *Jivanmukta*, a person who is supposed to be liberated while he is alive, a free man, in the Vedantic framework.

Before going into the details of *Jivanmukti*, however, I would like to say a few words here regarding another common aspect of Plotinus' and Sankara's thought. I do not think we can make much of the apparent resemblance between Plotinus' idea of unity and Sankara's idea of non-duality. In Advaita, non-duality is not the same as unity. Sankara is quite explicit about it. Moreover, the method by which Plotinus arrives at unity as the ultimate principle is not the same as the method adopted by Sankaracarya. I would therefore desist from highlighting these surface similarities between Plotinus and Sankara. But when we come to consider the life and conduct of a Sage, as envisaged by Plotinus, as also the life and conduct of a *Jivanmukta*, I think we are on surer grounds.

Whether one has his eye on unity as Plotinus envisages it or on the realization of the non-duality of one's own self as conceived in Sankara's Vedanta, one notices in both a unique equanimity and tranquility of mind very rarely found in ordinary human beings. Both the Sage and the *Jivanmukta* are happy under all possible circumstances. The above quotations from Plotinus speak for themselves; further Sankara in his *Vivekacudamani* says "*Sthitaprajna yatirayam yah sadanandamasnute*" ie., he being a man of equanimity is always in a state of happiness.

"*Istanistarthasampraptau samadarasitayatmani, ubhayatra-vikaritvam jivanimuktasya laksanam*" says Sankara; whether something desirable or otherwise comes on his way, the *Jivanmukta* is not affected thereby, because of his equanimity. The difference between the enlightened who is free and the unenlightened who is in bondage is that the former remains undisturbed and patient through his affliction due to *prarabdha*, whereas the latter is impatient and suffers on account of this,[5] Plotinus says, "Adverse fortune does not shake his felicity: The life so founded is stable ever". and yet, as Plotinus has aptly observed, "this does not make the Sage unfriendly and harsh: it is to himself and in his own great concern that he is the Sage; giving freely to his intimates of all he has to give, he will be the best of friends by his very union with the Intellectual Principle". According to Sankara *Jivanmukta* or the enlightened person is both *vimuktasanga* (devoid of attachment) and *Karunyasindhu* (ocean of mercy) or *Sadaparadayambuddhama* (for ever the boundless ocean of mercy).[6]

It may not be out of place here to point out that Russell's idea of emancipation, though not identical of course, bears a striking resemblance with the above ideals of the life of a Sage or a *Jivanmukta*. It may sound strange that the models of men set before us by a Plotinus or a Sankara should find an echo in the mind of an empiricist of the 20th Century, but one should not forget that Russell was after all a humanist also, a person who was very much concerned with human life and welfare. So when it comes to stipulating what constitutes the ideal life and conduct in human affairs, it is no wonder that a modern thinker's words should bear a striking resemblance to those of a Plotinus or of a Sankara when they refer to the life and conduct of a Sage or a Jivanmukta. This only speaks of a largely unfulfilled dream of mankind, or rather a dream that has been fulfilled only occasionally, if at all, in the unusual life and conduct of some extraordinary person.

The relevance of this model lies precisely in that it should serve as a beacon light for the entire humankind. "To abandon the struggle for private happiness, to expel all eagerness for (gratifying) temporary desire, not to burn with passion for external things"—this is emancipation or free man's worship as Russell[7] calls it; it is a beacon light, a model set before humans, irrespective of one's caste or creed, of the locality or time to which he may belong. This is true both in the case of the *Jivanmukta* of Sankara and the life of a Sage as Plotinus envisages it.

Whether it is the 'Sage' of Plotinus, the *Jivanmukta* of Sankara or an 'emancipated person' of Russell, these notions could be taken as performing only a regulative function in our discourse. If *'Jivanmukti'*, 'emancipation' and 'Sage-hood' are taken as regulative concepts, if this is their logical status, or to use the well known Rylian terminology, their logical geography, then it would be not very reasonable to search for a *Jivanmukta* or a Sage amidst ordinary living human beings. But Sankara does not take *'Jivanmukti'* as a mere regulative concept, for a *Jivanmukta* alone can be the teacher and the guide of the unenlightened in the ocean of samsara, according to him. The Guru or the guide whom the inquirer (*tattvajijnasu*) is supposed to approach is described in *Vivekacudamani* as *akamahatah* (unsmitten by desires), *Brahmavittamah* (a knower of *Brahman* par excellence), *brahmanyuparata* (one who has withdrawn himself into Brahman), *ahetuka dayasindhu* (a boundless reservoir of mercy that knows no cause), etc.[8]

There exist great and noble souls, says Sankara, calm and magnanimous, who do good to humanity as does the Spring season, (*Santa mahanto nivasanti santo, vasantavallokahitam carantah*), and who, having themselves crossed this dreadful ocean of birth and death, help others also to cross the same without any private motives whatsoever.[9] In this context, Sankara's words, *vasantavallokahitam carantah* (Doing good to humanity like the Spring) refer to the spontaneous goodness and kindheartedness of the enlightened, while they themselves remain unperturbed amidst pleasure and pain. This means that Sankara did not regard *Jivanmukti* as a mere regulatory concept. And there seems to be no sufficient reason to think that Plotinus regarded the concept of 'Sage' as a mere regulative concept either. I would therefore submit that all these thinkers took the concepts in question as having application in this world of ours; persons, according to them, should be judged in accordance with how near they got to such a perennial model of humanity, which though rare, is by no means non-existent.

Endnotes

1. *The Encyclopaedia Americana* (International Edition, Americana Corporation, 1980)
2. Stephen Hawking. *A Brief History of Time* (New York, 1989), p.185
3. Paul Davis. *The Mind of God* (Simon & Schuster, 1992)
4. Plotinus. *The Six Enneads*, translated by S. Mackenna and B. S. Page (Encyclopaedia Britannica, London 1952). All quotations from Plotinus cited in this paper are from *ibid*.
5. Cf. Vidyaranya, *Pancadasi*, "Na kleso jnanino dhairyanmudhah klisyatyadhairyatah".
6. Sankaracarya, *Vivekacudamani*, 35 & 486
7. Bertrand Russell. *A Free Man's Worship and other Essays* (Unwin Paperbacks, 1976), p.17.
8. Sankaracarya, *op.cit.*, 33.
9. *Ibid*, 37

Man's Predicament—The Unique Indian Experience and the Neoplatonic Tradition

Gopal Chandra Khan

Writing on the history of Greek philosophy Edward Zeller acknowledged that of all the people of antiquity, apart from the Greeks, only the Chinese and the Indians were philosophers, though there is no connection between the philosophical systems of the Chinese and the Indians, nor between theirs and that of the Greeks.[1] About Indian Philosophy he comments: "The Indians have indeed produced various philosophical systems, but Indian philosophy never lost contact with religion and never became independent. Its other-worldly character seems strange to our mind.[2] On the other hand, Greek philosophy, in Zeller's opinion, was built up by the strength of independent human thought, by the *logos*, which claimed to explain reality in a natural way.

Zeller, however, noticed the absence of this original feature of Greek philosophy to a large measure in Hellenistic Jewish philosophy, in Neo-Pythagoreanism, NeoSkepticism and Neoplatonism, all of which were conceived in Alexandria where the Greek and the Oriental world met and mingled. He therefore regarded these as not truly Greek Philosophy. In particular, "neoplatonism with its need of revelation instead of independent investigation carried to its limit the development begun in neo-Pythagoreanism and thus completed the suicide of philosophy."[3] To sum up: Neoplatonism is not wholly Greek and not wholly philosophy; its unphilosophical character is due to the presence of oriental influence in it. It is needless to say that the "Oriental influence" that Zeller here speaks of is the Indian influence, and thus goes history.

In this short space we do not wish to contest Zeller, we only explain one meaning of philosophy that the philosophers of ancient India upheld. This meaning we observe the Neoplatonists also discovered anew or endorsed. This appears strange to Zeller because he shares the original Greek view according to which all philosophy begins in wonder, and which Plato[4] and Aristotle[5] regarded as reason's divine discontentment, prompting human beings to enquire into the secret springs and principles of (the world regarded as) nature and thence acquiring philosophical wisdom. It is certainly true that philosophical wisdom (*sophia*) in the Greek sense included not only a theoretical understanding of the world, but also a certain attitude to life; but philosophical wisdom always influences life. For the Greek it was the pleasure of philosophical wisdom that mattered; it tasted so good that the philosopher was prepared to renounce other mundane pleasures of life for its sake, and it was this intellectual pleasure that sustained philosophical enquiry in the original Greek sense.

Indians of the ancient world with their very long tradition in philosophical quest and enquiry have, however, their own experience from which to speak. They found that philosophic reflection that began in wonder, as soon as it ran its course, seemed to end in despair. Thus, instead of giving rise to intellectual pleasure it created intense intellectual pain; instead of making philosophic living possible it made life unbearable. The world on which the Philosopher naturally lived from the beginning of his life seem to have ultimately receded to an inaccessible distance. Left thus utterly abandoned and disconsolate he developed a deep crisis in his inner existence. He was now in a fundamental predicament; he should either give up philosophy and return to uncritical living or live in an understanding of the emptiness of the world and still live in that world. For the philosopher it was a trying situation demanding a prompt and quick solution.

From all accounts it appears that the Skeptics among the philosophers of ancient Greece also came up against these problems of philosophy. They found a quick solution in executing an *epoche* with regard to all philosophy, which they claimed gave them the peace of *ataraxia*. It is however, difficult to conceive the real import of *epoche* or the meaning of that peace which *epoche* claimed to have produced. In any case, Immanuel Kant thought that Skepticism is a relapse into the uncritical or unphilosophical attitude of mind.

The Indians never advocated skepticism, and neither did the Neoplatonists. Both the Indian Sages and the Neoplatonists wanted to be positive towards philosophy, and proposed identical solutions to the problems confronted in the course of philosophizing. They pointed out that the problems of philosophy never remain mere theoretical difficulties, but enter into life in such ways as to constitute living experience. Thus in proposing solutions to the problems of philosophy they insisted upon a fundamentally new kind of experience. This new experience will come, they claimed, through a complete transformation of man's inner life.

It may not now be very difficult to see why philosophy was conceived as *mokshasastra*, or a discipline that leads to man's salvation. In India, they called it *paravidya* as distinguished from *aparavidya*. *Aparavidya* is mundane philosophy, or what Hegel regarded as 'thinking study of things'. It might well begin with wonder, but will ultimately end in chaos and confusion, getting life into its fundamental predicament and unresolved crisis.

Where *aparavidya* ends *paravidya* begins, for which crisis rather than wonder is the beginning. Its objective is not to satisfy man's intellectual curiosity but to bring relief to the tormented soul. The philosopher who exercises in *paravidya* is a lonely consciousness braving his way to recapture the world that once deserted him and threatened his existence. He succeeds in so far he truly expands or widens his inner life so that the whole of reality gets merged in it and nothing is left outside as the 'other'. Plotinus, the founder of the Neoplatonic tradition, also explained this possibility of man's inner development. He saw no possible limits to soul's possible expansion, no stopping place to fix its limits, and no demarcation line between itself and the 'All'.[6]

The older Greeks explained that wonder as reason's natural impulse pushes man into philosophy. But they did not further explain the significance of wonder in man's life, or for that matter admit any goal/fulfillment (*telos*) of reason. The Indians, on the other hand, explained man's philosophical enterprise as the soul's tryst with destiny. Man's life on earth is a journey towards truth. It is a painful and difficult journey, but reach the end of the journey he must; salvation through suffering is his destiny. Plotinus characterized it as soul's rough and arduous return journey, homecoming, as ascent to the union with the One, the All.[7]

The Indian experience says that man's life on earth is full of suffering. The opposite of suffering is bliss, but where is bliss in this world! There are only pleasures and pains. According to the natural tendency of the mind, pleasures are sought after and pains are sought to be avoided. But what initially appears to be pleasure ultimately proves to be pain in disguise. Actually, both pleasure and pain are suffering in different forms. Then, what is the meaning of a suffering life? The Indians explained that suffering is a constant reminder to the sufferer that as yet he lives in unfulfilled purpose. Since the man feels the urge to achieve his goal, but has no clear knowledge of what he is seeking for, he is perpetually in distress. In other words, man's inner greatness as coupled with his basic ignorance is what the Indians called *avidya* (a beginningless cosmic nescience), and what Plotinus regarded as soul's *tolma*—an illegitimate self-assertion and desire of movement for movement's sake, or the movement of passage from one form of living to another.[8] Through constant suffering and constant enterprise he returns to himself, is redeemed, and his ordeal is over. In the beginning of his earthly life a man works with his natural belief that all that he covets is to be found in the world out there. But the world never satisfies him. His desire gets aggravated, and he becomes more and more restless. In this restlessness he sometimes starts reflecting. Through intense reflection he may realize that everything in this world is transitory, and that what he is seeking for is something permanent. This creates frustration, and his faith in the world gets shaken. Thereupon he tries to find a new ground, and until he finds it he suffers a deep crisis in his inner experience. In this his hour of spiritual distress, philosophy as *paravidya* comes forward as guide and brings him permanent relief. It shows the way to man's inner greatness, his divinity, which is beyond any meanness of the world. As long as man lives in ignorance of his basic spiritual identity, and regards the world out there as the only reality, he finds himself identified with his body, a small entity occupying an insignificant corner of the world. But if he ever learns to see his spiritual identity in its proper light, he discovers the divine in him, his true and basic self which is vastly greater than the world and which, instead of being supported by the world really supports the world.

As Plotinus described his ecstatic soul-experience: The soul is not in the body, but the body is in the soul, penetrated and enveloped by it; the soul is not in the world but the world is in the soul, as in his great image floating like a net in the sea.[9] It is a truly great experience which removes every uncertainty from one's life and resolves one's crisis once for all.

Standing on the verge of a century, thinking of welcoming the next, the twenty-first, our mind is none the less filled with gloom. What kind of a world are we living in, and what kind of a culture are we projecting—boxer is a nation's great man, a mass-meeting attended by millions is a triumph, a political theory is a consumer theory, the relation between nation and nation is merely a trade relation, a presidential election is fought and won with a promise 'I give you my countrymen, more consumer goods', and such further nonsense! What stupid answers we give to the great philosophical question; what is Man?—Man is conceived as a mere creature of flesh and blood, a producer of consumer goods and a consumer.

But what will happen to this endless consumerism? What if no viable alternative source of energy comes up? What if population explosion continues unabated? What if the ozone layer goes on decaying this way? What if the planet becomes uninhabitable? Through all this turmoil, hopefully one question still arises in our mind: Why is man so lacking in himself? Is he born to be ever defeated? Our great ancestors showed us the way. We must be reborn in their philosophies and struggle to bring back the divine in man to the divine in the All. We shall resolve our crisis in the same way as the great Valmiki, the author of the Ramayana, the great Arjuna, the mighty warrior of the Mahabharata, and the great Siddhartha, who later became the Buddha, resolved the crisis of their lives.

Endnotes

1. Edward Zeller, *Outlines of the History of Greek Philosophy*, tr. L. R. Palmer, Routledge & Kegan Paul Ltd., London, 1955, p.2.
2. *Ibid.*, p.2.
3. *Ibid.*, p.291.
4. Plato, *Theaetetus*, 155 D
5. Aristotle, *Metaphvsica*, I,2,P 982 b.
6. Plotinus, Enneads, 6.5.7.
7. Cf. Plotinus' last words as recorded by his friend and physician Eustochius.
8. Plotinus Enneads 5.1.1; 3.7.11.
9. *Ibid.*, 4.3.9; 4.3.20.

Rationality and Ritual in Neoplatonism

Robert M. Berchman

Introduction

It has become the practice in the present day to regard Neoplatonic ritual as a sign of the decline of ancient philosophy into superstition.[1] In one form or another this interpretation has prevailed throughout this century.[2] In these approaches it is assumed that there is little about Neoplatonic ritual that reflects rationality.

Although there is much that can be learned from these studies, it is also the case that no one has paused to examine the adequacy of their particular notion of rationality for the separation and explanation of ritual, philosophy, and science. Very briefly: it is a hypothetical-deductive model of rationality with a notion of correspondence rules. It can be summed up as follows:

> According to this account, scientific theories, the foundation and success of modern knowledge, are based on a distinction between theoretical terms ("entities" or "forces") and observational terms ("observed happenings"). Correspondence rules (operational definitions, rules of interpretation) define the theoretical terms, guarantee the cognitive significance of theoretical terms, and specify the procedure for applying the theory to what is observed.[3]

It is on this model of scientific explanation that philosophical and scientific knowledge are marked off from religious thought.[4] Unobservable entities, mystical notions, or metaphysical entities are excluded by this model of rationality. Since they are beyond empirical verification or falsification, religious belief and rituals are judged as nonsense, or unintelligible.

This model has been thoroughly dismantled by contemporary philosophers of science on the basis of its notion of "correspondence rules," which relate invariant observational statements to unobservable entities in theoretical statements.[5] The very validity or coherence of correspondence rules marked the demise of the nomological-deductive model of science.

This fact is significant for the purposes of this study because it requires us to seriously question traditional approaches to rationality and ritual in Neoplatonism.[6] More significantly, it compels us to find another definition of rationality.[7]

Symbolic and rationalist attempts to define rationality argue that rationality is a means/ends decision-making process.[8] It is instrumental. For a belief or action to be rational all that is required is that there be good reasons, or a requirement of adequate evidential support for them. In short, rationality involves pursuing ends that are coherent, and employing means that are appropriate to those ends.[9]

A person is considered rational when (a) he pursues ends that are mutually coherent, and (b) he employs means that are appropriate to the ends pursued: "the critical appraisal implied by the attribution of rationality is, judged in light of the agent's belief, the action he decided upon constitutes a reasonable or appropriate choice of means for achieving his end."[10]

This means that if we are to choose a rational course of action in pursuit of given ends, we have to take into account all available information concerning such matters as the particular circumstances in which the action is to be taken; the different means by which, in these circumstances, the given ends might be attained; and the effects that may be expected from the use of the different available means in pursuit of ends.[11] Thus, to judge the rationality of a decision, we have to consider what information is available to the decision-maker, what reasons did he have for believing it true, and its suitability, judged by the information, for achieving its specified objective. Rationality can be adequately defined as a means/ends calculation. Rationality is instrumental, and the criteria of rationality are provided by the believer who culls them from his cultural system.

This definition of rationality allows Neoplatonic ritual action and belief into the domain of rationality.[12] It may well be that these ritual beliefs are mistaken, but this does not imply irrationality, or sheer non-rational expressiveness. For within its Neoplatonic cultural context ritual stands as an element within a wider rational system. Its means are appropriate, and its ends are coherent because for later Platonists ritual is among the best ways of accomplishing a series of intended objectives, such as the ascent of the soul and communion with the divine.

It is suggested that much can be drawn from this definition of rationality and approach to ritual for the study of cognition and magic in Neoplatonism. Plotinus, Porphyry, Iamblichus, and Proclus can be used to illustrate the extent to which ritual reflects a kind of rationality, for these Neoplatonists grounded much of their theurgical beliefs and practices on a means/end calculation.[13] What needs to be done is to describe and interpret the data available concerning theurgy. We need to know what these Neoplatonic agents believed about ritual, and why they thought it rationally plausible.

The issue addressed in the following pages is the examination of Neoplatonic views of the relationship between cognition and magic, culled from the writings of Iamblichus and Proclus. To keep this paper within appropriate limits and yet show the range of functions which rationality and ritual display in Neoplatonism, the discussion will concentrate on Neoplatonic views of cognition, their understandings of the means/end relationship between cognition and ritual, and their judgements concerning the rationality of ritual. These are largely based on epistemological and psychological grounds.

I. Thesis

Plotinus and his heirs stand at an important point in the history of the interpretation of the rationality of ritual. With caution the following can be said of later Platonic views of cognition, the relationship between cognition and ritual, and the rationality of ritual:

> A. The starting point for the study of rationality and ritual in early Neoplatonism is epistemology:
>
> - The notion that the mind perceptively imagines being erases a divided line which linked perception with particulars and intellection with universals.
> - The notion that a sensible thing instantiates being marks an inversion of an older Platonic paradigm which claims that a sense object imitates being.
>
> B. The reification of perception and imagination forms the basis for the legitimization of magic and theurgy by Neoplatonists:

- This intelligible world is instantiated in sensible objects such as statuary or in sensible things such as temples.
- Through perception one imaginatively gains entrance to the intelligible world, thereby attaining communion with the gods.
- Through perception the soul imaginatively grasps a divine world and gains salvation.
- Ritual and the salvation of the soul are intimately linked to one another. Attainment of the intelligible world and communion with the gods is effected through theurgy.

C. These notions constitute the main source from which a theory of the rationality of ritual are constructed:

- Ritual is efficacious in terms of means because there is adequate epistemological evidence to suggest that theurgy is suitable for achieving its specified objective—entrance into the intelligible world and communion with the gods.
- Ritual is done for certain reasons. It can be explained as a means to an end—the salvation of the soul.
- Ritual can be rationally explained and justified from within a massive network of philosophical postulates. It can be explained holistically as elements within a rational system.

II. Definition of Topic

What is implied in the simple Greek word *lagon*, hip? Historians of Neoplatonism can be trusted to ask such questions. The occasion is famous, the figure celebrated. Hecate's hip pours forth a divine oracle; Porphyry and later Proclus are suitably present ready to give the correct interpretation:

> About the cavity of the right hip is poured forth in abundance the plenteous liquid of the primordially generated soul who entirely ensouls the light, the fire, the ether of the worlds. In Hecate's left hip exists the source of virtue which remains wholly within and does not give away its virginity.[14]

If it is possible to imagine such hips you have entered the world of Neoplatonic philosophy and religion. For by (*lagon*) Porphyry and Proclus mean that Hecate's flanks symbolize cosmic order and virtue. One hip contains the signs (*symbola*) of the natural order and the other is the source of the sublunary virtues (*aretai*) the goddess dominates. Such hips require a brief summary of their significance.

Hecate clearly possesses hips worthy to be remembered. Yet what makes them so memorable? To appreciate the boldness of this later Platonic proposition we need only to contrast it with the earlier Platonic one.[15] For early Platonists a statue of Hecate visibly imitates transient becoming. For the Platonist *aisthesis* yields an opinioned reflection of the transient, physical arrangement of the sensibles, not a true perception of the ideas or the symbols of the gods. Consequently, her hips aesthetically symbolize particulars—they are mere icons of cosmic order and virtue.[16] For later Platonists a statue of Hecate visibly embodies ideal being. Her hips noetically symbolize universals—the right cosmic order and the left the source of virtue.

The notion that *aisthesis* deals only with particulars, while *noesis* only refers to universals, is called into question by this imaginative, Neoplatonic perception of Hecate's hips. For the Neoplatonist perception (*aisthesis*) provides entrance into an imaginative apparition of the fixed, noetic order of the intelligibles, even of the divine forms themselves. This understanding of the relation between perception and intellection is unknown in the early Academy.

The effects of this Neoplatonic proposition are considerable. If Hecate's hips had captivated Porphyry and Proclus merely in the manner they would have pleased Plato, we would not be reflecting on her statuesque anatomy in the manner of the two Romes, the old one on the Tiber and the new one on the Bosporus—but in the manner of classical Athens where Plato taught that rationality and ritual were not complementary, but exclusive notions.[17] This position is overturned, beginning with Plotinus.

I
Iamblichus

A. Aesthetic Pattern

At this point, Porphyry puts his finger on the central difficulty in all attempts to elevate *aisthesis* to the level of *noesis*. Beyond the indirect evidence of sense perception lies the solid evidence of the intellect. Knowledge of the intelligible world and union with the divine depends on intellection of the intelligibles, not perception of the sensible world and apperception of images of intelligible forms and the gods.[18]

Perception depends on the speculative interpretation of the imagination and this evidence has to be recognized for what it is. For Porphyry, like Plotinus, the difficulty with perception is an acute one. Little more can be made of its evidence than that it yields reasonable symbolic forms. Until some solid evidence was found to indicate that perception is intellection, then Platonists could do no more than ask how intelligible forms might appear in nature and so sketch the outlines of possible epiphanies. Thus even at the beginning of the Diocletian era, with the great period of ancient philosophical thought behind them, the men and women of Athens, Alexandria, and Rome knew little more than their predecessors about perception, or the remoter faculty imagination—and that was precious little.

So at the end of the third century, a vision of knowledge remained, fundamentally as Plato envisioned it. However, a way to break through the divided line had been conceived in the new extramissive epistemology. But until some principles were established to control and render nugatory arguments that perception remains opinion, until some reliable modes of inference had been worked out, by which the noetic barrier could be outflanked or overleaped—claims about the truth character of perception were necessarily speculative. For the theoretical possibilities they imagined far outran the facts available to them as evidence.

The flanking of the noetic barrier is evident from a glance at Hecate's thighs. The sheer extent of their symbols and virtues, which before the fourth century Platonists might guess but never prove, are accepted and proven afterwards.

B. The Descended Soul, the Vehicle of the Soul, and Divine Causality

This raises the question of motivation. Iamblichus' conception of a dynamic order of reality, its perceptive appropriation and manipulation, which played so large a part in later Platonism, was the product of two factors, each of which tended to strengthen the other. One of these was the acceptance of the theory of divine giving as the basis of ontology and epistemology:[19] the other was the adoption of the doctrine of the descent of the soul as the foundation of psychology.[20]

Taking these together, Iamblichus recognized that the state of the soul—her descent from the hypercosmic realm into generation in stages—resulted in subservience to fate.[21] The reversal of this situation of misfortune dominates Iamblichus' thought. This leads the philosopher to include a place for the vehicle of the soul in his explanation of the descent and reascent of the soul.[22]

To briefly describe Iamblichus' view of the soul's vehicle (*ochema*): it was created by the demiurge; it is not merely generated from portions of the bodies of the visible gods; it is not fated to remain in the material realm. For the philosopher, then, the vehicle has a divine origin; it is ethereal; and it is not subject to destruction or dissolution of any kind.[23]

The descent of the soul involves demiurgic sowing; her encosmicing with vehicle into the visible gods:[24]

> ....the demiurgic sowing of souls will be divided around the divine creations.[25]

This sowing has a major consequence for it makes each soul fall under its own saviour and patron god:

> But they (i.e., the souls) made their first descent when they have already been sown around the visible gods in order that they might have the gods as saviours (*soteras*) of their wandering around generation and that they might call upon them as their patrons (*prostasis*).[26]

Each created thing falls into four classes: the heavenly class of gods; the winged class that traverses the air; the class that lives in water; and the terrestrial class.[27]

Mortals are not joined to the gods but require intermediaries.[28] Since the sowing is not merely of human souls their vehicles and their own gods but also angels, daemons, and heroes, human souls can call upon these greater souls to aid them in their reascent.[29] Thus each soul has its own saviour god and patron powers.

Generative sowing involves the descent of the soul and its vehicle into matter.[30] This procession (*proodos*) from the mixing bowl determines each soul's cosmic rank.[31] From the place allotted to the soul in sowing, she makes her descent into generation. Embodied the soul is no longer a rational soul existing apart from its vehicle. She exists together with her vehicle in the sensible realm.[32]

According to Iamblichus each soul can project a *logos* (*logon probolai*)[33] and leads a life in harmony with a god.[34] For example, projecting a solar life means the soul takes on the *logos* of the physician and is connected with Asclepius or takes on the *logos* of the telestic and is associated with Apollo.

There appears to be a necessary law that requires the soul's descent.[35] Nonetheless, the soul can either assent and descend voluntarily or resist and be compelled to descend.[36]

Those who descend by choice are pure and perfect souls without passions and not deprived of intellect. They descend for the benefit of the sensible world. They remain in contact with the noetic realm and, thus, are purified from all stains and sin.[37] Some souls are so pure that their descent does not involve generation at all. Thus they enter the material realm and are not contaminated by it. These souls serve the lesser ones in the lower realm.

Souls also voluntarily descend to train and correct their characters.[38] These are souls between purity and impurity, impassivity and passivity who are given the opportunity to better themselves and become fully pure.

Those who resist descent and violate divine and cosmic law are souls who must descend for punishment and judgement of sins committed in a pervious life.[39] These impure and passionate souls are sent to Hades and rehabilitated. Upon completion of their sentence they can choose their next life.

With these aspects in mind Iamblichus makes the argument that it is theurgy and not contemplation that brings salvation to the soul. He builds his thesis on two foci: that happiness is union with the gods;[40] and that liberation from fate occurs through knowledge of the gods.[41]

Happiness and knowledge together is defined as wisdom (*gnosis*). This wisdom and union (*theia henosis*), the first road to happiness, is caused by theurgy.[42]

Theurgic rites purify the soul, liberate her from fate, and permit union with the gods.[43] Purification involves the cleansing of the vehicle of the soul.[44] Once purified the soul can associate with the gods. They shine (*epilampontai*) their light upon the soul, freeing her from passions and disorderly motion. Once illuminated the soul begins its elevation to the gods.

In ascent the soul is granted gifts which include health of body, virtue of soul, and purity of intellect.[45] The entities that bring about these purifications are the visible gods.[46] These are the soul's leader gods. Thus if the soul is mercurial her purifications are done by Mercury; if heliotic her purifications are undertaken by Apollo. Once reunited with its god, the soul joins its entourage.

With ascent the soul is also liberated from fate.[47] She separates and leaves her irrational part and vehicle behind in the cosmic realm.[48] These elements are the organs for the soul's lower functions. The irrational soul functions as appetite and desire; the vehicle as sense perception and imagination. Useless in the higher realms they could be detrimental to the soul's existence, binding her to fate.

For Iamblichus the irrational soul and vehicle remain in the divine entourage with the rational soul but only the rational soul beholds the forms in the noetic realm. This he pictures in his interpretation of the *Phaedrus*. The charioteer with his head views the forms in the noetic realm and then descends to rejoin his lower self.[49]

The vehicle's fate is to be reunited with the ethereal vehicle of the visible god, the soul's leader-god. Once accomplished the vehicle and irrational soul are purified and liberated from all irrational activity.[50] This permits the rational soul to ascend and unite with the demiurge and, perhaps, the hypercosmic gods, if not the One.[51] This, then, is how Iamblichus conceived of the descent and ascent of the soul. Even here, perhaps, we catch a glimpse of his defense of the faculties of perception (*aisthesis*) and imagination (*phantasia*).

C. The Aesthetic Imagination and Theurgy

It has been shown that the vehicle controls the functions of sense perception and imagination, the irrational soul functions as appetite and desire. However, the vehicle which also houses the rational soul can be purified by divine light. In the theurgic act the gods illuminate:

> ....the ethereal and luminous vehicle that surrounds the soul. From this (i.e., illumination) divine images take hold of the imaginative power (*phantastiken dynamin*) in us, images moved by the will of the gods.[52]

The vehicle of the soul (*ochema*) is illuminated by an evocation of light (*photagogia*). These divine apparitions (*phantasia*i) move the soul's active imagining perception (*hen en hemin phantastike dynamis*). Thus the divine vehicles are made visible through theurgy.[53]

When the vehicle is illuminated images of the god are impressed upon it. Normal sense perception (*aisthesis*), consciousness (*parakolouthesis*), and intuition (*epibole*) cease. In this state the vehicle's theurgic function is to be filled with divine images. Indeed by this means divination occurs.[54] For Iamblichus the imagination (*phantasia*) does not perceive mere material images or sense impressions. It grasps divine images directly. Plotinus' theory of the imagination is reinterpreted in a profound way.[55] For the soul's purification and ascent not only begins but ends in the sensible realm.

For Iamblichus it is theurgy and not contemplation that brings human salvation. Philosophy is secondary to ritual. The human soul cannot save itself but requires the help of the gods. Indeed, throughout the entire cycle of her existence, the human soul is in the hands of the gods. Sent to the earth by the gods, the soul requires their help to reascend. Thus:

> ....it is not thinking (*ennoia*) that unites theurgists to the gods...what hinders those philosophizing by contemplation (*theoretikos*) from having theurgic union with the gods? But such is not the case. Rather, the efficacy of ineffable acts accomplished divinely (*theoprepos*) beyond all intellection and the power of unspeakable symbols understood only by the gods impart theurgic union.[56]

Thus bit by bit, the derivative nature of perception, a principle upon which Platonic epistemology rested for half a millenium, was challenged. Now it would be dismantled. The ineffaceable character of intellection would be grounded in the intuitive nature of divinely given perception.

This dismantling emerges with Iamblichus:

The apparition of the gods gives us physical health and virtue of the soul, purity of mind, in short, an ascent of our whole inner existence towards its proper beginnings.[57]

The philosopher begins which the assumption that the gods are perceptible. Moreover their apparition brings to the soul a reversal of her situation of misfortune. The whole point of knowledge lay in its therapeutic and salvific content.[58] These two elements dovetail neatly together. Divine giving manifests itself apparatively. Its symbols are physical and psychological well being, intellectual purity, and union (*henosis*) with the gods.[59]

Other notions inherited from science, magic and ritual fit into Iamblichus' picture, like pieces in a jigsaw. Scientists in late antiquity assumed the familiar interaction of the heavens and the earth.[60] This assumption served as the basis for a system of sym*pathe*tic and homeopathic correspondances.[61] Each daemon and god was associated with particular plants, minerals, animals, and parts of the human body.[62] Therefore, Iamblichus concludes, matter is not necessarily evil.[63] Indeed, there is a kind of matter which is pure and divine and does not prevent us from communicating with the gods. It is a kind of receptacle for their manifestations on earth.

The interconnections which Stoic philosophers treated as links in a deterministic network were now transformed into channels for divine power. Every astral deity fills matter with its own power (*dynamis*). They, in turn, interact with higher, intelligible deities, who in turn, have their source in the hierarchy of Ones which are the ground of all reality.[64] Like some great source of invisible energy, the primal One directed its influence from the recesses of the intelligible world to the physical world, along the conducting paths established by these correspondences.

It is a short step from endowing the physical universe with divine power to assuming that sense perception (*aisthesis*) is in harmony with intellection (*noesis*). From the humblest and most imaginative of sense-perceptions at one end, up to the highest and most complex of intellections at the other, there extended a single divine, intelligible power. Therefore, perception like intellection has a truth character.

In this way, pieces from the whole corpus of ancient science and philosophy were brought together and combined to offer evidence of the truth character of perception. For the central question in Platonism stubbornly concerned the relationship between the divine and human minds. Since the world was an organism whose continued existence was sustained by divine intellection (*noesis*) and will (*boulesis*), it seemed natural to measure the value and authenticity of all human knowledge by tracing it back to its source.

For Iamblichus the sense of sight became a pre-eminent means by which to acquire knowledge and divine union.[65] Every aspect of sensation has its intelligible association. Sensible knowledge, then, is the starting point of a more refined and potent intelligence. It no longer is a mere imaginative reflection of reason.

D. Perception and Salvation

The full consequences of this reformulation have not always been appreciated.[66] Certainly the epistemologies of Plato and even Plotinus have been left far behind. But in their place stands a theory of knowledge that fit the reasons, fears, and ambitions of later Roman men and women.

As a rule, active, immaterial properties are associated with material things. Moreover such relationships are knowable, at least initially, through sense perception. If communication is desired with the source of these properties then prayers, formulas, and epithetai bring the supernatural being before the invocator. Moreover language and its symbols (*symbola*) and tokens (*synthemata*) represent the supernatural powers invoked.[67]

Iamblichus, therefore, distinguishes three kinds of ritual prayer: the one that brings together (*synagogon*); the one that ties together (*syndetikon*); and the union (*henosis*).[68] Hieratic utterances function as a path to knowledge. This idea that discourse depends on the capacity for analogy exemplifies the kind of metaphoric theory of language held by the philosopher.

Discourse accommodates purpose. Thus the uttering of the names of the gods, the invocation of ritual prayers and the use of divine symbols make the ascent of the soul possible. For such discourse results in the appearance of a daemon or god which leads, hopefully, to communion if not union with the divine.

This accommodation of language and purpose is a darling of Iamblichus. He found in this analogy the kind of metaphoric thinking knowledge requires in order to achieve the ascent of the soul. What is required are:

> ....hierartic supplications...(and a) ritual which involves...admirable signs (for) the ineffable expresses itself in unutterable symbols...[69]

These symbols and signs placed in the hollow statues of the gods animate them at the right moment and bring an apparition of the deity before its supplicants.[70] An intangible and incorporeal spirit appears and surrounds, as if in a circle, those present. Initially it is not perceived or registered as it enters. Then it swishes and this noise (*roizos*), the sound of a whistling arrow, is symbolically interpreted as the divine spirit approaching the human soul.[71] This pneumatic noise has its corollary. It is also the sound made by the stars in their celestial revolutions.[72]

Clearly, hieratic discourse represents the supernatural powers to be invoked; the statue establishes a firm and direct link between the god and his followers.[73] These pneumatic statues were channels through which humans could tap divine power thereby achieving salvation. If not that at least through such *paredroi theoi* ancient Mediterranean men and women attained protection of self, house, city, or country.[74] Although the statue of a god is a material object, Iamblichus reminds us, matter (*hyle*) is also offered by the gods for it is congenial (*symphyes*) to them. Pure and divine its is their receptacle for their manifestations on earth.[75]

Thus a new ingredient enters an ancient equation. Divine sympathy pullulating throughout the universe not only manifests itself universally but also particularly in matter. Although Plotinus accepted this notion, in theory, he saw any manipulation (*goetein*) of cosmic sympathy: "the sum of love and hatred in the universe".[76] Moreover such manipulation of natural sympathy diverts the soul from intelligible to sensible activities. Since these are intrinsically deceptive and incapable of elevating the soul to a knowledge of intelligible reality, Plotinus rejects the proposition that manipulation of natural sympathy leads the soul to the divine. Contemplation (*theoria*) is sufficient to free the soul and catapult her to the gods.[77] Porphyry also noted these facts and was wary for they led to the use and abuse of the gods.[78] Iamblichus, however had fewer reservations. Theurgy replaces and supercedes all philosophy and theology.[79]

These objections to magic and theurgy had to do with their theoretical assumptions. Beliefs about the interaction between the intelligible and sensible worlds, sensible and intelligible knowledge, however, were only the starting points. It was the ambition of magic and theurgy that kept them under a cloud. Both were suspect, as being excessively presumptuous. The theurgist was attempting to sense and manipulate what the intellect alone could know. Moreover, the theurgist aimed at power over the soul and nature of a kind reserved for the intellect and the gods.

Moreover the natural world pictured by Iamblichus, of symbols (*symbola*) and conventions (*synthemata*) which link every physical thing 'here' with intelligible principles 'there', was impossible.[80] Scattered throughout the material universe by the gods they were known to theurgists who used them achieve union with the gods.[81]

Yet, as Plotinus and Porphyry proposed, this axiom could not be easily reconciled with Platonic teachings on knowledge and being. The theurgists of late antiquity were hard pressed to match their sym*pathe*tic view of nature and the fallen soul with earlier Platonic formulations.

The compromise eventually achieved by Iamblichus depended on making the doctrine of knowledge a matter for initiation rather than reason. Plato had not really proved that sense-perception could not attain epistemic veracity.[82] Rather he had demonstrated that intellect proved to be a more credible instrument of knowledge.[83] If this were so, reason alone could not establish either. Thus, the veracity of sense-knowledge was not one to be argued out rationally but had to be decided by other means—and these Neoplatonists were fortunate, in having the question settled for them in the Chaldaean Oracles, collections of *logia* in Greek hexameter.[84] Known to the third century Platonists Porphyry and Iamblichus,[85] they became so influential that Proclus saw their source in Plato and Plotinus.[86]

II
Proclus

A. Aesthetic Pattern

The compromise eventually established by Iamblichus and Proclus was achieved only at a price. Questions about theurgy opened its assumptions to scientific and philosophical discussion. The full consequences of this fact have long been recognized but misunderstood.[87] To characterize Proclus as exhibiting an incurable weakness for the occult and his Platonism as an example of a decline in the Greek rationalist tradition would be to take too one-sided, if not anachronistic view of their thought.[88]

Theurgic Neoplatonism is not so much evidence of a decline into the irrational, the triumph of superstition over reason, reflecting the general malaise of later Roman society,[89] as it was an attempt by some to expand Platonic theory beyond the frontiers of Plotinianism.[90]

It was in Hellenic Neoplatonism that the hold of theurgic tradition on men and women's minds proved most tenacious and long lasting.[91] In their minds supernatural power is inherent in the world of the phenomena that surrounds us. Divine power can be activated and theurgy is the theory and practice of divine activation.[92] Consequently, a vision of reality emerged, fueled by the fall of the soul, her purification, and her ascent that reconciled Platonism and the theurgic mysteries.

Porphyry and Iamblichus had taken crucial steps towards legitimizing theurgic Platonism. In Iamblichus' eyes theurgy was a divine phenomenon to which there was no higher counterpart. Proclus agreed and his works were the first sustained systematic attempt to complete this account of reality. Thus by the early fourth century Platonism had solidified its interaction with theurgy. From the second half of the fourth through the late fifth century philosophical debate had replaced the Plotinian view of reality with a Proclean one that would survive another millenium.

B. Hieratic Art and Allegorical Physics

Taken separately, few of Proclus' chief steps were entirely new. What distinguished Proclus was the cumulative weight of his whole system. He drew together into a unified whole theories that had previously developed almost randomly. His strength was that he patiently settled down to work out the actual interrelationship demanded by such metaphysical and theurgical premises. After painstaking research he concluded that theurgy:

> ....is a power higher than all human wisdom, embracing the blessings of divination, the purifying powers of initiation, and in a word, all the operations of divine possession.[93]

How and why he reached this conclusion must be examined. Both questions involve issues central to aesthetics. They are mediated through Proclus' physics, epistemology, and psychology.

Convinced that the hieratic art leads to the union of the human soul with the One, Proclus understood theurgy as a process of deification which completes, and does not render nugatory, contemplation.[94] Indeed as the crown of contemplation, theurgy is a supremely noetic act, encompassing all the contemplative and active attributes of worship.

The hieratic art is possible to know and to practice because divine power pullulates through the universe and is inherent in the natural phenomena that surrounds humanity. This vision allowed philosophical issues a more significant place in theurgic Platonism than is generally recognized.[95] Proclus attempted to place the practice of theurgy on a theoretical plane by hard-wiring it into the first principles of natural philosophy.

He made the familiar interaction between the noetic and physical worlds the basis for a complete system of correspondences whose interconnections were understood as channels for divine power. Taking over from the ancient Ptolemaic astronomers the theory of the heavens comprised of some sixty concentric translucent spheres, the earth being at the center and the sphere of fixed stars enclosing the whole system, Proclus allegorized this picture to symbolize the degrees of reality and perfection between matter and the ineffable One.

The poetic value of astral religion was reinforced by his Neoplatonic interpretation of Aristotle's 'quintessence'—the imperishable substance of the heavens—exempt from the change and decay afflicting terrestrial things. With Proclus an astronomical nest of crystalline spheres became the accepted symbol for the scale of cosmic perfection. Things on earth were lowest, both in location and worth. The passage upward through the spheres of the moon, sun, successive planets to the outermost heavens, and then through the crystalline barrier to the hypercosmic gods, represented a soul's journey from corruption to perfection.

The natural world was an organism whose continued existence was sustained by a divine noetic act, thus it seemed essential to describe and measure the channels of divine power by tracing them back to their supreme source. This became the point of a great deal of metaphysical debate which was a stimulus to novel developments in Neoplatonic epistemology, psychology, and physics.

Seen against this background the intellectual preoccupations of Proclus are understandable. Neoplatonic epistemology and psychology were reinterpreted in a similar allegorical way. For his central question concerned the relationship between the divine and human intellects and the union of the human soul with the One.

C. Perception, Imagination, and Theurgy

Proclus, for example, came to recognize sight as the pre-eminent means by which we acquire knowledge of the supernatural power immanent in the world. He identified light as the spiritual bond linking the human intellect to its divine origin. Consequently he valued sense perception as the mental faculty responsible for receiving, integrating, and interpreting the photogenic images and forms presented to the intellect.

To Psellus we owe a number of valuable notes and comments from Proclus on this branch of aesthetics.[96] He studied the conditions under which invocations (*kleseis*) take place and the locations where they were performed. He noted that before and during rituals the participants avoid any activity which interferes with the arrival of the gods. They also maintain absolute quiet.

Again and again he was drawn to the phenomenon of divine light, its shapes and symbols (*schemata tauta kai theia synthemata*). Some appear to be lifeless objects, others living beings. Some are endowed with reason (*empsycha logika*), are not (*empsycha alogika*). Statues are filled with divine light when inspired by a god or daemon and deliver oracles.

When supernatural beings self-manifest (*autophaneia*) in statuary they appear in shapes and forms perceptible to the senses. Proclus reports that although divine beings are incorporeal:

....bodies were attached for your (sic. gods) sake to the self-revealed manifestations, as you are grafted upon a corporeal nature.[97]

They may appear in symbols (*symbola*) associated with the divine being. For example, Hecate's symbol is the Iynx. She often manifests herself in a top (*sgrophalos*). Clearly, the art object is linked per analogiam to the goddess. Once manifest in her plastic image she has made that journey from her abode at the acme of the celestial sphere to a locus in the terrestrial sphere.

Proclus reports this is represented symbolically. A disc of the moon was located on the statue's back. Proclus tells us this symbol represents the power the goddess wields over the intra-mundane regions. For this heavenly sphere, called nature, is the abode of Hecate. For she is the ruler of the visible world and resides at its acme as the self-manifesting image of nature.

Proclus even clinically examined those who saw such light. They receive the divine spirit and are possessed by it (*katochoi ginontai, theoleptoi kalountai*). The philosopher noted that this experience was always spontaneous (*aoristios*) even though with some it was continuous and with others intermittent. Some mediums are unconsciously ecstatic, others are consciously possessed. Spiritual light was thought to confer a special radiance on its possessor, which in turn could be transmitted to others.

This is what Proclus means when he says that there is a contemplative prelude to theurgy. Before one can practice theurgy one must understand its physical environment; its psychological and epistemological contexts. Moreover, these studies were no stumbling block between the Platonist and salvation. Indeed, they were a necessary propadeutic. Philosophy had much more to do than fetch and carry for the wisdom of the Chaldaean oracles. Theurgy, therefore, was a scientific art based on observation where the theurgist applied sensible knowledge towards a particular goal—the activation of divine power in the universe.

For Proclus theurgy has two foci: it is an activity, an operation, a technique dealing with the gods based on observable principles; it is also the worship of the gods. Consequently, it is a priestly art (*hieratike techne*).[98]

It purpose is to evoke a god (*theagogia*) by evoking its light (*photagogia*). This evocation of light illuminates the vehicle of the soul (*ochema*). The result is divine apparitions (*phantasia*i) move the soul's active imagining perception (*hen en hemin phantastike dynamis*) and the shiny vehicles of the gods are seen.[99]

D. The Descended Soul, The Vehicle of the Soul, and Divine Causality

To appreciate the weight that theurgy had upon the perceptions and imaginations of later Roman men and women requires us to return to a psychological problematic—the fall of the soul. By Proclus' time the fall of the soul had become accepted as a symbol for the individual's plight.[100] Her reascent, her journey from corruption to perfection was, for Proclus, a matter of aesthetics.

Proclus, like Porphyry and Iamblichus, maintained the theory of the descended soul. The process of descent is familiar. Proclus sees the soul's movement from the hypercosmic realm to generation as occurring in stages. First the soul is above fate and then upon embodiment becomes subservient to it. There are a series of stages between freedom and slavery.[101] There is the first hypostasis, the distribution, the sowing, the assignment of allotments, and then the descent.[102]

The first hypostasis refers to the soul's hypercosmic life when it is separated from the cosmos and her vehicle.[103] The distribution is the allotting of souls under divine circulations, or the hypercosmic gods.[104] The sowing represents the establishment of the soul and her vehicle into the circulation of the soul's cosmic or visible god.[105] This represents her placement in the heavenly lexis from which the soul either rises to the noetic or descends to the sensible realm.[106] Descent entails the soul's placement of the soul into the four different classes of living things: the heavenly, the winged, the watery, and the terrestrial.[107]

The soul's initial genesis, or sowing, represents her descent from the noetic to the physical realm.[108] Allotted to a visible god the soul takes on the characteristics of her patron and chooses a life.[109] This is what Proclus means by logon probolai.[110] However, the soul can choose to life this life rightly or wrongly.

Since Proclus understands this sowing to occur under the young gods, it places the soul under the aegis of the earth, the moon, and other organs of time.[111] Consequently, this sowing involves the soul together with its vehicle. Together they are arranged under the circulations of the celestial gods. This effects a two-fold connection between human souls and the gods. The soul's power is encompassed by the soul's god and the soul's vehicle is filled by the god's vehicle. Thus the human soul and vehicle are filled by the god's personal nature.[112] Divine and human soul and vehicle are conjoined. Next Proclus states that the sowing occurs in each element (*stoicheion*) under the moon. This includes the four regions divided into the four elements. This explains the difference between different human souls. They are coupled to distinct comic deities.[113] Then the souls hear their fated laws.[114]

At this point the human soul is separate from the divine. Nonetheless, the demiurge:

> ....himself generates the vehicle of the soul and every life in it, to which the young god's weave the mortal form of life.[115]

Thus, the conditions for the possibility of reascent to the noetic exist for the embodied soul and her vehicle. The rational soul and vehicle are immortal and can attain union with their creator. This will be discussed momentarily.

The reasons for the soul's descent again are familiar. For Proclus there is no part of the soul that does not descend. Descent is necessary but the soul may assent and descend or resist and be forced to descend. Assentive souls make a pure descent; dissident souls an impure descent. Pure souls are impassionate, sinless, and benefit the terrestrial realm; impure souls are passionate, sinful, and wreck havoc in the earthly world.[116]

Unlike the impure soul, the pure soul maintains a connection to the noetic realm while embodied. Purified of all stains and sin this soul serve a religious-theurgic purpose. This soul is the one which invokes the gods and makes it possible for purified souls to encounter the holy and begin an ascent through the heavenly spheres to their leader gods and eventually their maker—the hypercosmic demiurge.[117]

For Proclus a strict metaphysical hierarchy exists in which the noetic gods and the good beyond them are accessible to humans only through the intervention of heroes, daemons, and the visible gods.[118] Nonetheless, from purified human souls to the visible gods and beyond to the hypercosmic deities and the demiurge there is one continuity, one chain of being that links embodied souls with their source.

This means each human soul is allotted a leader god to which it is connected by a series of higher entities—pure souls, heroes, and daemons.[119] The soul's salvation depends on these intermediary entities which can be reached only through theurgy.

From the doctrine of the soul's increasing materiality in descent, the vehicle of the soul (*ochema*) obtains its theurgic function.[120] Once the vehicle of the soul is purified the soul to be able to imagine those symbols and rites presented to her by the gods. This occurs when an individual is initiated into the divine mysteries of theurgy.

Although the immortal vehicle is tied up with the irrational soul it is capable of an existence apart from it.[121] The vehicle's ultimate goal is to be reunited with the ethereal vehicle of the visible god, the soul's leader god. There the vehicle and the irrational soul remain, purified, and perhaps, the rational soul ascends even higher to the noetic realm.

Once initiated and consecrated the vehicle of the soul can be filled with divine images. They prevent any material images or sense-impressions from occurring within the vehicle, thereby blocking out any irrational activities. The rational soul can now operate on the noetic level.

> Whenever the partial (i.e., human) soul attaches itself to the whole (i.e., the divine soul), its vehicle also follows the vehicle of the divine soul, and just as the soul imitates the intellection of the divine soul, so also its body imitates the movement of the divine body.[122]

Indeed the vehicle is purified and elevated by the divine light from the soul's leader god. Thus its function is to be illuminated. This occurs through initiation.

E. Aesthetic Symbols and the Arts

Proclus, therefore, set out three degrees of initiation: initiation (*telete*); consecration (*myesis*); and vision (*epopteia*).[123] Telestic and consecratic initiation constitute the purifying stages for the vehicle.

Marinus reports that Proclus was initiated into the Mysteries of the Great Nestorius by Asclepigeneia, the daughter of the theurgist and thaumaturge Plutarchus, son of Nestorius.[124] Having studied his teacher Syrianus and:

> ....the many works of Porphyry and Iamblichus and the writings of the Chaldaeans which belong to the same order of ideas and thus, nourished by divine oracles, he rose to the highest level of the... theurgical virtues.[125]

For the philosopher the last initiation, vision, is a liberation of the soul effected by the gods that brings things together. It is to this image we turn. What does this vision (*epopteia*) bring with it? This question brings us back to the symbolics of this essay. We return to the immortal symbol of Hecate's thighs:

> About the cavity of the right hip poured forth an abundance of plenteous liquid of the first generated soul, who entirely ensouls the light, the fire, the aether, and the worlds. In Hecate's left hip exists the source of virtue, which remains wholly within and does not give away its virginity.[126]

Since the goddess ensouls the sublunary world her hips symbolize the cosmic orders dominated by her. The right flank represents the potency of this cosmic soul. She is a power who ensouls the totality of the physical cosmos—its elements of light, fire, aether, and worlds. These correlate to *Aion*, the Father begotten light; *Pyr*, the Empyrian realm, *Aether*, the region of the fixed stars, and *Kosmoi*, the zone of the planets and the terrestrial world.

The orifice on Hecate's left hip does not discharge any water for its symbolizes the source of virtue. The goddess is unwilling to imperil its purity by contact with the sublunary world. Accordingly her remains within Hecate and is accessible to those souls capable of rising to the intramundane realm where the goddess resides.

To acquire these powers and the virginal virtue associated with them the soul must approach her left thigh. Although Hecate is unwilling to reveal them on a terrestrial level, she will willingly reveal her charms to those souls who ascend to the aethereal realm. This, however, requires an ascent of the soul to the moon, to Hecate.

For Proclus, art functions as an instrument of the divine intellect. It triggers and actuates the rational soul and her vehicle. Indeed, when Hecate self-manifests in her statue in an apparition perceptible to the imagination human and divine souls and vehicles move in consort together. When the human elements grasp the activity of the divine elements they turn outward to receive the deity and discover their eternal link with the divine. *Aisthesis* is an *antilepsis*, a coming to consciousness of a higher self, and a divine source. For Proclus this is only possible through aesthetics and the symbolics of the hieratic art.

III
Rationality, Ritual, and Culture

A. Aesthetic Pattern as Culture Pattern

For ancient Mediterranean men and women the pilgrimage of the soul to intellect and to deity is cast in terms of divine giving.[127] Later Roman men and women treasured the arts and aesthetic perception. The arts transmuted psychological and ontological distance into the deep joy of proximity to self and to the gods. Aesthetics contributed to a network of interpersonal acts that carried the full over-tones of the later Roman cultural traits of love, power, sympathy, patronage and salvation.[128] Perception and the arts functioned as one of the cements of their social world.

B. Later Platonic Symbols and Roman Culture

The remains of this aesthetic pattern pullulate through the writings of later Platonism. Its instantiation lay in the *Truemmerfeld* of temple sites and statuary that ring the Mediterranean basin. To the ancient eye these surfaces and solids reveal images of an ideal world of symmetry, harmony, and beauty for an intelligible beauty could be grasped through the narrow apertures of its temples and the formal qualities of its statues. Architecture and statuary present images of ideal being vivified. Masonry and marble symbolize needs satisfied and long distances overcome.

What does an ancient theory formation tell us about an ancient aesthetic pattern? An elusive question to ask, let alone answer. Plotinus has suggested that beauty manifested itself to the Roman in buildings dedicated to the gods; that the beautiful shimmered in the statues formed to their images. Perhaps by localizing intelligible beauty in art these Romans recognized the presence of the divine in the visible, fed on the joys of its proximity, and thereby tempered their fears of distance from self and from their gods.

The human craftsman like the cosmic demiurge fashions a world. Artistic creation makes one aware of the attainability in the visible world of an intellectual beauty whose abode is the intelligible world. Distance is overcome, the beautiful is proximate in temple and statue. The visible fact of the beautiful points to the instantiation of the eternal in the temporal, the formal in the material.

Hic locus est—is the refrain that runs through these monuments of a lost age. The intelligible is accessible aesthetically. Through art the lower self communes with the forms, gains union with the higher self, and eventually with the beautiful. For in temples and statuary beauty dwells. Temples are theomorphic sanctuaries; statuary theomorphic beings. Loci for gods and goddesses they become a focus for the image-making faculty of the soul, even perhaps, places where one's daemon appears.

Clearly temples are places where souls meet *daemons* and gods. Porphyry tells how Amelius visited temples at the New Moon and the Feasts of the Gods happily offering sacrifices (*philothutes*).[129] He asked Plotinus to come along. The master answered: "They ought to come to me not I to them". His refusal to accompany Amelius probably means he did not expect to find any of the higher gods waiting for him in their temples, only lower gods or daemons. Thus, he refused to go. This does not mean, however, that Plotinus thought temples devoid of higher beings.

Porphyry reports that Plotinus encountered a god at an *Isis* temple in Rome.[130] The spirit was summoned (*kletheis*) to appear (*eis autophian*). The deity visually appears and the philosopher assesses it through his faculty of sense perception (*aisthesis*). Statues also are vehicles for the manifestation of the image of the form of beauty.[131] Plotinus claims that the perception of the form of beauty instantiated in the statue leads the mind to an understanding of intelligible beauty and, perhaps, to the beautiful (*he kallone*).[132] Since the beautiful is divine, statuary clearly are concrete manifestations (*algamata*) of divine beauty itself.[133]

Thus Plotinus assumes the physical presence of the divine and the beautiful in architecture and statuary. Their beauty and symmetry guarantee the presence of divinity and beauty in their midst. Most significantly, however, he maintains an aesthetic theory that makes their presence in art meaningful. The philosopher was, after all, a mind that grasped these divine and formal images; a soul aware of its undescended self; a figure who knew the intelligible world of the forms; and even succeeded in rising to the highest god four times.[134]

By the fourth century the strictly noetic way of access to the intelligible world, tied to the presence of the ideal world in the act of intellection, had come to be irreversibly modified in Platonism.[135] Indeed an aesthetic way opened up, legitimized by an axiological shift in the value of perception and imagination, and heralded by the Neoplatonic view of the instantiation of the divine forms in statues and icons, temples and churches.

The great building projects of Constantine and the rededication of temples by Julian reflect this new awareness.[136] A sense of divine grace lies at the root of the building, making, and translation of art objects by the Roman upper class.[137]

As members of an inherited elite Neoplatonists were in a strong position to encourage the translation of the arts, to appropriate and give the stamp of legitimacy to these channels of the holy. For their theories of knowledge, the soul, and reality rendered intelligible the constant presence of the divine in nature and within art.

In the demi-monde of Hellenic Neoplatonism the dark mood cast over the soul due to her fall and separation from the intelligible world was ameliorated aesthetically.[138] For art served as a visible gesture of divine access to the unconscious and descended soul. Aesthetic knowledge and theurgic practice represented a replication of interpersonal relations between humanity and divinity thought lost because of the tragic nature and destiny of the soul.[139]

The ceremony that surrounds the arts in later Platonism, thus, guarantees good happenings in a world cluttered by bad ones. Theurgic rites represent a carefully articulated model of the new aesthetic relationship between humanity and divinity. Art symbolized for the Neoplatonist contact with ancient gods and goddesses, aesthetic knowledge and theurgic action solidarity with their own empire-wide class.

By the fifth century the philosopher and theurgist are indistinguishable.[140] As the knower of divine wisdom and the doer of the hieratic arts, this figure becomes a supernatural extension of divine power (*dynamis*) and love (*eros*) in the universe. Thriving on the tenacious bond of aesthetic friendship (*philia*) their knowledge and activity offered a mantel of divine patronage (*prostateia*) and the possibility of divine salvation (*sotereia*) to all who fell within their orbit. Indeed, the philosophers use and transfer of divine power to their clients rendered accessible the proprietary relationship with the gods thought lost because of the fall of the soul.[141]

C. The Philosopher as Cultural Symbol

Mortals are not immediately joined to the gods but require greater kinds of intermediaries ranging from the cosmic gods and their angels to heroes and sages. Philostratus, Damascius, Marinus, Eunapius, Sozomen, and Zosimus present the lives of wise men and women who effectively brokered this patron-client relationship.

Asclepiodorus and Heraiscus spent long periods of their lives in temples, Damascius resided in a cave under a temple devoted to Cybele near Hierapolis.[142] Each communed with the gods and goddesses who appeared at such places. Venturing forth they became privileged agents and administrators of divine power, love, patronage, and salvation to a wider Roman world.

Hypatia of Alexandria and Sosipatra of Pergamon were higher souls protected and guided by blessed daemons and heroes.[143] Not only philosophers of high repute—Hypatia was the teacher of Synesius and the author of a famous treatise on numbers and Sosipatra was the instructor of countless students and wrote commentaries on the dialogues of Plato—they were practicing theurgists. Using a statue Hypatia telestically cured a man who fell in love with her while Sosipatra victim of a love-spell cast on her by Philometer had it reversed by Maximus, the pupil of Aedesius and teacher of the Emperor Julian.[144] Other women like Asclepigenia and Anthusa of Cilicia joined men like Plutarch and Hermias to contact, fathom, and translate the divine presence and hallowing in statues to aristocratic clients in city, town, and country throughout the Empire.[145] The inverted magnitudes of temples and statues resided n their souls. Consequently they were able to bring to seance and seminar their condensed solidarity with the divine world.

This map of divine love and power correlates with another symbolized by divine patronage and salvation. Both coalesce around Neoplatonic aesthetic patterns and later Roman cultural patterns. It is easy to be misled by the heritable traits of later Platonic aesthetics and Roman culture.[146]

So often presented as expressions of those who somnambulated in a utopian world many have lost view that this coalescence of aesthetic pattern and culture pattern functioned to enlist and register the participation of listeners (*akroates*) in the manifestation (*autophania*) of the gods in the physical world.[147]

Since matter is not evil it does not prevent communication with the gods. The statue of a god is a material object and matter (*hyle*) is offered (*didomai*) by the gods. Thus, it is congenial (*symphyes*) to them.[148] Thus to make and consecrate statues to the gods is the aesthetic way of communing with the divine:

> Create a statue, purified in the manner I shall teach you. Make the body of mountain rue (*peganon agrion*)[149] and adorn it with little animals, with domestic lizards, and when you have crushed a mixture of myrrh, gum (*sturaz*), and frankincense, blend it with these creatures, go out to the open air under a waxing moon and perform the rite by saying the prayer...[150]

Porphyry says:

> You consecrate a statue of Hecate in the following way: Produce a certain kind of fillet; grind lizards together with fragrant essences and burn all that; say a certain prayer in the open air under a waxing moon; do all this to consecrate the statue of Hecate. The she will appear to you in your sleep.[151]

Buildings and statues, herbs and stones, incantations and formulas, gestures and dancing were included in the categories of symbols (*symbola*) and tokens (*synthemata*) that established contact between a human being and a god. Tools like the bull-roarer (*rombosstromphalos*)[152]. Marinus reports that Proclus used the rhombos wheel to communicate with the gods.[153] Syllabic utterances (*voces mysticae*) were also employed to render the gods visible.[154]

A divine light (*autophia*) often appeared with the manifestation (*autophania*) of the deity. Sometimes the mediator, the philosopher-theurgist, would radiate divine light.[155] While lecturing Proclus would project such light for he communicated with luminous apparitions of Hecate and saw the goddess herself.[156] Not only gods appear; a parousia of nature appears, preceded by a whole choir of daemons, angels, and spirits. They are gracious, kind, and give beneficence to the person who evoked them as well to those whom the theurgist initiates into their mysteries.[157]

Through symbols and tokens the god would recognize the theurgist as a legitimate practitioner, and the theurgist the god as a real god.[158] Scattered throughout the universe through the kindness of the gods they work without our knowledge[159] but they are known to the higher soul. Known to them they were used to achieve union with the gods.[160] Spoken or unspeakable, concealed within the statues of the gods, they assure the presence and intervention of the gods known only to the *telestai*.[161]

A sacred fire that shines without shape speaks to the theurgist:[162]

> For your sake, bodies have been attached to our autophanies (*autoptois; phasmasin*).[163]

The theurgist becomes a medium (*docheus*) for the presence of the divine in the world.[164] Eunapius reports that Maximus assembled a large number of friends in the temple of Hecate and burned a grain of incense, reciting to himself the text of a hymn. The goddesses smiled, then laughed, and finally the torches she held burst into flames, into a blaze of light.[165] Wise men and women, therefore, brought a divine presence into the world and the divine power embraced their human community, reintegrating each human soul with her divine source.

Buildings, statues, natural objects, and language became the visible companions that crowded around the men and women of late antiquity. Pullulating with divine expressions of access and friendship they explain the ancient map of relations between deity and humanity in the age of the later Caesars. Neoplatonists were convinced that gods, goddesses, daemons, and angels revealed their natures and names through those special men and women whose primordial sowing linked them eternally with the divine. Aesthetic perception and the arts enabled the imagination to project a structure of a clearly defined reality onto a known social world and to define personal relationships.

D. Aesthetic Symbol as Cultural Symbol

Art, in late antiquity therefore, did more than decorate a landscape with imposing temples and sublime statues. It was an expression of piety exquisitely adapted to enable ancient Mediterranean men and women to articulate and render intelligible urgent questions on the nature and destiny of the soul. Art revealed the continuity between the self and the divine, serving to establish a sense of the stability of the identity. It permits the soul to turn her back on the towering disparity between the different orders of the universe and to seek reassurance in the tight web of her imagination, in the stability of the well-known human relationships of patron and client.

Against this immemorial backdrop, later Romans turned to discover their divine, unconscious selves. Objects of art provided the soul with recognizable forms of divine beings whose self-presentations were rendered aesthetically intelligible through theurgy.

Neoplatonic aesthetics makes clear the metaphysical structure of patronage and the solidarities that bound together the aristocratic classes of the Roman Empire, in these last pagan centuries. Aesthetic theory established the presence of divine love and power in the world, their accessibility, and, therefore, consolidated the Platonic philosopher at the acme of a divinely sanctioned *patrocinium*.

Thus, art, becomes part of a universe increasingly marked by implicit and explicit patronage. The divine has its network; holy men and women tapped into it by building patronage networks of their own. As a result the theurgist was placed at the forefront of later Roman society as the fulcrum of a wide-ranging social *patrocinium*. As patrons divine men and women emerged to resolve the gulf between self and deity through an aesthetic therapy of proximity. The theurgist emerges as the leader of a *patrona communis* who sees the different levels of the self and the manifold levels between the self and god and resolves them. The aesthetic pilgrimage of the soul to intellect and beyond overcomes distance and alienation. Integral to this Odyssey of the soul is the detachment of the arts from a mimetic context and its attachment to a hypostatic context. Through art the divine communes with the human. Moreover it becomes a locus of a network of "interpersonal acts" between gods and humans that carries with it the full overtones of later Platonic epistemological, psychological, and reality theories as well as later Roman understandings of generosity, inter-dependence, and solidarity.

With Plotinus' concession, Platonic aesthetics at last comes to terms with the cultural world of the later Roman Empire. As Plotinus insisted, the absolute certainty characteristic of the intelligible world manifests itself in the sensible world. The world of ideas is self-contained, cogent, and certain. It is accessible because the natural world is deliberately fashioned so that our minds can move freely and confidently within it to capture the divine essence that creates and sustains it.

Everything in the natural world may be in flux, while certainty belongs to the intelligible world. Nonetheless, Plotinus, Porphyry, Iamblichus, and Proclus postulate a fixed framework within nature as a necessary mark of its rationality. The arts provide access into a clearly defined structure of reality within which everything and everyone has a lucidly defined relationship.

Earlier Platonic assumptions, that only a fixed order of being could be intelligible, are proved groundless. The divine order is aesthetically intelligible. In Neoplatonic terms, we understand the world not less, but more completely through nature and the arts. We also understand interpersonal relationships in a new way. Later Romans drew intellectual strength from these facts.

For these ancient Mediterranean men and women Hecate beckons:

> Bats are now beginning their short strutting flights against the sky. In the east the color is washing out the world, leaving room for the great copper-colored moon which will soon rise over Epirus. It is the magic hour between two unrealized states of being—the day-world expiring in its last hot tones of amber and lemon, and the night-world gathering with its ink-blue shadows and silver moonlight.
>
> 'Watch for her,' says the Count, 'behind the mountains there.' The air tastes faintly of damp. 'She will be rising in a few moments.'
>
> 'I am thinking,' says Zarian, 'how nothing is ever solved finally. In every age, from every angle, we are facing the same set of natural phenomena, moonlight, death, religion, laughter, fear. We make idolatrous attempts to enclose them in a conceptual frame. And all the time they change under our very noses.'
>
> 'To admit that,' says the Count oracularly, is to admit happiness—or peace of mind, if you like. Never to imagine that any of these generalizations we make about gods or men is valid, but to cherish them because they carry in them the fallibility of our own minds.'

Conclusion

Plotinus, Porphyry, Iamblichus, Proclus: the list would probably have puzzled my grandfather and his generation. It makes sense now; it symbolizes changes in our historical perspective. We can face, more or less from the same angle, thought communities which seem far apart; and we can find something in common among them through the rationality and the rituals of the social organizations that produced such facts.

For the most part these men did not know one another. No obvious external link connects most of them with each other. Yet all of them gave new meanings to prophecy, divination, and magic in later Platonism, and brought about profound changes in the societies to which they belonged.

We have been led to ask the philosophical and cultural questions that will interpret the teachings of the later Platonists in order to make them more socially perceptible. We have asked what conditioned the appearance of so many kindred understandings of prophecy, knowledge, reality, and the soul within relatively wide chronological limits. We have inquired how indeed were prophecy, divination, and magic interpreted in so many different ways within relatively narrow cultural limits We have examined why there is a relation between the religious and philosophical ideas of later Platonism and the social messages these thought communities conveyed.

The very nature of the questions that have come to our minds indicates the essence of our new position towards these men and women. Instead of seeing each later Platonist as representatives of specific religions and schools, we now see all of them as participants in a general cultural system. They have explained themselves to us directly by their own words. We have done our part by commenting on their words. Given the necessary knowledge of languages and texts, we may presume that at some future date we shall understand Porphyry and Proclus in the same way as we comprehend Philo and Origen.

Until then firm conclusions about the relation between individual minds and social institutions can be drawn only when all the evidence has been collected and analyzed. Nonetheless, it is possible, even now, to make a few preliminary observations about prophecy, divination, and magic in Later Platonism and their relation to social facts.

> A. Later Platonists established a connection between rationality and ritual. This linkage underscores the ontological, epistemological, psychological, ethical, and soteriological significance of occult knowledge and practices.

B. Later Platonists utilize the pneumatic/noetic link between oracular and scientific knowledge to resolve a series of ontological and psychological problematic endemic to their degree of reality metaphysics and the fall of the soul. This is clear from the extensive use later Platonists make of the technical terminology of ontology, epistemology, and psychology. This permits later Platonists to lift ritual out of the *arcana mundi* to which it was consigned.

C. Later Platonic understandings of rationality and ritual suggest a relationship between individual minds and social institutions. This association resolves itself in four main points:

- Later Platonic cognitive processes reflect later ancient social arrangements. This is largely clear in the relationship between later ancient metaphysical theory and later Roman patronage and kinship systems. Knowledge reflects and builds social solidarity.
- The proposition that philosophical facts are social facts suggests that knowledge is essentially social. Key activities of thinking such as the conferring of identity, the positing of similarity relationships, and the classification of divine and natural kinds are shaped by the cultural and institutional contexts in which they occur.
- Later Platonic knowledge processes and practices underpin institutions. Thought communities are social institutions. The fact-generating activity of later Platonism and later ancient cultural complexes get shaped together. To constitute a version of reality is at the same time to constitute a society.
- The thesis that knowledge acquisition and sharing shows how institutions and knowledge get shaped together effectively limits those who are committed to rational choice theory and its assumption that individuals act as autonomous rational calculators. Rational choice theory cannot fully explain the relationships between metaphysical thinking and the social arrangements it reflects. The difficulty lies in rational choice theory's neglect of the prior problem of how knowledge systems come into being.

To view later Platonic rationality and ritual from these perspectives is to connect them with their proper contextual worlds and to explain how ritual was legitimized rationally and socially. If this study has shed light on the relationship between knowledge and society and stimulates others to investigate these connections further, it will have more than fulfilled its purpose.

Endnotes

1. Especially, E.R. Dodds, "Theurgy," in *The Greeks and the Irrational*, Berkeley, CA: University of California Press, 1951, pp. 283-311. cf. Pierre Boyance, "Theurgie et telestique neoplatonicienne," *RSR* 47 (1955), pp. 189ff.; Samson Eitrem, "La Theurgie chez Neoplatoniciens et dans les papyrus magiques," *Symbolensis Osloensis* 22 (1942), pp. 22f.
2. See, Georg Luck, "Theurgy and Forms of Worship in Neoplatonism," *Religion, Science, and Magic In Concert and in Conflict*, New York, NY: Oxford University Press, 1989, pp. 185-228.
3. Fredrick Suppe, *The Structure of Scientific Theories*, Urbana: University of Illinois Press, 1977, p. 17.
4. In this sense the model of rationality used by Dodds is implicitly logical positivist. This model for theoretical explanations is elaborated on and critiqued by Carnap, Hempel, Nagel, and Braithwaite.
5. See, Hans H. Penner, "Rationality and Religion: Problems in the Comparison of Modes of Thought," *Journal of the American Academy of Religion LIV* 4 (1986), pp. 646-671.
6. Such as those of E.R. Dodds. cf. e.g., *The Greeks and the Irrational*, Berkeley, CA: University of California Press, 1951, pp. 283-311.
7. On the question of rationality, ritual, and science. cf. Hans H. Penner, "Rationality, Ritual, and Science," *Religion, Science, and Magic In Concert and In Conflict*, New York, NY: Oxford University Press, 1989, pp. 11-24.
8. This definition received its classical sociological analysis in the works of Max Weber. For more recent definitions. cf. Steven Lukes, *Essays in Social Theory*, London: Macmillan, 1977, p. 54; Maurice Godelier, *Rationality and Irrationality in Economics*, New York, NY: New Left Books, 1972, p. 12.
9. *op. cit.*, p. 22.
10. In Carl Hempel, *Aspects of Scientific Explanation*, New York, NY: Free Press, 1965, pp. 463-465.
11. *Ibid.*, p. 464
12. Following, Hans H. Penner, "Rationality, Ritual, and Science," *Religion, Science, and Magic In Concert and In Conflict*, New York, NY: Oxford University Press, 1989, pp. 20-24.
13. This is not to suggest that Plotinus was a practicing magician. cf. Philip Merlan, "Plotinus and Magic," *Isis* 44 (1953), pp. 341ff.; and the response to Merlan's positive thesis. cf. A. Hilary Armstrong, "Was Plotinus a Magician," *Phronesis* I (1955), pp. 73ff. It is to suggest that Plotinus was instrumental in establishing a series of epistemological and psychological formulations that were used by later Platonists to ground ritual upon rational grounds. Plotinus rejects magic, not because he denies the existence of ritual. He abjures magic because it does not fit his own definition of rationality. cf. *Vit. Plot.*, 10ff.

14. Porphyry, *Phil Orac.*, 1.152.7; Proclus, *Remp.*, 2.201.10ff.
15. Cf. *Laws* 10.888e; *Phaedrus*, 249c; Ep. 7.341c. Also see *Sym.*, 210e. However this figure is not the craftsman of the plastic arts who is an imitative artist, cf. *Gorg.*, 450c. For Plato on art see, Paul Friedlaender, *Platon* I, Berlin: De Gruyter, 1964, pp. 59-84; Whitney J. Oates, *Plato's View of Art*, New York, NY: Charles Scribner's Sons 1972, pp. 28; 48-62.
16. For Plato the arts are a mere imitation of nature which is but an imitation of being. cf. P. Friedlaender, *Platon* I, Berlin: De Gruyter, 1964, pp. 60ff. Plato, consequently, places the imitative artist in class vi of viii classes among knowers of the ideas, cf. *Rep.* 7.522b; and the plastic arts among the lowest of the imitative arts, cf. *Rep.* 3.401ab.
17. For Plato on the mantic arts, see E.R. Dodds, *The Greeks and the Irrational*, Berkeley, CA: University of California Press, 1951, pp. 207-235.
18. *Enn.*, 2.9.14; 4.4.40-44. On Plotinus and magic (*goeteia*) see, A. Hilary Armstrong, "Was Plotinus a Magician," *Phronesis* 1 (1955), pp. 73ff.; Philip Merlan, "Plotinus and Magic," *Isis* 44 (1953), pp. 341ff.
19. *De Reg. An.*, fr. 7, 11, 2.
20. *De Myst.*, 43.3; 44.14. For this theory in Iamblichus see, A. Smith, *Porphyry's Place in Neoplatonism*, The Hague: Brill, 1974, pp. 100-110.
21. The soul's descent is discussed in *De An.*, 1.377,13-380,29. cf. A.J. Festugiere, *La revelation d'Hermes Trismegiste*, III, Societe l'Edition "Les Belles Lettres," 1953, pp. 69-73; 216-223; James F. Finamore, *Iamblichus and the Theory of the Vehicle of the Soul*, Chico, CA: Scholars Press, 1985, pp. 59-124. *De An.*, 1.375,5-18; 378,19-379,10; 380,6-29. cf. *In Tim.*, fr. 87. Also see, James F. Finamore, *Iamblichus and the Theory of the Vehicle of the Soul*, Chico, CA: Scholars Press, pp. 94-114.
22. ap. Proclus, *In Tim.*, 275,26-29.
23. *Ibid.*, 276,5-11.
24. Each position stands in contrast to those of Porphyry, cf. James F. Finamore, *Iamblichus and the Theory of the Vehicle of the Soul*, Chico, CA: Scholars Press, 1985, pp. 11-27.
25. *De An.*, 1.377.18.
26. *Ibid.*, 1.377.19-21. cf. James F. Finamore, *Iamblichus and the Theory of the Vehicle of the Soul*, Chico, CA: Scholars Press, 1985, p. 63 n. 8.
27. ap. Proclus, *In Tim.*, 3.280,19-21.
28. *Ibid.*, 3.280,22-32.
29. *Ibid.*, 3.107,30-108,1.
30. *In Parm.*, fr. 2.
31. *De An.*, 1.377,16-17.
32. *Ibid.*, 1.377,23-25.
33. *Ibid.*, 1.377, 18-29. This is its cosmic allotment lexin.
34. *De Myst.*, 1.8.
35. ap. Proclus, *In Tim.*, 3.279,11-30.

36. *De An.*, 1.378,21-379,6.
37. *Ibid.*, 1.379,7-10.
38. *Ibid.*, 1.379,2; 22-25; 1.380,7-9; In Phaed., fr. 5.
39. *De An.*, 1.380,9-12.
40. *Ibid.*, 1.380,12-14.
41. *De Myst.*, 10.1, 286,3-11.
42. *Ibid.*, 10.5, 290,16-17.
43. *Ibid.*, 10.5, 291,10-12.
44. For the association with Chaldaean thought see, Hans Lewy, *Chaldaean Oracles and Theurgy*, Cairo, Impr. l'Institut Francais d'Archeologie Orientale, 1956, pp. 178-184.
45. *De Myst.*, 3.31.
46. *Ibid.*, 2.6.
47. *De An.*, 1.455,1-4.
48. ap. Proclus, *In Tim.,* 3.266,16.
49. *De An.*, 1.384,26-27; 1.457,13-14.
50. *In Tim.*, fr. 87.
51. ap. Proclus, *In Tim.,* 3.276,19-22.
52. *De Myst.*, 5.20; 5.22; 10.7.; *In Phaedonem*, fr. 5.
53. *De Myst.,,.*, 3.14.132,11-17.
54. *Ibid.*, 3.14.
55. *Ibid.*, 3.11; 14.
56. For Iamblichus the imagination perceives divine images directly. For Plotinus the imagination grasps only images of the forms. cf. *Enn.*, 4.8.4,28-31.
57. *De An.*, 2.11.
58. *De Myst.*, 2.6.
59. *Ibid.*, 10.4ff.
60. *Ibid.*, 1.11f.; 15; 21; 2.11.
61. On this notion see, Martin P. Nilsson, *Die Geschichte der griechischen Religion* 2, Muenchen: 1969, pp. 14ff.
62. On this theory see, Albert Berthelot C.E. Ruelle, *Collection des anciens alchimistes grecs*, Paris: Steinheil, 1888; J. R. Harris, *Lexigraphical Studies in Ancient Egyptian Minerals*, (Deutsche Akademie der Wissenschaften zu Berlin. Institut fuer Orientforschung 54), Berlin: Akademie Verlag, 1961; Georg Luck, *Arcana Mundi: Magic and the Occult in the Greek and Roman Worlds*, Baltimore-London: The Johns Hopkins University Press, 1985, pp. 361-366.
63. See, Pliny, *Nat. Hist.*, s.v *fauna, flora et al.*
64. *De Myst.*, 5.23.
65. This association is explained in Olymp. *Met.*, 3.59. cf. M. W. Gundel-H. G. Gundel, *Astrologumena. Die astrologische Literatur in der Antike und Ihre Geschichte*, Wiesbaden: Steiner Verlag, 1966.; W. Gundel, *Dekane und Dekansternbilder*, Darmstadt: Wissenschaftliche Buchgesellschaft, 1969.
66. *De Myst.*, 2.6; 1.11f.; 15; 21; 2.11.

67. See, E. R. Dodds, *The Greeks and the Irrational*, Berkeley, CA: University of California Press, 1951, pp. 287ff.
68. See, F. Dornseif, *Das Alphabet in Mystik und Magie*, Leipzig: Teubner, 1925; Karl Preisigke, *Namenbuch*, Heidelberg: Selbstverlag des Herausgebers, 1922.
69. *De Myst.*, 5.26.
70. *Ibid.*, 2.6.
71. Cf. E.R. Dodds, *The Greeks and the Irrational*, Berkeley: CA, The University of California Press, 1951, p. 292.
72. *De Myst.*, 3.2.
73. *Ibid.*, 3.9. cf. Eduard des Places, *Oracles Chaldaiques*, Paris: Editions du Cerf, 1971, p. 109 n. 2.; 126.
74. These notions are also illustrated in the Greek Magical Papyri. Precise directions are given for making a figure of Helios appear. A formula is uttered which causes the god to enter the statue. He begins to communicate through the icon sending dreams, curing insomnia, and exorcizing evil daemons. cf. *PGM.*, 4.88-93.
75. Sulla carried an image of Apollo with him and Nero one of the Dea Syria, cf. Seutonius, *Vit.*, 30; 56.
76. *De Myst.*, 5.23.
77. *Enn.*, 2.9.3.
78. *Ibid.*, 4.4.44.
79. *De Reg. An.*, fr. 2
80. *De Myst.*, 2.11.
81. For both Plotinus and Porphyry such symbols and tokens link physical things, at best, and not sensibles with intelligibles. cf. *Enn.*, 2.9.3; *De Reg. An.*, J. Bidez, *Vie de Porphyre*, Ghent: E. van Goethem, 1913, fr. 4.
82. *De Myst.*, 5.23.
83. *Phaedrus*, 249d-250c.
84. *Tim.*, 27d-28e; 29b; 48e.
85. Edited with translation and notes by Eduard des Places, *Oracles Chaldaiques*, Paris: Edition du Cerf, 1971.
86. By the early fourth century the Oracles were considered authoritative scripture by some Neoplatonists. They are quoted extsensively by Porphyry in his *Phil Orac.*, and *De Reg. An.* cf. Hans Lewy, *Chaldaean Oracles*, Cairo: Impr. de l'Institut Francais d'Archeologie Orientale, 1978, pp. 449-456. According to the Suida Porphyry also wrote a commentary on them, cf. J. Bidez, *Vie de Porphyre*, Ghent: E. van Goethem, 1913, frr. 52*18; 70*50. For Iamblichus see, Julian, Epistula in Bidez's colllection of his works. cf. 1924, p. 19; pp. 73ff.; Eduard des Places, *Oracles Chaldaiques*, Paris: Edition du Cerf, 1971, p. 44.

87. See, Proclus, *In Tim.*, 2.255.26ff. cf. *Enn.*, 4.9.11. On this interpretation see, Pierre Boyance, "Theurgie et telestique neoplatonicienne," *RSR* 47 (1955), pp. 195ff.
88. See, E. R. Dodds, *The Greeks and the Irrational*, Berkeley, CA: University of California Press, 1951, pp. 283-311.
89. *Ibid.*, pp. 19-20.
90. See the review of E.R. Dodds, *The Greeks and the Irrational*, Berkeley, CA: University of California Press, 1951, 327 pages. Peter Brown. cf. EHR (1968), pp. 542-558.
91. Cf. Carlos G. Steel, *The Changing Self: A Study on the Soul in Later Platonism*, Brussels: Paleis Academien, 1978, pp. 34-56.
92. As noted Proclus went to great lengths to make Plato and Plotinus good theurgists. cf. *In Tim.*, 2.225.26ff.
93. *Theol. Plat.*, 1.26.63.
94. *Ibid.*, 1.26.63. cf. Iambl. *De Myst.*, 10.4ff.
95. On theurgy in Proclus cf. e.g., E. J. Festugiere, *Commentaire sur le Timee*, Paris: Societe l'Edition "Les Belles Lettres," 1968, pp. 17ff.
96. Cf. E. R. Dodds, Proclus: *The Elements of Theology*, Oxford: Oxford University Press, 1963, pp. iff.
97. They are collected by Eduard des Places, *Oracles Chaldaiques*, Paris: Edition du Cerf, 1971, pp. 219ff.
98. *Remp.*, 2.242.8.
99. *El. Theol.*, xx.
100. See, J. Trouillard, *L'un et l'ame selon Proclus*, Paris: Societe l'Edition "Les Belles Lettres," 1972, pp. 186ff. cf. Iambl. *De Myst.*, 3.14.
101. See, James F. Finamore, *Iamblichus and the Theory of the Vehicle of the Soul*, Chico, CA: Scholars Press, 1985, pp. 59-123.
102. *In Tim.*, 3.276,5-11..
103. *Ibid.*, 3.263,22-265,12.
104. *Ibid.*, 3.275,26-31.
105. *Ibid.*, 3.276,8-9.
106. *Ibid.*, 3.280,22-32.
107. *Ibid.*, 3.280,22-32.
108. *Ibid.*, 3.107,30-108,1.
109. *Ibid.*, 3.278,31-32.
110. *Ibid.*, 3.279,15.
111. *Ibid.*, 3.279.17-20.
112. *Ibid.*, 3.304,30-305,11.
113. *Ibid.*, 3.305,7-10.
114. *Ibid.*, 3.307,26-308,7.
115. *Ibid.*, 3.266,11-14.
116. *Ibid.*, 3.233,26-28.

117. See, James F. Finamore, *Iamblichus and the Theory of the Vehicle of the Soul*, Chico, CA: Scholars Press, 1985, pp. 59-124.
118. See, E. R. Dodds, *Proclus: The Elements of Theology*, Oxford: Oxford University Press, 1963, pp. xxff.
119. See, R. T. Wallis, *Neoplatonism*, London: Duckworth, 1972, s.v. Proclus.
120. In *Tim.*, 3.280,19-21. Here Proclus refers to such intermediaries as saviours (*soteras*) and patrons (*prostasis*).
121. *El. Theol.*, prop. 209.
122. *In Tim.*, fr. 81.
123. *Ibid.*, 3.276,19-22.
124. *Theol. Plat.*, 4.16.
125. *Vit. Proc.*, 28.
126. *Ibid.*, 26.
127. *Remp.*, 2.201.10.
128. On this concept in later Platonism see, A. Smith, *Porphyry's Place in Neoplatonism*, The Hague: Brill, 1974, pp. 100-110.
129. Proclus explains what is at issue in *In Tim.*, 3.280.19-21.
130. *Vit Plot.*, 10. On this encounter see, A. Hilary Armstrong, "Was Plotinus a Magician," *Phronesis* 1 (1955), pp. 73ff.; Philip Merlan, "Plotinus and Magic," *Isis* 44 (1953), pp. 341ff. Most discussion of this passage focuses on the issue of Plotinus and magic.
131. *Vit. Plot.*, 10.
132. *Enn.*, 5.8.1.
133. *Ibid.*, 1.6.5.
134. *Ibid.*, 1.6.3.
135. Porph. *Vit. Plot.*, 23.
136. See, A. Smith, *Porphyry's Place in Neoplatonism*, The Hague: Brill, 1974, pp. 123-141.
137. See, A.H.M. Jones, *The Later Roman Empire*, 2 Vols. Oxford: Basil Blackwell, 1986, 2.1012-1024.
138. See, Peter Brown, *The Cult of the Saints*, Chicago, IL: University of Chicago Press, 1981, pp. 106-126.
139. The insights of Evans-Pritchard concerning the function of magic apply as well to theurgy. It reverses a situation of misfortune. cf. E. E. Evans-Pritchard, *Witchcraft, Oracles, and Magic Among the Azande*, Oxford: Oxford University Press, 1976, pp. 1-55; For the use of this model for late antiquity, cf. Peter Brown, *Religion and Society in the Age of Saint Augustine*. New York, NY: Harper and Row, 1974, pp. 119-146.
140. This seems to be born out in reports from Porphyry about Plotinus, cf. *Vit. Plot.*, 10; and from Eunapius about Sosipatra, cf. *Vit. Soph.*, 466-467. Each had to counter spells cast on them by opponents or lovers. Fallen souls were under the aegis of fate. Only contact with a power higher than fate insured escape from

daemonic powers, cf. Peter Brown, *Religion and Society in the Age of Saint Augustine*, New York, NY: Harper and Row, 1974, pp. 119-146.
141. Also see, E. R. Dodds, *The Greeks and the Irrational*, Berkeley, CA: University of California Press, 1951, pp. 283-311.
142. For a more recent study on this phenomenon see, Eugene V. Gallagher, *Divine Man or Magician? Celsus and Origen on Jesus*, Chico, CA: Scholars Press, 1982.
143. Cf. Zosimus, *Epistula*, 5.46.3f.
144. Cf. Sozomen, *Hist.*, 9.8
145. *Ibid.*
146. A portrait of the mood is nicely given by Augustine, cf. *Civ. dei*, 5.23.235.28ff.
147. Cf. e.g., E. R. Dodds, Proclus: *The Elements of Theology*, Oxford: Oxford University Press, 1962.
148. Iambl. *De Myst.*, 5.23; cf. Oracles, fr. 101 {des Places}.
149. Iambl. *De Myst.*, 5.23.
150. According to Dioscorides, 3.45-46 this is the herb molly = *ruta halepensis*.
151. *Oracles*, fr. 224. {des Places}.
152. *Phil Orac.*, 7.130ff. {Wolf}.
153. This is the golden ball of Hecate enclosing a saphire, covered with magical characters, and placed at the end of a strap made of bull hide. See, Psellus, *Oracles*, fr. 206, 170; cf. Theocritus, 2.30.
154. *Vit. Proc.*, 28. They hung from the ceiling of the palatial hall in Babylon. cf. Phil. Vit. Apoll., 1.25.6.
155. Psellus, *Oracles*, 221f. {des Places}.
156. *Oracles*, fr. 147. {des Places}.
157. Iambl. *De Myst.*, 2.4; cf. 1.12; 2.5; 3.6.
158. *Ibid.*, 2.4,7; Psellus, Oracles fr. 88. 175. {des Places}.
159. Psellus, *Oracles*, fr. 149, p. 184. {des Places}.
160. Iambl., *De Myst.*, 5.23; 2.11.
161. Proc., *Elem. Theol.*, 223 {Dodds}.
162. *Ibid.* Also see, *In Tim.*, 1.273d. cf. E. R. Dodds, *Proclus: The Elements of Theology*, Oxford: Oxford University Press, 1963, p. 292 n.34; Pierre Boyance, "Theurgie et telestique neoplatonicienne," *RSR* 47 (1955), p. 196 n. 2.
163. *Oracles.*, fr. 148, 173 {des Places}.
164. *Ibid.*, fr. 101.; cf. Iambl. *De Myst.*, 5.23.
165. *Psellus*, 1.249 K-D.

Participants

Dr. J. P. Atreya, Editor, "Darshana International", Diwan Bazaar, Moradabad, 244 001 India
Professor R. Balasubramaniam, Chairman, Indian Council of Philosophical Research, 210 Deen Dayal Upadhyaya Marg, New Delhi 110 002, India
Professor Arabinda Basu, Sri Aurobindo Ashram, Pondicherry, 605 002, India
Dr. Robert M. Berchman (absent), Department of Philosophy, Dowling College, Oakdale, New York 11769-1999, USA
Dr. D. R. Bhandari, Joint Secretary, Akhil Bharatiya Darshan Parishad, Jodhpur University, Jodhpur, India
Professor S. R. Bhatt, Department of Philosophy, Delhi University, Delhi 110 007, India
Professor Henry J. Blumenthal, Head, Department of Classics and Ancient History, University of Liverpool, Liverpool L69 3BX, United Kingdom
Professor Bhuvan Chandel, Member-Secretary, ICPR, New Delhi 110 002, India
Professor D. P. Chattopadhyaya, Former President, ICPR, Jadavpur University, Calcutta 700 032
Dr. Roman T. Ciapalo, Department of Philosophy, Loras College, 1450 Alta Vista, Dubuque, Iowa 52004-0178 USA
Dr. Christos Evangeliou, Department of Philosophy & Religion, Towson University, Towson, Maryland 21204, USA
Professor Lloyd P. Gerson, Department of Philosophy, St. Michael's College, University of Toronto, 81 St. Mary St., Toronto, Ontario M5S IJ4, Canada
Dr. Ranjan K. Ghosh, (Organising Secretary), Director, ICPR, New Delhi 110 002, India
Dr. Paulos Mar Gregorios, (Co-Chair), Director, Sarva Dharma Nilaya, 2 Tughlakabad Institution Area, New Delhi 110 062, India.
Professor Robert Helm, Worrell Professor of Philosophy, Wake Forest University, Winston-Salem, NC 27106, USA

Dr. **Mani Jacob**, General Secretary, All India Association for Christian Higher Education, 39 Institutional Area, D Block, Janakpuri, New Delhi 110 058, India.

Dr. **Daniel Kealey**, Department of Philosophy and Religion, Towson University, Towson, MD 21204, USA.

Dr. **Gopal Chandra Khan**, Department of Philosophy, University of Burdwan, Burdwan 731 104, West Bengal, India.

Professor **Ravindra Kumar**, Director, Nehru Memorial Museum and Library, Teen Murti Bhavan, New Delhi, India

Dr. **David Lea**, Department of Psychology & Philosophy, University of Papua-New Guinea, Papua-New Guinea, Pacific Islands

Professor **John R. A. Mayer** (Co-Chair), Department of Philosophy Brock University, St. Catharine's, Ontario L2S 3Al, Canada

Professor **P. K. Mukhopadhyaya**, Department of Philosophy, Jadavpur University, Calcutta 700 032.

Professor **K. Satchidananda Murty**, Executive Chairman, Indian Philosophical Congress, Aparajita, Sangam Jagarlamudi, Guntur Dt. Andhra Pradesh 522 213

Professor **G. C. Nayak**, Department of Buddhist Studies & Philosophy, Nagarjuna University, Nagarjuna Nagar, 522 510, AP, India

Professor **M. Rafique**, Department of Philosophy, Aligarh Muslim University, Aligarh 202 002, India

Professor **A. Rahman**, Tower A, Flat 30, Zakir Bagh, Moulana Mohammad Ali Rd, New Delhi 110 025, India

Dr. **Frederic M. Schroeder**, Department of Classics, Queen's University, Kingston, Ontario. K7L 3N6, Canada

Manav Dayal Dr. I. C. Sharma, Manavata Mandir, Hoshiarpur Punjab, India.

Dr. **Raj Singh**, Department of Philosophy, Brock University, St. Catharine's Ontario, Canada.

Professor **Richard Sorabji**, Professor of Ancient Philosophy, King's College, London, UK, 17 Cobden Crescent, Oxford OXI 4LJ, United Kingdom

Dr. **Atsushi Sumi**, 30 Yakake-cho, Saiin, Ukyo-ku, Kyoto, 615, Japan.

Dr. **P. B. Vidyarthi**, Nagartoli, Ranchi 834 001, Bihar, India

Dr. **Girija Vyas**, Minister of State, Department of Information & Broadcasting, Government of India, New Delhi.

Dr. **A. Yajnik,** Director, University School of Psychology, Education, and Philosophy, Gujarat University, Ahmedabad 380 009, Gujarat, India

Sponsoring Organizations

1. International Society for Neoplatonic Studies, USA
2. Indian Council of Philosophical Research, India
3. Indian Philosophical Congress, India
4. Nehru Memorial Museum and Library, New Delhi
5. Indira Gandhi National Centre for the Arts, India
6. Jamia Millia Hamdard, New Delhi
7. Akhil Bharatiya Darshan Parishad, India
8. International Society for Indian Philosophy, India
9. All India Association for Christian Higher Education
10. Manavata Mandir, Hoshiarpur, India
11. Sarva Dharma Nilaya, New Delhi

Contributors

Arabinda Basu, editor, GAVESANA, Review of Philosophy and Yoga; has taught and lectured on Comparative Philosophy and Religion at Universities in India, Europe, U.S.A. and Israel.

Robert Berchman is Associate Professor of Philosophy at Dowling College. He is the author and editor of books and articles in later ancient philosophy with particular focus on Philo of Alexandria, Origen of Alexandria, and Plotinus.

S. R. Blatt is a senior Professor of Philosophy in Delhi University. Author of several books and numerous research papers, his research interests include Indian Philosophy, Philosophy of Religion, Social and Political Philosophy and Philosophy of Education.

D. P. Chattopadhyaya is Professor of Philosophy in Jadavpur University, Calcutta, and a former president of the Indian Council for Philosophical Research.

Roman T. Ciapalo is Associate Professor of Philosophy at Loras College, Dubuque, Iowa. He has lectured extensively in the United States and internationally in New Delhi, Bratislava, and Ukraine. He has published articles on Neoplatonism and is currently working on an English translation of the 18'h century Ukrainian philosopheer, Hryhorij Skovoroda

Christos Evangeliou is Professor of Philosophy in Towson University, Towson, Maryland and the Vice-President of the International Society for Neoplatonic Studies. He is the author of two books, Aristotle's *Categories and Porphyry*, and *The Hellenic Philosophy: Between Europe, Asia, and Africa* and forty scholarly papers.

Lloyd P. Gerson is Professor of Philosophy in the University of Toronto. He is the author of two books: *Plotinus, Arguments of the Philosopher*, and *God and Greek Philosophy* and the editor of *The Cambridge Companion to Plotinus*, the co-editor of *Hellenistic Philosophy* and *Aristotle's Politics*, and the author of many articles in Ancient Philosophy.

Paulos Mar Gregorios, recently deceased, was Syrian Orthodox Metropolitan of North India and the President of The

International Society for Neoplatonic Studies in India. He was a former President of the Indian Philosophical Congress and the World Council of Christian Churches.

R. Baine Harris is Eminent Professor of Philosophy Emeritus in Old Dominion University in Norfolk, Virginia and Honorary President of The International Society for Neoplatonic Studies. He is the General Editor of Studies in Neoplatonism: Ancient and Modern (12 volumes) and one of the founders of ISNS, and served as its Executive-Director for twenty-four years.

Gopal Chandra Khan is a senior Professor of Philosophy at Burdwan University, Burdwan, India

John R. A. Mayer is Professor of Philosophy Emeritus in Brock University, in St. Catharines, Ontario. He was the sponsor of the first ISNS conference on Neoplatonism and Indian Thought, and has been an active supporter of the society since its founding.

P. K. Mukhopadhyaya is Professor of Philosophy in Jadavpur University in Calcutta. His fields of interest and expertise include Indian Philosophy, especially Nyaya, and in Western Philosophy Philosophical logic and Philosophy of Science. He is a founder member of the Calcutta Centre of Advanced Study in Science and Philosophy and an Editor of the journal Science Philosophy Interface.

G. C. Nayak is U.G.C. Emeritus Fellow in the Department of Philosophy and Religion of Banaras Hindu University in Varanasi (India). Some of his main books in English are: *Evil and the Retributive Hypothesis, Philosophical Enterprise and the Scientific Spirit, Philosophical Reflections, Essays in Analytical Philosophy, and Understanding Religious Phenomenon.*

Frederic M. Schroeder, Department of Classics, Queen's University, Kingston, Ontario, Canada K7L 3N6, is the author of *Form and Transformation. A Study in the Philosophy of Plotinus* (Montreal and Kingston, London, Buffolo: McGill-Queen's Press, 1992) and numerous articles and book chapters on Plotinus.

I. C. Sharma, Manav Dayal is spiritual leader of Manavata Mandir, Hoshiarpur, Punjab, India. He was a former professor of Philosophy in a number of universities in India and the United States and a past president of the Indian Philosophical Congress. He has been a strong supporter of the work of ISNS both in India and North America from the early years of its founding.

Atsushi Sumi is Lecturer of General Education at Hanazono University in Kyoto, Japan. He is the author of several articles on Plotinus, Plato, and Whitehead in both English and Japanese.